a change of appetite

WHERE HEALTHY MEETS DELICIOUS

DIANA HENRY

MITCHELL BEAZLEY

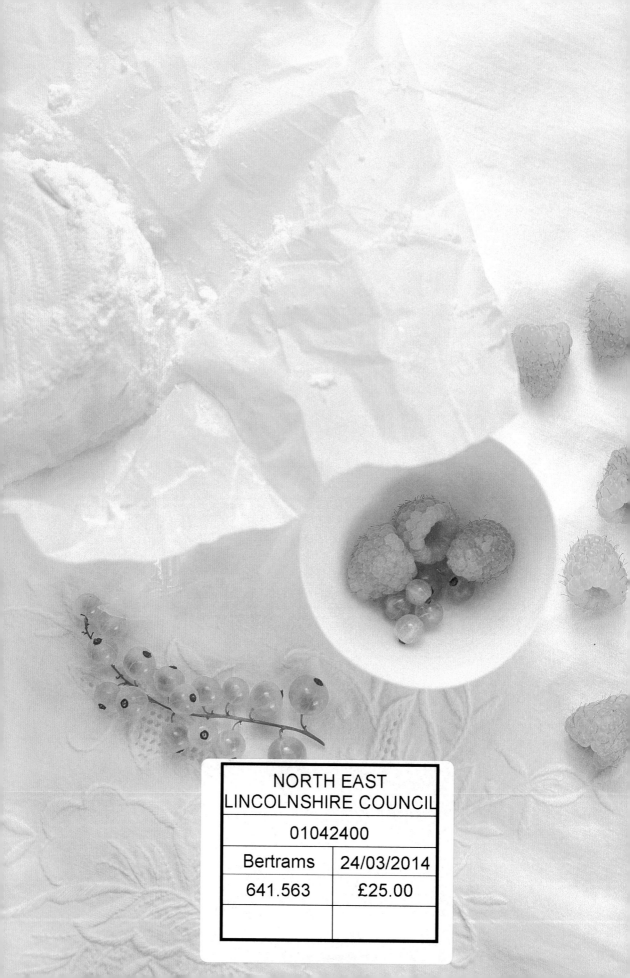

contents

introduction

Stand in any newsagent and look at the magazine covers. The advice on how to eat – to fight cancer, to lose weight, to achieve glowing skin – is all-pervasive. And a lot of it is telling you what you *can't* eat. We angst about food and health all the time… and yet there is clearly something very wrong with the Western diet. Rates of obesity and type-2 diabetes are soaring; heart disease and cancer are commonplace.

Against this background I gradually realized that friends weren't asking me for recipes for cakes any longer, but for advice on what to do with a tuna steak and how to cook quinoa. They wanted to eat more healthily, cook more vegetables, lose a bit of weight and cut their intake of red meat. When they told me what they were cooking – trying to think of sixteen exciting things to do with turkey breast – it sounded grim. Round about the same time, my doctor was urging me to get my blood pressure down and lose some weight. Perhaps I needed to take stock of my own eating as well.

I don't, by any stretch of the imagination, have a 'bad' diet. I don't eat ready meals or fast food, though I'll admit to the occasional Indian takeaway. The only processed stuff in the house is canned tomatoes and beans and the odd packet of biscuits. But I love food. And I have a few weaknesses. One is sugar, particularly in pastries. There is not much I wouldn't do to get my hands on an almond croissant or a little *tarte aux pommes* at four o'clock in the afternoon. I also love bread – crusty baguette, rich, golden brioche – as well as healthier whole grain loaves. (I may have been born in Ireland but I'm clearly French. And refined carbohydrates are my *bêtes noires*.) So I decided to explore what a 'healthy diet' actually is and come up with dishes that were so good (and good *for* you, too, but first of all delicious) that you wouldn't feel you were missing out.

My biggest problem was thinking about food in terms of 'healthy' or 'unhealthy'. I can't think of meals as sets of nutrients. A meal is a colourful assembly of foods – many of which we don't quite understand in terms of health – that should be, first and foremost, enjoyable. The term 'healthy' does negative things to me (in fact I struggled with whether to put the word on the front of this book). It makes me think of miserable, beige food. It also smacks of preciousness. While at university, I briefly shared a house with a girl who was tremendously into 'healthy' food. It was all nuts, seeds and little bowls of Iceberg lettuce. Not only was she one of the most joyless people I have known, she was also self-obsessed. (American journalist Michael Pollan uses the term 'orthorexia' to describe an all-consuming and destructive interest in healthy food. He claims it's a growing problem in the USA.)

I'm much more into living life to the full than I am into thinking of my body as a temple. About ten years ago I wrote a book about dining pubs, for which I travelled the length and breadth of Britain, meeting great chefs and food producers. The joy and care with which they approached their food and their work was so life-affirming that it put me on a high every day of my journey. To fret about whether you are getting enough omega-3 and vitamin B when you eat seems to me the anxious, hand-wringing opposite of this.

I settled on two terms that I liked that would guide me. First, I was going to eat food that was 'accidentally healthy'. It had to be delicious, healthiness was a bonus. Second, I was going to practice 'considered eating': find out what fats were okay; if I should be cutting down on cheese; whether whole grains were better for me… so I would think about what I was consuming, but I wasn't going to be slavish.

My eating had already changed quite a lot, especially compared to the way I ate twenty years ago. There were a lot more vegetables and whole grains, the more robust the better. And I wasn't prepared to declare anything off limits. Food is one of the greatest pleasures in life, so I wouldn't advise anyone to completely give up steak with béarnaise sauce or gratin dauphinoise. Just don't eat them very often (they're rich anyway, so you wouldn't want to).

When I started to put together lists of 'accidentally healthy' dishes, I found they were the kind I wanted to eat anyway. My love of Middle Eastern food goes way back, and that's a healthy place to start, but I also plundered the cuisines of Japan, Thailand and Vietnam.

As I cooked different dishes, I started to read about food and health as well. One of the very frustrating things about trying to eat 'healthily' (and one reason why I had largely ignored it) is the competing claims, the 'superfoods', the misinformation. I read lots of stuff that was contradictory, discovered that some 'beliefs' had long since changed (I really thought eggs were bad for your cholesterol, for example, though the thinking on that altered quite a long time ago) and got angry about how much we had been misled (go and read about all those 'healthy' low-fat spreads we were encouraged to eat in the 1970s, they were way worse than the butter they were designed to replace).

How did I choose what advice to follow? Common sense and my own experience. (There's an extensive bibliography in this book if you want to do your own reading.) Even my kids joined in. Telling them they had to cut down on sugar was one thing. Sitting them down in front of Robert Lustig (obesity expert and anti-sugar campaigner) on youtube was another. They started to understand why sugar wasn't good for them and why, contrary to what they'd been taught at school (which seems to lump all carbohydrates together), you don't need the white stuff for energy. Learning about sugar, and the negative impact it's having on our diet and health *worldwide*, was the most fascinating and shocking research I did. The arguments as to why calorie counting doesn't work (I should know, I've done enough of it) were convincing too, and I gradually understood the current thinking on fats and on phytochemicals, the compounds found in plants that may act upon our own biology.

I am not keen on 'nutritionism'. Seeing foods just in terms of health – for what they can potentially do for us rather than simply being delicious – makes us all that much more anxious, and pressurizes us to buy things we don't need. Any food that has had something added, I leave on the shelf. These are 'functional' foods, created in factories and sold by marketeers to take advantage of our worries. (You can't slap a sticker on a bunch of carrots, but they'll do you more good than a carton of carrot juice that has 'extras' added.) But I was glad to find that some of the things I love – such as roast tomatoes – are good for you as well. (They contain lycopene, which appears to protect against heart disease and breast cancer.) Eventually I came up with answers about what was healthy (or at least what was probably healthy, as far as we actually *know*), as well as a collection of dishes I really loved.

The main thing you can do for good health is to eat proper home-cooked food, limit anything processed, really keep an eye on refined carbohydrates (especially sugar), switch to whole grains for at least some meals and up your vegetable intake.

None of the recipes here are 'cranky' or punishing (or I wouldn't eat them). There's a lot of olive oil and veg. There's a bit of red meat, but not loads. Oily fish pop up again and again, as do whole grains. There's some sugar; it's in cakes, sorbets and other puddings that are part of largely healthy 'menus' and are meant to be kept for treats, not eaten every day. There's also sugar in some dressings, especially those from South-east Asia that depend on the balance of hot, sour, salty and sweet tastes. I think that's okay. The problem isn't with what you eat at one meal, but what you eat *across the board*.

Initially I intended to put together a book of recipes to eat during the week, assuming most people would revert to less healthy eating at the weekend. Then I stopped seeing the distinction. This food was so good I wanted to give it to friends when they came round for supper, so I put celebratory seasonal menus into the book too.

I have undergone a change of appetite. I'm eating better, I feel better. My way forward has been to reduce refined carbohydrates (I only eat them at the weekend) and significantly increase the range of veg I eat. You might use the knowledge in this book and settle on a different path. The biggest surprise for me has been how much friends and family like the food. There are lots of big front-of-mouth flavours, such as chilli, ginger and lime, the kind of thing you want when you aren't eating starchy or rich food. It's food that makes you feel revitalized and energetic. Deprivation is not on the menu. If you cook the dishes in this book you'll eat really well and happily and you shouldn't notice that you're eating more 'healthily'; neither will your friends, on being served any of the menus, think you've become a health food nut. This is good food for people who love eating. It's a happy bonus that it's good *for* you as well.

spring

eating in spring

We feel ourselves to be part of something bigger when spring arrives. Without making any conscious decision, we find we want different foods: greener, cleaner, sprightlier flavours. Spinach, spring onions and radishes are all abundant but I also want lime, which somehow tastes 'greener' than lemon, mint, lemon grass, dill, ginger and tangy goat's cheeses.

It doesn't pay to be impatient. It's easy to rush on to summer and start buying red peppers… but resist and you will eat more interesting food. We're drawn to different cooking techniques in spring, too. I always feel like poaching and steaming, and turn out griddled skewers of meat with big salads and bright sauces. It's not time to crank up the barbecue yet, but getting your hands messy while eating is as liberating as the warming weather.

This kind of cooking requires more care and attention than wintry braises and roasts that are just bunged in the oven, but you're more alert in the kitchen in spring than in November. If you hold on to what your body seems to crave – bright, light food – the climb towards summer brings good eating that is also good for you.

early spring

broccoli
carrots
cauliflower
kale
leeks
nettles
purple-sprouting broccoli
spinach
spring onions
watercress

blood oranges
kiwi fruit
lemons
oranges
passion fruit
pineapples
rhubarb

dover sole
lemon sole
gurnard
mussels
red mullet
salmon
shrimp

mid spring

asparagus
globe artichokes
jersey royals
lettuces
radishes
rocket
spring cabbages

basil
chives
dill
sorrel

lamb

crab
plaice
prawns
sea trout

late spring

new potatoes
peas

chervil
oregano
mint
tarragon

haddock

persian salad

We don't think about putting herbs into salads, except as an afterthought. But, in the Middle East, they can *be* the salad. And this one is beautiful, though it depends on top quality leaves and flowers as well as herbs. I like the flowers to be all blue and white, that way it has the same colour palette, but see what you can get. Obviously, the flowers need to be unsprayed. Even some supermarkets seem to be doing various colours of radish – purple and mauve as well as pink – but, again, see what you can find; just use pink and it will still look gorgeous, as long as everything is absolutely perky and fresh.

SERVES 6

FOR THE SALAD

12 radishes (different colours if you can get them)

½ ridge cucumber (use ½ regular cucumber if you can't find that)

75g (2¾oz) salad leaves (baby spinach, watercress, lamb's lettuce and any red-veined leaves you can find)

20g (¾oz) dill fronds

25g (1oz) mint leaves

15g (½oz) basil leaves

15g (½oz) flat-leaf parsley leaves

edible flowers and petals

FOR THE DRESSING

4 tbsp extra virgin olive oil

1 tbsp white balsamic vinegar

good squeeze of lemon

salt and pepper

If the radishes have really fresh leaves, remove them, wash and pat dry. They can go into the salad, too. Either quarter or shave the radishes, whichever you think will look best. Peel the cucumber, remove the seeds and cut the flesh into chunks.

Mix all the dressing ingredients together and season well.

Toss all the elements together and serve.

goat's curd, blueberries and watercress

Goat's curd – which tastes like light, creamy, almost 'unformed' goat's cheese – is quite hard to find unless you live near a top-notch cheesemonger. But it's a cinch to make. It doesn't have to be made into a 'proper' dish, either. Spread it on bread then drizzle with olive oil, or a little flower honey.

This salad is lovely with added spelt (see page 224 for how to cook it, you'll need just 50g/1¾oz raw weight). Toss it in some of the dressing and scatter in the bowl or on the plates before you add everything else. You'll need to increase the quantity of dressing a little, too. The vinegar I use for this, made by A l'Olivier, contains raspberry pulp and is stocked at Waitrose.

The recipe for the goat's curd is from my good friend, the food writer Xanthe Clay. It makes about 175g (6oz) of goat's curd.

SERVES 4

FOR THE GOAT'S CURD

1 litre (1¾ pints) whole goat's milk (pasteurized is fine)

1 tbsp rennet

2 tbsp lemon juice

salt

FOR THE DRESSING

1 tbsp raspberry vinegar

2 tbsp hazelnut oil

2 tbsp extra virgin olive oil

½ tsp runny honey (optional)

pepper

FOR THE SALAD

100g (3½oz) watercress, coarse stalks removed

100g (3½oz) blueberries

150g (5½oz) goat's curd

20g (¾oz) pistachios, or toasted hazelnuts or almonds, coarsely chopped

15g (½oz) microleaves (red amaranth is especially lovely), if you can get them

To make the goat's curd, heat the milk to 25°C (77°F). Stir in the rennet and lemon juice, cover and leave for an hour.

Line a colander with muslin and place it over a bowl. Strain the mixture through the muslin. Gather the corners to make a kind of bag and hang this to drip for a couple of hours (use the tap over the sink, or a door handle where it can drip into a bowl). It should be thick, but if you'd like it thicker, just leave to drip for longer.

Tip the cheese out of the muslin and into a bowl. Season with salt and gently mix this in. Cover and keep in the fridge.

Whisk all the dressing ingredients together with a fork, adding salt to taste. Toss the watercress and berries with this, then put into a broad shallow bowl (or arrange on plates) and dot with the goat's curd. Sprinkle with the nuts and microleaves (if using), then serve.

another idea… Slice 350g (12oz) sweet tomatoes (mixed colours if possible) and put in a bowl with the torn leaves from a bunch of basil. Drizzle with extra virgin oil and lemon juice, season and dot nuggets of 175g (6oz) goat's curd on top. This also works with cooked farro dressed with oil and lemon (see page 223, you'll need 50g/1¾oz raw weight). Serves 4. The curd is delicious with fruit as well. Use it instead of ricotta for the recipe on page 149.

spring menu longing for brightness

feta and orange salad | persian saffron and mint chicken | greek yogurt and apricot ice cream

Winter eating has its benefits. It can be rich and deep but, particularly as it gets towards the end of winter and the start of spring, I yearn for juiciness, crunch, colour. I especially want greenness. This menu is an antidote to all the winter cooking and eating you're leaving behind. Feta, honey and sprightly green leaves all shout 'spring'.

feta and orange salad with honeyed almonds

Fresh. Just what you want come April, though this is good in the winter as well, especially when blood oranges are around.

SERVES 4 AS A STARTER,
2 AS A LIGHT MEAL

FOR THE DRESSING

1 tbsp white wine vinegar

½ tbsp orange juice

salt and pepper

5 tbsp extra virgin olive oil

about ½ tsp runny honey

leaves from 1 sprig of thyme

FOR THE ALMONDS

½ tbsp olive oil

50g (1¾oz) blanched almonds

1 tbsp runny honey

⅛ tsp smoked paprika

⅛ tsp ground cumin

FOR THE SALAD

3 oranges

1 small or ½ large fennel bulb

60g (2oz) watercress

100g (3½oz) feta (preferably barrel-aged), broken into chunks

10g (¼oz) mint leaves, torn

Make the dressing by whisking all the ingredients together. Taste to check the seasoning, then pour into a broad shallow bowl.

To make the almonds, heat the olive oil in a small frying pan and add the almonds. Fry them over a medium heat until they are toasted – keep an eye on them to make sure they don't burn – then add the honey and spices and cook until the honey is bubbling and almost caramelized. Spoon the hot honeyed almonds on to a non-stick baking sheet or some baking parchment. Leave to cool a little. You can chop these very roughly or leave them whole.

Cut a slice off the bottom and top of each orange so they have a flat base on which to sit. Using a very sharp knife, cut the peel and pith off each orange, working around the fruit and cutting the peel away in broad strips from top to bottom. Slice the oranges into rounds and flick out any seeds you see. Set aside.

Trim the fennel, reserving any feathery bits, and remove the tough outer leaves. Quarter the bulb lengthways (or cut the half bulb in half) and cut out the core. Slice very finely (a mandoline is best) and throw into the dressing. Finely chop any feathery bits you pulled off and add them, too. Discard any coarse watercress stalks.

Put the oranges, watercress, feta and mint into the bowl as well and toss gently. Add the almonds and serve immediately.

persian saffron and mint chicken with spring couscous

A really pretty dish. Change the couscous according to what you have (even using fresh cherries when they're in season instead of dried ones). It just has to be fresh and green, so keep plenty of herbs in it. You can also use the marinade for whole chickens or poussins instead of thighs.

SERVES 4

FOR THE CHICKEN

about ¼ tsp saffron stamens

juice of 2 lemons and finely grated zest of 1

2 garlic cloves, roughly chopped

2 red chillies, deseeded and roughly chopped

2 tbsp olive oil

leaves from 1 small bunch of mint

8 skinless boneless chicken thighs

FOR THE COUSCOUS

20g (¾oz) dried sour cherries

200g (7oz) wholemeal couscous

200ml (7fl oz) boiling chicken stock or water

2 tbsp olive oil

1 garlic clove, crushed

juice of ½ lemon and finely grated zest of 1

2 tbsp extra virgin olive oil

salt and pepper

2 tbsp each chopped flat-leaf parsley and mint leaves

2 spring onions, trimmed and finely chopped

25g (1oz) pistachios, chopped

handful of pea shoots (or other small salad leaves)

FOR THE YOGURT SAUCE

200g (7oz) Greek yogurt

3 tbsp extra virgin olive oil

1 small garlic clove, grated

microleaves, such as amaranth, or 3 radishes, julienned

For the chicken, put the saffron and lemon juice in a small pan, heat gently and stir to help the saffron stamens dissolve. Remove from the heat and mix with the zest, garlic, chillies and olive oil. Tear the mint leaves into the pan. Put the chicken thighs into a broad, shallow non-reactive dish and pour the marinade over. Turn them over to make sure they get completely coated, then cover with cling film and put in the fridge to marinate. Leave for about 30 minutes.

At the same time, pour boiling water over the cherries for the couscous and leave them to plump up for 30 minutes.

Sprinkle the couscous into a bowl, pour over the stock or water and the olive oil. Leave for 15 minutes. Fork it through to separate the grains, then add the garlic, lemon juice and zest, extra virgin oil, salt and pepper. Stir in the herbs, spring onions, pistachios, pea shoots and drained cherries.

To make the yogurt sauce, mix the yogurt with the extra virgin oil and garlic and place in a serving dish. Sprinkle the microleaves or radish matchsticks on top.

Heat a griddle pan until it is really hot. Lift the chicken out of the marinade and griddle it (you will have to do it in two batches if your pan is small), turning frequently. You want to get a good dark golden colour on each side. Make sure the chicken is cooked (cut into the underside to check: the juices should run clear with no trace of pink). Serve it with the couscous and yogurt sauce.

greek yogurt and apricot ice cream

It's really important to sieve the apricot purée, otherwise you end up with an ice cream that has little bits in it. (Though don't use a sieve with too fine a mesh, or you won't be able to push it through.) You can also use regular plain yogurt rather than Greek stuff, it's just slightly tarter. Don't use low-fat yogurt, though, it sets very hard. Even with this full-fat version you need to bring it out of the freezer and let it defrost a little before serving.

SERVES 8 (HALVE THE QUANTITIES IF YOU PREFER)

300g (10½oz) dried apricots

300ml (½ pint) apple juice

4 tbsp golden caster sugar

400g (14oz) Greek yogurt

4 tbsp crème fraîche

2 tbsp runny honey

Put the apricots into a saucepan with the apple juice and sugar and pour in 100ml (3½fl oz) of water. Set over a medium heat and bring to just under the boil. Take the pan off the heat and leave to plump up overnight (turn the fruit over every so often to make sure all sides are getting soaked).

Put the apricots and their liquid in a food processor and whizz to a purée. You need to get it as fine as you can, so keep puréeing. Push this through a sieve (with not too fine a mesh), pressing hard to get as much of the mixture through as possible. You shouldn't end up with that much left in the sieve.

Stir the apricot purée into the yogurt, completely incorporating it, then mix in the crème fraîche. Taste for sweetness.

Pour into an ice-cream machine and churn according to the manufacturer's instructions. While it's churning, add the honey. If you don't have an ice-cream machine, pour the mixture into a broad, shallow freezer-proof container and put into the freezer. You need to break the mixture up – the easiest way is to whizz it in a food processor – three or four times during the freezing process so the ice crystals are broken down for a smooth ice cream. Add the honey during the last time you beat the mixture.

there are calories and *calories*

Most women I know can reel off the calorie count of a glass of white wine, an apple, or a bag of salted peanuts. I have even taken the decision – when young and foolish – to 'treat' myself to a calorie-free cigarette instead of more wine, or another handful of those nuts. All experienced dieters – and that means most of us – number crunch. The received wisdom is, 'If you eat it you better burn it, otherwise you are going to store it'. And if you've ever dieted you'll have beaten yourself up, even when restricting your calories severely, if you don't lose weight. ('I should have done another hour at the gym.')

The battle, both in the UK and the US, against our spiralling weight (we are twenty five pounds heavier than we were thirty years ago) has been fought on the calories in <-> calories out principle. It has led us to believe that people who are either overweight or obese have only themselves to blame; they eat too much and don't exercise enough. Because we believe all calories are equal, we conclude that 200 calories of cola and 200 calories of fish will do the same thing to our weight. (If you've ever decided to skip dinner because you succumbed to a doughnut at 4pm, that will have been your reasoning.)

I know from experience that the calories in <-> calories out model doesn't work. I'll bet we could all produce anecdotal evidence against it. Now scientific research shows all calories are *not* equal. Highly processed carbohydrates and starches, such as sugar, potatoes and white flour, are treated differently by our bodies than are green vegetables and fish. Refined carbs cause spikes both in blood sugar and the hormone, insulin. Our bodies need insulin, but producing too much of it, basically, makes us fat. Protein also stimulates insulin production but to a lesser degree, and stimulates another hormone, glucagon, that mitigates the fat-forming effects of insulin. Fat, it appears, does not stimulate insulin.

The form calories come in is very important. The differing effects of the three 'macronutrients' – carbs, protein and fat – on key hormones means they have different fattening potentials. This is important to know not just to help you lose weight but, crucially, to help you maintain a healthy size once you get there.

Watching your weight has been further complicated by the fat issue. Since the 1970s we have been taught that fat, especially saturated fat, is bad and will lead to heart disease. Low-fat diets, low-fat spreads, we went mad for them. The net result of eating less fat – and we have successfully reduced our fat intake – is that we consume more carbohydrates, especially highly processed carbohydrates. We cut the fat and put on weight.

There are many studies where different diets have been followed – the same calories consumed but in different ratios of fat, carbs and protein – and most of them show that low-fat diets don't help you lose weight (and don't help prevent heart disease either) and that high-protein low-carb diets (such as the Atkins diet) do help you lose weight. But as with all diets, you need the whole story. One of the most recent pieces of diet research was conducted in 2012 by Cara Ebbeling and David Ludwig of Boston's Children's Hospital.

They put three groups of people on diets with the aim of losing ten to fifteen per cent of their body weight. One group followed a standard low-fat diet: sixty per cent of calories from carbs (with an emphasis on fruits, vegetables and whole grains), twenty per cent from protein and twenty per cent from fat. This is the kind of diet we've been told is good for us.

The second group followed a very low-carb diet (similar to Atkins), with ten per cent of calories from carbs, sixty per cent from fat and thirty per cent from protein. The third diet tested was a low glycaemic diet, with forty per cent carbs ('good carbs' such as whole grains, pulses, fruits and vegetables), forty per cent fat and twenty per cent protein.

The results were clear. Those on the low-carb Atkins-type diet burned 350 calories more each day than those on the standard low-fat diet. Those on the low-glycaemic diet burned 150 calories more. So where your calories come from *does matter*. Ludwig concluded that 'the low-fat diet that has been the primary approach for more than a generation is actually the worst for most outcomes'. And this is what The Harvard School of Public Health says: 'Over time, eating lots of "fast carbs" can raise the risk of heart disease and diabetes as much as – or more than – eating too much saturated fat.'

Let's look at the low-carb high-fat regimes that 'worked'. Disciples of Atkins-type diets are vehement anti-carbists. They believe that even what we regard as 'good carbs' (pulses and whole grains) should be kept to a minimum (if eaten at all). They further argue that, nutritionally, carbohydrates are of little value, that you can find all the nutrients you need elsewhere. They're not bothered about fibre, because you get that in vegetables. They don't believe that meat, or a high intake of fat, is bad for you.

But even if they are correct, that's far from the whole story; you have to look at what else diets do to the body other than succeeding in shedding weight. In the same experiment, research showed that a low-carb high-fat diet produced problems when followed for a sustained period. It raised the stress hormone, cortisol, and levels of something called c-reactive protein, which is a measure of chronic inflammation. Ludwig states that both of these are 'tightly linked to long-term heart risk and mortality'. So the low-carb diet, though it seems the most successful for weight loss, has long-term downsides.

Pro-carb proponents only advocate 'good carbs', not the refined carbs or starches found in sugar, sodas, white bread and potatoes (because, by God, do they vary). The differences between carbs can be seen in their glycaemic index (GI) scores. The glycaemic index is a scaling system that rates, from zero to one hundred, how quickly a food raises blood sugar levels. The higher the GI, the more it affects blood sugar levels. An abundance of high-GI carbohydrates (and you get plenty in a plate of pasta) in the system triggers the release of insulin, which will move these carbs into cells where they can be stored as fat. Foods with lower GIs (fifty five or less) don't provoke such a high insulin response, so they don't lead to the fat deposits that high-GI foods (seventy or more) do.

High-protein, low-carb, high-fat diets work spectacularly for weight loss. (I have followed them myself.) But eating like this is hard to maintain. It's expensive, it's tough to refuse fruit (fruits contain good things but are also full of sugar) and it's difficult to stay away from grains and pulses. Even without looking at the research on what this kind of diet can do, it feels unhealthy to eat a lot of meat and fat. (I'm not against it as a way of losing a lot of weight, but you have to change your way of eating afterwards.)

David Ludwig concluded that the low-glycaemic diet seemed to work best because you didn't eliminate an entire class of food; you could have 'good' carbs. I'm with him. When I think back to my childhood – the 1970s, before we all became obsessed with saturated fat – my mum kept an eye on my dad's weight by cutting his potatoes (and pudding). We knew that sweet and starchy foods didn't do you any favours. Somehow that wisdom got lost.

I wanted to know what happens when you severely restrict calories (the kind of dieting I've done again and again). The Minnesota Experiment, conducted more than sixty years ago, is one of the most significant pieces of research in this area. It took thirty six healthy men and examined what happened to them over fifty six weeks, first eating 'regularly', then while on a low-calorie ('semi-starvation') diet, then a 'restricted' eating period (calories went up slightly) and finally an unrestricted phase (they could eat whatever they wanted).

The men lost one-fifth to one-quarter of their body weight while on the low-calorie phase, but energy expenditure dropped by almost forty per cent. They also became depressed, withdrawn, couldn't concentrate, and thought about food incessantly. Maybe you'll tolerate that to lose weight. But here's the rub. Once the Minnesota men were allowed to eat whatever they wanted – no calorie restrictions – they stuffed themselves, often eating four thousand calories a day. And the more weight the individuals had lost while dieting, the more they wanted to eat. Participants ended up with fat levels seventy five per cent higher than when they started dieting.

When we cut calories severely, our bodies fight. We hold on to our weight. Our drive to eat is not wholly determined by what's in our stomachs, but also by hormones that tell the body how well stocked it is with fat. Conventional dieting (calorie counting) might not just be ineffective, it might be worse than doing nothing at all. *It's where you get your calories from that counts.*

Forget counting calories, that only makes you cross (or smoke). It's refined carbs, especially sugar, that are your enemies.

asparagus, veneto style

This sounds very ordinary, but it ain't. A DIY dish, it's a real pleasure to do some mixing at the table. You can smell the olive oil as soon as it hits the warm egg and asparagus. Go easy on the vinegar, and season carefully.

SERVES 6

1.25kg (2lb 12oz) asparagus spears

6 eggs

very good extra virgin olive oil

salt and pepper

red wine vinegar

Break or cut any woody ends off the asparagus and put the eggs on to boil. When the eggs have cooked for seven minutes, drain and plunge them into cold water. Leave to cool a little, but only until they are cool enough to handle. Put them into a wire basket or a bowl lined with a tea towel, pulling the tea towel round the eggs to keep them warm.

Meanwhile, cook the asparagus either in an asparagus pan, or in a regular pan (covered) with the base of the stems in about 5cm (2in) of boiling water and the rest of the stalks and the tips propped up against the side. It should take four to six minutes and the spears should be just tender when pierced with the point of a knife. Lift the asparagus out of the water, briefly pat dry with a tea towel, put on a platter and drizzle with extra virgin oil and season with salt and pepper.

Take the bottle of oil to the table with the red wine vinegar and seasoning. Each person should peel and mash their egg, adding vinegar and extra virgin oil (about 1 tsp vinegar and 2 tbsp oil per person is about right).

more spears... **asparagus with prawns and dill** Prepare and cook 1.5kg (3lb 5oz) asparagus in the same way as above. While it's cooking, melt 75g (2¾oz) butter in a frying pan and gently warm 200g (7oz) cooked, shelled and deveined prawns (ideally organic) with the chopped fronds from 6 sprigs of dill. Divide the asparagus between plates (or serve on a large platter). Spoon some prawns and dill butter over each serving and season. Serves 8.

asparagus mimosa

'Mimosa' is the term applied to dishes garnished with hard-boiled egg pushed through a sieve. This version is a bit more rustic. You can treat leeks in the same way (steam them until they are completely tender; how long that takes depends on the thickness of the leeks).

SERVES 6

2 tbsp lemon juice, or to taste

smidgen of Dijon mustard

salt and pepper

8 tbsp extra virgin olive oil, or to taste, plus more to serve

1½ tbsp very finely chopped flat-leaf parsley leaves

1½ tbsp capers, rinsed and chopped

4 eggs

700g (1lb 9oz) asparagus

Make the dressing by mixing the lemon juice, mustard and salt and pepper in a cup and whisking in the extra virgin oil. Stir in the parsley and capers and taste. You may want more lemon or oil.

Put the eggs into boiling water and cook for seven minutes, then briefly run cold water over them. Trim the base off each asparagus stalk and finely peel off any the skin that looks tough. Boil or steam the asparagus until just tender (four to six minutes).

When the eggs are cool enough to handle but still warm, quickly remove the shells and chop the yolks and whites together.

As soon as the asparagus is cooked, drain it and divide between six plates. Season with salt and pepper and spoon the dressing on top, then put the chopped egg across the middle of the asparagus. Drizzle with some more extra virgin oil and serve.

other ways… Look at the ideas for broccoli on page 49; asparagus can be used in just the same ways. Also try it with Watercress pesto (see page 282) – just spoon it over – and top with a poached egg. Fantastic.

soft-boiled eggs with antipasti

An easy and rather splendid 'bits and pieces' lunch dish. Put the egg cup in the centre of a plate and surround it with a mixture of bought and home-cooked foods. To the selection below you can add cooked asparagus, roast beetroot, smoked mackerel, prawns… whatever you fancy. The idea is to eat the warm egg along with mouthfuls of the antipasti. Each diner gets his or her own feast.

Get the dishes ready in advance, then cook your soft-boiled eggs when you want to eat.

SERVES 8

FOR THE DRESSING

1 tbsp white wine vinegar

1 tsp Dijon mustard

4 tbsp extra virgin olive oil

pinch of caster sugar

salt and pepper

FOR THE LENTIL SALAD

225g (8oz) Puy or Umbrian lentils

½ small onion, very finely chopped

½ celery stick, very finely chopped

2 tbsp olive oil

2 tbsp finely chopped flat-leaf parsley leaves

½ small red onion, cut wafer-thin

FOR THE BROCCOLI

250g (9oz) purple-sprouting broccoli

50g can anchovies in olive oil

1½ tbsp extra virgin olive oil, plus more to serve

2 garlic cloves, finely sliced

good pinch of chilli flakes

juice of ½ lemon

FOR THE RADISH SALAD

bunch of French Breakfast radishes

2 tsp capers, rinsed and drained

1 small garlic clove, finely chopped

2 spring onions, finely chopped

leaves from 4 sprigs of mint, torn

1 tbsp lemon juice

2 tbsp extra virgin olive oil

handful of microleaves (optional)

lentilles en salade

Make the dressing by whisking all the ingredients together. Rinse the lentils, then cover them with cold water, bring to the boil and cook until tender but still holding their shape (15–30 minutes, depending on their age).

Meanwhile, gently sauté the onion and celery in the oil until they are soft but not coloured. Drain the lentils, add them to the onion mixture and stir them round to coat in the cooking juices. Add the dressing and parsley and season really well, then gently stir in the red onion.

purple-sprouting broccoli with melting anchovies

Trim the broccoli stalks and steam until just tender; it will take four or five minutes.

Drain the anchovies and gently heat the extra virgin oil in a small frying pan. Add the garlic and chilli and cook for a few minutes until the garlic is a very pale gold. Add the anchovies and press them with the back of a wooden spoon to break them up; the heat of the oil makes them melt into a sauce. Toss the warm broccoli with this, adding lemon and pepper. Serve with a drizzle more extra virgin oil over the top.

radish and caper salad

Trim the radishes and cut them into very thin slices lengthways (a mandoline is good for this). Toss with all the other ingredients and taste for seasoning.

silken tofu, prawn and chive soup

You might think you don't like tofu, but give it a go. Having it in a brothy soup is a good introduction, it takes on the flavour of the stock and melts as you eat it.

SERVES 4

1.2 litres (2 pints) good chicken or fish stock

3cm (generous 1in) root ginger, peeled and sliced

4 spring onions

2 garlic cloves, chopped

small handful of coriander stalks

350g (12oz) raw tiger prawns, shelled and deveined (preferably organic)

160g (5¾oz) tofu, cut into bite-sized cubes

salt and pepper

juice of 1 lime, or more to taste

10g (¼oz) chives, chopped

2 tbsp chopped coriander leaves

Put the stock into a saucepan with the ginger. Finely slice the spring onions on the diagonal and separate the green bits from the white. Reserve the green bits. Crush the white bits in a mortar and pestle with the garlic. Add to the stock with the coriander stalks. Bring the stock to the boil, then reduce the heat and simmer for about 30 minutes. If you have time, leave the stock to sit so that the flavours can infuse. Strain.

Return the stock to the boil, then reduce the heat to a simmer. Add the prawns, tofu and seasoning and simmer for one minute, then squeeze in the lime juice and check for seasoning. Serve in soup bowls, dividing the chives and coriander leaves between each bowl. This doesn't reheat brilliantly – it is much less fresh and the tofu makes the whole thing look a bit cloudy – so it's best eaten when just made.

for something different This doesn't just have to be made with prawns. You can also use small 'queen' scallops – halve them horizontally – or cubes of salmon. Or try shredded cooked chicken. And there doesn't even have to be any meat or fish; in season, green beans and asparagus tips can be used, too: cook them in the stock for as long as it takes them to become tender, then add the tofu and cook for another minute.

peruvian chicken soup

Brothy chicken soup can be found the world over and this is the Peruvian version, though it is often eaten there for breakfast rather than supper. Peruvians include egg noodles as well as potatoes, but I don't like the double starch. You could replace the potatoes with quinoa, it's better for you and, as a south American grain, seems totally apt. Just prepare it as on page 224 and spoon it into the soup, or serve on the side. The avocado is not authentic but it does go very well.

SERVES 8

2.25kg (5lb) chicken

2 leeks, roughly chopped

2 celery sticks, roughly chopped

2 carrots, roughly chopped

4cm (1½in) root ginger, peeled and sliced

1 bulb of garlic, halved horizontally

8 waxy potatoes (peeled or not, as you like)

6 eggs

small bunch of coriander leaves, roughly chopped

4 spring onions, chopped

2 red chillies, deseeded and finely sliced

juice of 1–2 limes, to taste, plus lime wedges to serve

slices of avocado, seasoned, with lime squeezed on top, to serve

Put the chicken into a large saucepan with the leeks, celery, carrots, ginger and garlic. Cover completely with water and bring to the boil. Immediately reduce the heat to a gentle simmer and slowly cook for about three hours, skimming the surface every so often to remove impurities and fat. The chicken should be just tender and the broth around it golden.

Carefully lift the chicken out on to a platter and strain the stock. Skim the surface of fat (you can throw a handful of ice cubes into it which will make the fat rise to the surface). Taste and reduce the stock by boiling if you want it to taste stronger.

Put the potatoes into the stock and cook for about 25 minutes, until tender. Boil the eggs for seven minutes, then cover with cold water and peel once they are cool enough to handle.

Meanwhile, take the meat off the chicken (or you can serve it whole and in the pot in which it was cooked). If you are cutting it up, you want to end up with eight nice big bits of meat, one for each person, or the equivalent in small pieces.

When the potatoes are cooked, return the chicken pieces (or whole bird) to the broth to warm through. Take off the heat and stir in the coriander, spring onions, chillies and lime juice to taste. Serve with the avocado. Each plate should have a halved hard-boiled egg and lime wedges.

beetroot, radish and goat's cheese salad

It might seem odd to put yogurt dressing on a salad that contains goat's cheese, but it seems to work. Buttermilk dressing (see page 96) is good too and a little lighter. Leave the beetroot raw if you want – cut it into very fine slices – and replace the lamb's lettuce with watercress if it's easier. A little spelt (see page 224 for how to cook it) is good alongside.

SERVES 6 AS A LIGHT LUNCH

FOR THE SALAD

600g (1lb 5oz) small raw beetroots

salt and pepper

2 tbsp olive oil

1 very small red onion, very finely sliced

125ml (4fl oz) cider vinegar

35g (1¼oz) granulated sugar

125g (4½oz) radishes

150g (5½oz) lamb's lettuce

small handful of mint leaves

1½ tbsp extra virgin olive oil (use a light, fruity one)

good squeeze of lemon juice

175g (6oz) goat's cheese, crumbled

FOR THE YOGURT DRESSING

100g (3½oz) Greek yogurt

2 tbsp extra virgin olive oil

1 garlic clove, crushed

Preheat the oven to 180°C/350°F/gas mark 4. Cut the stalks and leaves from the beetroots and trim the tufty tail off too (if the leaves are nice and fresh wash them, shred them and add to the salad, they have a great colour). Wash the beetroots really well and put them into a double layer of foil set in a roasting tin (the foil has to be large enough to be pulled loosely up round the beetroots to make a 'tent'). Season them and drizzle with the oil, turning them to make sure they are well coated. Pull the foil around the beetroots to make a parcel and put into the hot oven. If you have managed to get small beetroots they should be tender to the point of a small sharp knife in about 30 minutes; larger ones can take as long as 1½ hours. As you are eating them cold you can cook the beetroots well in advance, so the cooking time won't be a problem.

Put the onion into a saucepan with the vinegar and sugar. Bring gently to the boil, then pull off the heat and leave for 30 minutes. The onions will lightly pickle. Drain.

Top and tail the radishes – only take off the very longest bit of the tail – then cut them, lengthways, into thin slices.

To make the dressing, mix everything well with 2 tbsp of water.

When the beetroots are tender and cool enough to handle, carefully peel them. Either cut them into rounds or wedges. Toss the lamb's lettuce, mint and radishes with the extra virgin oil, lemon and seasoning, then divide between six plates. Spoon on the pickled onions and arrange the beetroot and goat's cheese on top. Drizzle with the dressing and serve immediately.

artichoke and ricotta salad with honeyed preserved lemon dressing

You can vary this by adding cooked and skinned broad beans, peas, asparagus or roasted peppers. They would all work well with the artichokes and ricotta. You can use canned instead of the more expensive jarred artichokes; they will need to be marinated first (see page 90).

SERVES 4

FOR THE DRESSING

2 shop-bought preserved lemons (1 if home-made, as they will be larger)

1 tbsp white wine vinegar, or to taste

1 tbsp runny honey, or to taste

1½ tsp juice from the jar of preserved lemons

leaves from 4 sprigs of mint, torn

4 tbsp extra virgin olive oil

salt and pepper

FOR THE SALAD

400g (14oz) artichoke hearts from a jar, drained of oil (about 6 per person)

50g (1¾oz) salad leaves (lamb's lettuce or watercress, or a mixture)

150g (5½oz) cherry tomatoes, halved

250g (9oz) ricotta, fresh if possible, crumbled into chunks

2 red chillies, deseeded and cut into slivers

35g (1¼oz) blanched almonds, toasted and roughly chopped

40g (1½oz) good-quality green or black olives

leaves from 15g (½oz) mint

Make the dressing first. Remove the flesh from the preserved lemons and discard it. Cut the skin into slivers. Mix the rest of the dressing ingredients together, season to taste and add the preserved lemon. Taste for seasoning and sweet-sour balance, adding more vinegar or honey to correct it to your taste.

Put the artichokes into a bowl and pour the dressing over them (this helps their flavour and texture). Cover and set aside until you want to serve (ideally leave them for at least an hour).

Lift the artichokes out of the dressing and shake off the excess. Arrange them on four plates with the other ingredients. Spoon the dressing over the top. Grind on some black pepper and serve.

pure and white

We go through a kilo of yogurt a week in our house. I love its cleanness, its snowy whiteness, its gentle sourness. It's not just for breakfast but is also a dipper or a sauce with mint, garlic or olive oil stirred in. I add my own fruit; that way I know how much sugar I'm adding. But is yogurt really 'good' for us? Like milk, yogurt is filling, a good source of protein and calcium and is associated with anti-inflammatory effects, immune system support and a lower prevalence of bowel cancer. Fruit yogurts are trickier. Read the label: you may be surprised how much sugar is added, especially to low-fat varieties. Natural yogurt isn't that high in fat anyway. Whole cow's milk yogurt contains a meagre 3.7% fat. I buy full-fat yogurt: it's filling, contains all the nutrients of the milk and has a good flavour. And what about 'live' and 'probiotic'? All yogurt is 'live' and has probiotics unless it's pasteurized. According to the World Health Organization, probiotics are live micro-organisms that can confer health benefits. They can increase bacteria that aid digestion, boosting our natural defences. But there are thousands of probiotics and only a handful have been shown to benefit us when eaten regularly. So yogurt is a good food (but read the label on low-fat pots), which may have extra perks. It's staying in my shopping basket.

middle eastern leeks with yogurt, dill and sumac

Somehow, for us, leeks don't quite fit the image of sun and blue skies, but leeks are much loved in the Middle East. Delicious either warm or at room temperature.

SERVES 4

6 leeks

6 tbsp extra virgin olive oil

really good squeeze of lemon juice (not quite ½ lemon)

salt and pepper

75g (2½oz) Greek yogurt

2 garlic cloves, crushed

1 tbsp chopped dill fronds

2 tsp Dijon mustard

ground sumac, to serve

Remove the tough outer leaves from the leeks and discard. Trim and cut into 4cm (1½in) lengths. Wash really well, then steam over boiling water for four to six minutes. They should be completely tender to the middle; test with the tip of a sharp knife.

Tip them on to a clean tea towel and gently pat them to soak up excess water. Immediately put them into a bowl and, while they are still hot, add half the olive oil and all the lemon juice. Season.

Mix the yogurt with the garlic, the rest of the oil, the dill, mustard, salt and pepper. You can thin this sauce further by adding water or milk (I love buttermilk in it, if I have any in the fridge). Either pour the sauce on to the leeks and leave it, or gently toss the leeks in the sauce. Either way, sprinkle with sumac just before serving.

spring menu clean and hot

rice paper rolls with nuoc cham | japanese rice bowl | fruits with mint and rose

This is a particularly good menu for serving to friends who fret about their weight. It's light and bright but still filling, and has all those 'front-of-mouth' zingy flavours that you really need if you are watching what you eat (the thrill comes from strong flavours, rather than the satisfaction you get from rich, starch-heavy dishes). The rice bowl has filling raw fish and 'good' carbs and the whole meal is beautiful to look at. For an alternative pudding, serve Citrus compote with ginger snow (see page 200).

rice paper rolls with nuoc cham

The Vietnamese dipping sauce, nuoc cham, is addictive. These look lovely but are a bit of a fiddle; worth it if you have friends for dinner, though. Be patient as you put them together. I often eat the filling on its own as a main course, with the dipping sauce and warm brown rice or rice noodles.

SERVES 6 (MAKES 18)

FOR THE ROLLS

18 rice paper wrappers

150g (5½oz) cooked, shelled and deveined prawns (ideally organic)

100g (3½oz) Iceberg lettuce, shredded

75g (2¾oz) carrot, in matchsticks

1 cheek of peeled green mango, cut in batons (optional but lovely)

40g (1½oz) beansprouts

leaves from 10g (¼oz) each of mint, basil and coriander

FOR THE NUOC CHAM

4 garlic cloves, chopped

1 red chilli, deseeded, chopped

6 tsp caster sugar

juice of 2 limes, or as needed

6 tbsp fish sauce

Put the rice papers, two or three at a time, into a bowl of water and let them soften for a few seconds. Don't leave them soaking or they will become too sticky to handle. Lift them out on to a damp tea towel. Leave them to dry a little and become flexible; they should look dimpled. If you try to roll them before they are ready, they will split.

Everything else for the rolls is their filling. Making sure each roll gets some of all the components, lay some filling down the centre of each roll. Wet your hands so they don't stick to the paper, then roll the paper tightly round the filling, tucking in the sides as you go. Put them on a plate as you finish them, seam-side down, and cover with damp kitchen paper. If you're not going to serve them immediately, they will sit fine for about 12 hours in the fridge.

To make the nuoc cham, put the garlic and chilli into a mortar and pound them with the pestle. Gradually add the sugar, lime juice and fish sauce, pounding as you do so.

Serve the rice paper rolls with the dipping sauce.

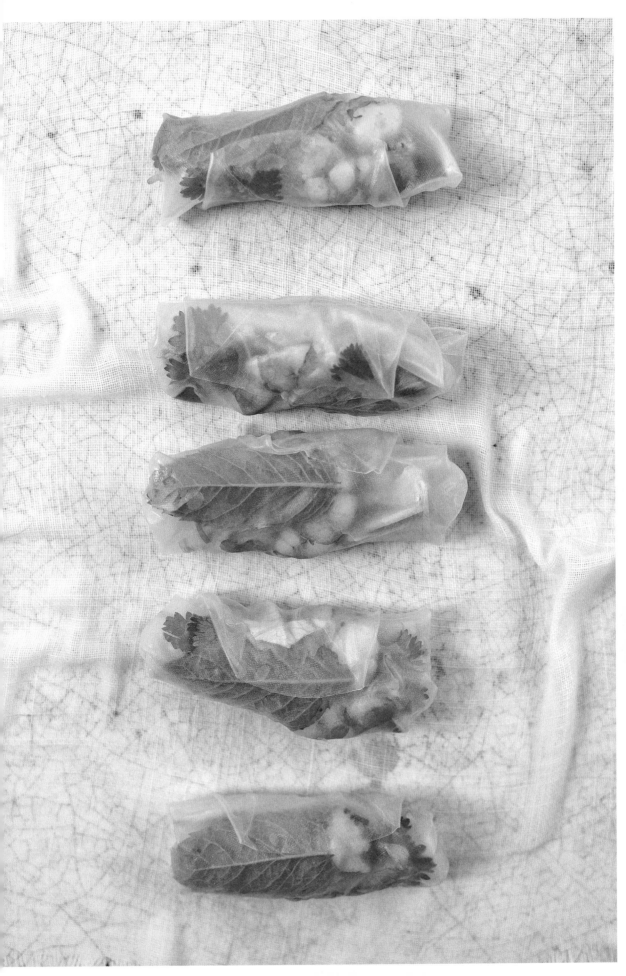

japanese rice bowl

Rice bowls are common dishes in Japan. Generally they have warm, simmered ingredients spooned over the top, such as braised beef. They are called 'donburi', which is both the name of the bowl in which they are served and also of the dish. This is a modern interpretation and a perfect recipe if you are watching both weight and health, with its whole grain rice, vegetables and raw fish. And the flavour is satisfyingly strong, because of the dressing. It also seems, perhaps because it is a beautiful dish, very centring to eat. There's nothing to cut or wrestle with. It's just you, simple food, a bowl and some chopsticks.

Make it spicy by adding chilli to the dressing, or serving wasabi on the side.

SERVES 6

FOR THE DRESSING
juice of 3 limes
3 tbsp rice vinegar
3 tbsp caster sugar
1½ tbsp tamari soy sauce

FOR THE RICE BOWL
375g (13oz) brown rice
150g (5½oz) edamame beans
150g (5½oz) sugar snap peas
½ ridge cucumber (ideally a thin one), or regular cucumber
525g (1lb 3oz) very fresh sushi-grade tuna
40g (1¼oz) pea shoots
6 spring onions, trimmed and chopped on the diagonal
4½ tbsp pickled ginger slices
2 tbsp black sesame seeds

Make the dressing by mixing all the ingredients together.

Cook the brown rice in plenty of boiling water until it is tender (it will still have a little bite in the centre of each grain), then drain and immediately stir in half the dressing. Cook the edamame and sugar snaps in boiling water for about two minutes, then drain and run cold water through them. Halve the sugar snaps lengthways.

Half-peel the cucumber (so it has stripes down it), halve and scoop out the seeds. Cut the flesh into slices about ½cm (¼in) thick.

Cut the tuna into slices about 3mm (⅛in) thick. Divide the rice between six bowls and top with the beans and sugar snaps, the cucumber, tuna, pea shoots and spring onions. Spoon the rest of the dressing over the top and add the ginger and sesame seeds. Serve immediately.

ringing the changes… The variations on this are endless and you can make really pretty combinations. Crunch is nice, so a version with matchsticks of carrots, beansprouts and radishes is good. You can also add fried tofu with soy sauce, purple-sprouting broccoli, fried shiitake or oyster mushrooms, slivers of avocado, raw salmon or mackerel, or cooked chicken. And while it isn't authentic, I sometimes use a South-east Asian dressing rather than a Japanese one (see page 103).

fruits with mint and rose

This is scented, but you can change the scent. Use orange flower water instead of rose, or basil or lemon thyme instead of mint (leave out the flower water if using the different herbs). And of course use whatever fruits are in season and available. They just all have to be ripe and in perfect condition. Try to cut the fruit irregularly. A bowl of chunks looks, well, just like a bowl of chunks…

SERVES 6

FOR THE SYRUP

175 (6oz) granulated sugar

2 broad strips of lime zest, plus the juice of 2 limes

leaves from a small bunch of mint, plus small sprigs of mint to serve (optional)

2 tsp rose water, or to taste

FOR THE FRUITS

1 large orange or 1 pink grapefruit

½ small pineapple, carefully peeled, core and 'eyes' removed, cut into small pieces

½ just-ripe mango, peeled, pitted and cut into irregular pieces

½ small Charentais or Ogen melon, skinned and deseeded, cut into cubes or small slices

12 lychees, peeled and carefully pitted (or you can use drained canned fruit)

little rose petals, to serve (optional)

To make the syrup, put the sugar in a pan, pour in 450ml (16fl oz) of water and add the lime zest. Slowly bring to the boil, stirring from time to time to help the sugar dissolve. Boil for four minutes. Remove from the heat, add the lime juice and mint leaves and leave to cool. Once it's cold, add the rose water a little at a time, they vary in strength and you don't want this too scented. Strain out the mint leaves.

Cut a slice off the bottom and top of the citrus fruit so it has a flat base on which to sit. Using a very sharp knife, cut off the peel and pith, working around the fruit and cutting it away in broad strips from top to bottom. Working over a bowl, slip a sharp fine-bladed knife in between the membrane on either side of each segment and ease it out. (If you don't want to do this, just slice the citrus fruits into rounds, but don't make them too thick and use a sharp knife. Flick out all the seeds you see.)

Put all the fruit into a large bowl – or individual bowls – and add enough syrup to coat it. (You don't want to drown it.) Chill before serving with sprigs of mint or rose petals, if you like.

spring barley couscous with harissa and buttermilk sauce

A dish that is so full of young vegetables it could have come out of Mr McGregor's garden. It is also very good made with two-thirds barley couscous and one-third pearl barley (see page 223 for how to cook that). Just toss the two together once cooked or plumped up. It is excellent with a pot-roast chicken (use the cooking juices instead of the stock here as your broth and mix the harissa with it).

Belazu sell barley couscous and it has a slightly different flavour to the wheat version (see page 328 for where you can buy it). It is one of a variety of couscous products; there is also wholemeal couscous and kamut couscous. For any couscous, just pour boiling water or stock over, cover and leave for 15 minutes. As a general rule, use 270ml (9½fl oz) liquid to 200g (7oz) couscous to serve four people as a side dish, but with an important caveat: you'll need less liquid if you are adding 'wet' ingredients, such as tomatoes, to the couscous. Finish with olive oil and seasoning and fork through to aerate the couscous grains.

SERVES 8 AS A SIDE DISH, 4 AS A MAIN COURSE

FOR THE COUSCOUS

200g (7oz) broad beans, podded weight

300g (10½oz) barley couscous

2 tbsp extra virgin olive oil, plus more to serve

finely grated zest of 1 lemon, removed with a zester, plus a generous squeeze of lemon juice

salt and pepper

200g (7oz) baby carrots

200g (7oz) peas, podded weight

200g (7oz) baby leeks

1 tbsp roughly chopped flat-leaf parsley leaves

350ml (12fl oz) vegetable or chicken stock

1–2 tsp harissa (have more to hand)

FOR THE BUTTERMILK SAUCE

½ onion, finely chopped

½ tbsp olive oil

½ tsp ground cumin

300ml (½ pint) buttermilk

2 tbsp Greek yogurt

2 tbsp chopped coriander leaves

Cook the broad beans in boiling water until just tender, five to seven minutes. Drain. When the broad beans are cool enough to handle, slip off their skins (laborious – it really is time-consuming – but worth it).

Put the barley couscous in a bowl and cover with 400ml (14fl oz) of boiling water. Add the extra virgin oil, lemon juice and salt and pepper. Cover with cling film and leave to plump up in the water for 15 minutes.

Meanwhile, cook the rest of the vegetables. Simmer the carrots and peas in separate pans until tender; the carrots will take about 15 minutes, the peas about seven. Quickly steam the leeks for four minutes, then immediately drain them into a colander and run cold water over them to keep them a bright colour.

Meanwhile, make the buttermilk sauce. Sauté the onion in the regular olive oil until soft but not coloured. Add the cumin and cook for a minute, then add the buttermilk, yogurt and seasoning. Heat but don't boil, then season and add the coriander.

Put the broad beans in a colander and run boiling water through them to reheat. Fork through the couscous to fluff it up, add the lemon zest and parsley and put it on a serving platter. Arrange all the hot vegetables on top and drizzle with extra virgin oil.

Bring the stock to the boil, add the harissa and serve this in a jug or bowl with a small ladle or spoon. Serve the warm buttermilk sauce on the side as well.

beautiful broccoli

Brassicas, along with watercress, are the foods there seems to be the most agreement on among nutritionists and doctors. They are – quite simply – really good for you. As well as being packed full of vitamins C and K, they contain minerals and phytochemicals that are believed to have a strong anti-cancer action, as well as an anti-inflammatory effect that may help reduce the risk of heart disease and stroke. You can never have too many ideas for how to cook broccoli, so here's a bunch of suggestions. I prefer purple-sprouting to any other kind, but eat the regular type the rest of the year.

jersey royals, purple-sprouting broccoli, quail's eggs, anchovy cream

This is lovely with salmon, or serve it with another vegetable dish to make a main course. (And add a bunch of radishes. This is wonderful served with radishes. Pure spring). The sauce is also great with roast peppers; it's the salty anchovies against the sweet peppers that is so good.

SERVES 6 AS A SIDE DISH

1 tbsp olive oil

3 shallots, finely sliced lengthways

12 quail's eggs

350g (12oz) Jersey Royals

salt and pepper

400g (14oz) purple-sprouting broccoli

2 tbsp extra virgin olive oil (a light one)

1 tbsp lemon juice

2 tbsp very finely chopped flat-leaf parsley leaves

FOR THE ANCHOVY CREAM

55g can anchovies in olive oil

2 garlic cloves

55g (2oz) pine nuts or blanched almonds

100ml (3½fl oz) extra virgin olive oil (fruity or buttery rather than grassy)

juice of ½ lemon, or to taste

Heat the regular olive oil in a frying pan and gently sauté the shallots until they are soft but not coloured.

Hard-boil the quail's eggs for four minutes, then drain.

To make the garlic and anchovy cream, put the anchovies, garlic and nuts into a food processor. Turn it on and start adding the extra virgin oil in a steady stream. Taste, add the lemon juice, then taste again. You want a mixture that has the texture of double cream so, if it seems too thick, add some water to let it down.

Boil the Jersey Royals in lightly salted water until tender.

Meanwhile, trim the base of each stalk of broccoli – they can be a little dry and rough – then steam them, timing them to be ready at the same time as the potatoes.

Drain the potatoes and gently mix them in a bowl with the broccoli, extra virgin oil, lemon juice, parsley, sautéed shallots, salt and pepper.

Peel and halve the eggs and gently mix into the other ingredients. Drizzle on some anchovy cream (don't drown the dish, serve the rest in a jug). Serve warm, as it is, or at room temperature.

broccoli, second helpings

These recipes are easy but, I hope, unexpected. When purple-sprouting broccoli is out of season, substitute Tenderstem or regular broccoli.

FOR THE PURPLE-SPROUTING
WITH RICOTTA

300g (10½oz) purple-sprouting
broccoli

175g (6oz) ricotta

50g (1¾oz) Parmesan

finely grated zest of ½ lemon,
plus the juice of 1

salt and pepper

8 tbsp extra virgin olive oil

FOR THE BROCCOLI
STRASCINATI

3 tbsp extra virgin olive oil, plus
more to serve

450g (1lb) broccoli or
purple-sprouting broccoli

3 garlic cloves, finely chopped

½ tsp chilli flakes

squeeze of lemon juice

FOR THE PURPLE-SPROUTING
WITH CHINESE FLAVOURS

450g (1lb) purple-sprouting
broccoli

2 garlic cloves, finely sliced

2cm (¾in) root ginger, peeled
and shredded

1 tbsp groundnut oil

2 spring onions, finely chopped

6 tbsp oyster sauce

purple-sprouting with ricotta, lemon and parmesan

Light and unfussy, so you can really taste the broccoli. You can also treat asparagus this way. Trim the broccoli stalks at the base if they need it – they may be a little dry – and steam until just tender, four to five minutes. Meanwhile, break the ricotta into lumps and shave the Parmesan with a vegetable peeler. Put the hot broccoli on plates and dot with the ricotta. Sprinkle on the lemon zest and spoon over the juice. Season. Scatter Parmesan over each serving, drizzle with the oil and serve. Serves 4 as a starter or side dish.

broccoli strascinati

Heat the extra virgin oil in a frying pan and add the broccoli (in florets if it's regular, the whole stems if it's purple-sprouting). Cook for six to eight minutes, until lightly browned. Add 3 tbsp of water and the garlic. Cook gently until the water disappears, then add the chilli flakes and cook until the broccoli is just tender and the garlic golden. Season and serve with a little more extra virgin oil and the lemon juice. Serves 6 as a side dish.

stir-fried purple-sprouting with chinese flavours

Steam the broccoli until only just tender. Meanwhile, sauté the garlic and ginger in the oil until golden and soft. Add the broccoli, spring onions and oyster sauce. Gently heat through and serve with brown rice. Serves 6 as a side dish.

also try... Toss cooked broccoli with Puy lentils or strips of roast red pepper and drizzle with Anchovy cream or Tahini dressing (see opposite and page 135).

Stir steamed broccoli into Kale pesto with wholewheat linguine (see page 282) for a double hit of brilliant brassicas.

Add a little more chilli to Calabrian pesto (see page 282) and serve steamed broccoli with this, or toss both with wholewheat linguine.

crab with chilli and garlic

Of course you can eat crab cold, but it does make me reach for the mayo (and rather a lot of mayo). And you don't always want it cold. This is a real treat for four (or use just one crab and have it as a special meal for two). You can buy ready-cooked crab for it, but I prefer to cook it myself and deal with warm crabs. To dispatch the crabs humanely, have a look at how the redoubtable Mitch Tonks does it (www.mitchtonks.co.uk/recipes/south-devon-crab). Serve this with a green salad and some good sourdough bread.

SERVES 4

2 medium-sized live crabs

sea salt and pepper

2 tbsp extra virgin olive oil (fruity rather than grassy), plus a splash more to serve

1–2 red chillies, deseeded and chopped, depending on how hot you want it

2 garlic cloves, finely chopped

1 lemon, plus lemon wedges to serve

leaves from a small bunch (15g/½oz) of flat-leaf parsley, roughly chopped

Fill a very big saucepan, large enough to take both crabs, with water. Bring to the boil and add 1 tbsp of salt. Put the crabs in, return to the boil and cook for 15 minutes, then lift them out.

When the crabs are cool enough to handle, put them on their backs on a chopping board and pull the legs and claws off. Remove and discard the triangular- or wedge-shaped tail flap and ease the top and bottom of the shell apart (you might need to insert a knife and twist it to help you). Remove and discard the stomach sac (you'll find it behind the mouth) and the translucent white/pale green, pointed gills ('deadman's fingers'). Scoop the brown meat out of the upper shell and place in a bowl. Split the body in half by giving it a good whack with something heavy. Carefully remove all the white meat (you will need a proper crab pick or skewer to get all the meat out of the internal tunnels). Give the claws one blow each to crack them enough for the chilli and garlic flavours to penetrate (the back of a cleaver is good for this).

Heat the extra virgin oil in a large frying or sauté pan, then add the chillies and garlic. Cook gently for a few minutes, then add the brown crab meat, the claws and the legs. Heat through, then add the white meat, seasoning, a good squeeze of lemon juice and the parsley. Add another good splash of the extra virgin oil. Serve immediately with lemon wedges. You'll need something heavy at the table for people to crack the legs with. Supply lots of paper napkins too, it's messy eating.

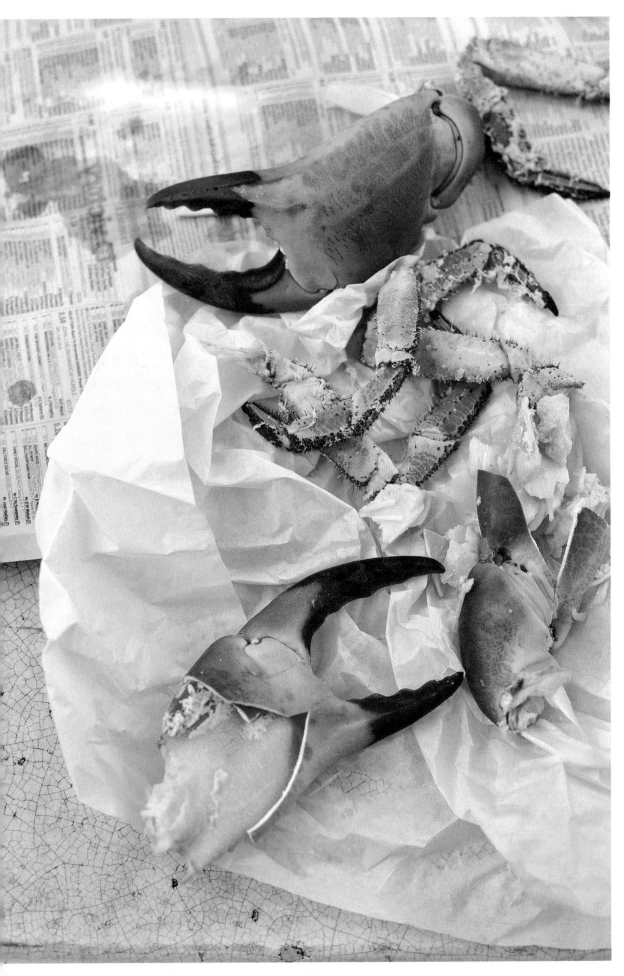

salmon tartare with pickled cucumber and rye crackers

Fresh Scandinavian fare. If you don't want to make rye crackers, serve rye bread or a spelt salad tossed with watercress (see page 224 for how to cook spelt). This recipe makes more rye crackers than you need, but there's no point not making a decent-sized batch. When I'm cooking for myself I eat the salmon tartare on its own with just rye crackers or salad, but if I'm doing it for friends I add the dilled yogurt, too.

SERVES 4

FOR THE RYE CRACKERS

250g (9oz) rye flour, plus more to dust

1 tsp salt

1 tsp soft light brown sugar

½ tsp baking powder

25g (¾oz) cold butter, cut into cubes

150ml (5fl oz) whole milk

FOR THE SWEET AND SOUR CUCUMBER

1 cucumber

1 tbsp sea salt flakes

2 tbsp rice vinegar

2 tbsp caster sugar

1 tbsp chopped dill fronds

FOR THE SALMON AND DILLED YOGURT

200g (7oz) salmon fillet, skinned

1 tbsp capers, rinsed, patted dry and finely chopped

1 small shallot, very finely chopped

2 tbsp very finely chopped flat-leaf parsley leaves

1 tbsp lemon juice

2 tbsp extra virgin olive oil

freshly ground black pepper

6 tbsp Greek yogurt

¼ tbsp chopped dill fronds

For the rye crackers, preheat the oven to 200°C/400°F/gas mark 6. Lightly flour a large – or two medium – non-stick baking sheets.

Put the flour, salt, sugar, baking powder and butter into a bowl and rub the butter in with your fingertips. Using a butter knife, mix in the milk, then use your hands to pull everything together into a soft dough. It will be sticky but don't panic, it will get easier to work with, so resist adding more flour.

Lightly dust a work surface with flour, then roll chunks of the dough into very thin, irregular rounds. These need to be thinner than any pastry you have ever made, basically thinner than you can measure. As you form each cracker, transfer it to the prepared baking sheet(s). Prick a few holes in each of the rounds with the tines of a fork. Bake for 10 minutes; do keep an eye on them as they burn very easily. Transfer the crackers to a wire rack as soon as they are cool enough to handle and leave until cold.

For the sweet and sour cucumber, cut the ends off the cucumber and peel it. Halve it lengthways and scoop out the seeds with a teaspoon (discard them). Cut the flesh into very fine – almost transparent – slices, either across the cucumber or lengthways so that you end up with ribbons. Layer in a colander with the salt, place a plate on top and set over a bowl so the juices can run out. Leave for two hours. Rinse the cucumber and carefully pat dry. Mix the cucumber with the rest of the ingredients and keep, covered, in the fridge until you are ready to serve.

To make the salmon tartare, cut the salmon flesh into really small dice, about 5mm (¼in) square. Put this in a bowl with the capers, shallot, parsley, lemon juice, oil and pepper. Mix and taste; you will probably find you don't need salt because of the lemon and capers. Cover and chill in the fridge. Mix the yogurt with the dill.

Serve the salmon tartare with the dilled yogurt, cucumber salad and rye crackers.

white fish, saffron and dill couscous pilaf

This recipe really is a boon. It is made in the time it takes couscous to plump up in hot stock (15 minutes), so it's a wonderful supper after a long day, or an unusual midweek dish for friends. When they're in season, broad beans (slip the skins off after cooking), are a lovely addition to the dish, though they make it more labour intensive.

SERVES 4

1 tbsp olive oil

1 onion, finely chopped

2 garlic cloves, finely chopped

4 cardamom pods, crushed

200g (7oz) wholemeal couscous

275ml (9½fl oz) fish stock

⅛ tsp saffron stamens

400g (14oz) white fish fillet (cod, haddock, gurnard, pollack), skinned

salt and pepper

juice of ½ lemon

4 tbsp chopped dill fronds

1½ tbsp chopped pistachios

a few golden rose petals, torn

Heat the olive oil in a saucepan and sauté the onion until it is soft but not coloured. Add the garlic and cook for another two minutes, then add the cardamom pods and cook for another minute. Add the couscous and stir it round in the oil. Remove from the heat.

In another pan, bring the fish stock to the boil and add the saffron, stirring. Reduce the heat to a very gentle simmer and add the fish. Poach gently for about four minutes (it will cook more when it is mixed with the couscous). Lift the fish out with a slotted spoon and break it up into big chunks.

Return the stock to the boil, then pour it on to the couscous, season and fork through. Place the fish on top, cover with foil and a lid. Leave for 15 minutes.

Carefully fork through the lemon juice, dill and pistachios. Put this into a warm serving dish and sprinkle the rose petals on top. Serve immediately.

plenty more fish... You don't have to make this only with white fish. You can change its character and make it with mackerel instead – it's oilier and richer – and use coriander and toasted hazelnuts instead of dill and pistachios. Leave out the roses in colder weather and instead add some dried barberries or a handful of chopped dried apricots or raisins. Some shreds of preserved lemon zest would be great in this, too.

you can go everywhere on an egg

As a child I used to have eggs, shelled and mashed with a knob of butter which melted into them, in a tea cup. They were my ultimate comfort food. Then, suddenly, we were forbidden eggs because their yolks contain cholesterol. A wilderness of uncertainty set in; most of us didn't know whether we should eat eggs or not. Now it's increasingly accepted that eating cholesterol doesn't lead to heart disease and eggs are back (mine mashed in a tea cup). Some still think you shouldn't eat them with abandon, but you wouldn't want to as they're so filling (a brilliant source of protein, the macronutrient that best satisfies hunger). When I'm sick of fancy food, an egg (and a pink grapefruit) is what I want. A pleasing lunch is a warm boiled egg broken up with a fork, seasoned, drizzled with olive oil, with tomatoes or purple-sprouting alongside. Or chop warm hard-boiled eggs and stir into a vinaigrette with herbs and capers; good with greens and fish. And there are a million more ways to eat them... they're great with spices and smoked salt, earthy with pulses, an endless provider of easy meals. And, of course, they are excellent for going to work on.

good son-in-law eggs

In authentic son-in-law eggs, hard-boiled eggs are fried before being sauced. It contributes to the texture, but I'll forego that to eat something that hasn't been fried and yet offers wonderful contrasts. These are eggs you would give a good son-in-law (because you want him to be healthy).

SERVES 8

8 eggs

2 tbsp groundnut oil

6 shallots, finely sliced

2 tbsp tamarind paste

2 tbsp fish sauce

2 tbsp soft light brown sugar

3 tbsp chopped coriander leaves

2 red chillies, deseeded and finely chopped

Hard-boil the eggs for seven minutes, drain, and leave sitting in the warm pan with a lid on.

Meanwhile, heat the oil and cook the shallots over a medium heat until golden and slightly crispy. Set half aside. To the other half add the tamarind, fish sauce, sugar and 100ml (3½fl oz) of water. Bring to the boil and cook for about three minutes; the sauce will reduce and become slightly syrupy.

Shell the eggs and put them in bowls. Spoon some sauce over and scatter with the remaining shallots, the coriander and chillies.

You are supposed to serve these with jasmine rice (and they are fab) but they're also good with brown rice. I love to top the rice with stir-fried greens or baby spinach or watercress (the leaves wilt in the heat of the sauce), to make a more complete meal.

japanese lessons

For me, discovering Japanese food was like being a reasonably good painter who suddenly finds a whole school of artists whose work is breathtaking. I had never looked beyond sushi when I won a haiku competition, the prize for which was a meal in a Michelin-starred Japanese restaurant in London. Going to Umu was like unlocking a secret. First, I literally couldn't find the way in. There didn't appear to be a door, though I knew I had the right address. I had to stand on the other side of the street and watch to see how other diners entered. One eventually came along, waved his hand over a sunken panel and the door opened. It was prophetic.

Umu is expensive but not glitzy. It is serene. The Japanese food experts I was with did the ordering… and it was a revelation. Each dish, served on plates and bowls of various textures, had a kind of quiet perfection, a completeness. There were expensive 'wow' dishes such as wagyu beef (which redefines the term 'melting') and a trembling custard of crab and ginger, but the dish I adored was the most simple: dashi, Japanese stock, with tofu that the chef had made himself. The tofu was like silk; the dashi like a liquid that had washed over seashells. As this meal went on, I became more and more happy. The best thing I get from my time in the kitchen is a gentle joy that things work, that dishes balance, come out harmoniously. But my cooking has big flavours and bright colours. Here was food that was quiet, that you approached in a micro eating style – you homed in on each texture, each colour – the tingle of a shiso leaf, the heat of a dab of wasabi. Appropriately, it was like eating a series of haiku.

You might think this was because I was in a Michelin-starred restaurant but, some months later, I dined with – and took cooking instruction from – a Japanese food photographer called Yuki Sugiura. It was a drab day, filled with pewter-coloured drizzle. Yuki is not quiet and Zen-like – she is warm and excitable – yet her flat had the same peace as the restaurant. There was a big jug of rosehips on the table and the place was uncluttered. I sat down to another meal where texture, colour, taste and balance were key. There was freshly made dashi, an octopus salad with rice vinegar, carrots with a black sesame paste that Yuki had energetically pounded in a *suribachi* (a Japanese mortar), crunchy sweet-pickled lotus root, a wooden drum of warm rice. The incredible thing, though, was the cooked chrysanthemums. They are a much-loved seasonal treat in Japan, so I sat on a rainy day in south London at a table redolent with the flavours, textures and colours of a Japanese autumn.

There are only a few Japanese dishes in this book – and they have been changed to suit my kitchen – but I urge you to try more. In its use of vegetables and fish it's a very healthy cuisine. And there is something in Japanese cooking that you can apply in your kitchen no matter what you're making; it's a particular psychological approach to food. There is an intense appreciation of detail. One of the tenets of Japanese cooking is to try to have balance across a meal. The ideal is to have five colours within one meal. Texture is vital and that doesn't just come from the foods themselves, but from the way they are cooked.

Again, the Japanese ideal is to include five different cooking methods in one meal, so you might have griddled, poached, steamed, braised and fried food all at once. I'm not suggesting you specifically do this, of course, but that you think about the various components of a meal, bearing in mind a contrasting variety of colours and textures.

There are also considerations of setting and attitude. I read about these in *Washoku*, a fascinating cookbook by Elizabeth Andoh, an American who went to live in Japan. Two rather elevated phrases, coined by Sen no Rikyū, the sixteenth century philosopher credited with refining the world of tea and the food served at the tea ceremony, sounded worth considering in all cooking. The first is *ichi go, ichi é* (one moment, one meeting) which is about creating pleasure at one particular meal, a fleeting but special experience of shared cooking and eating. The other, which rings even truer to me, is *wabi sabi* (charm of the ordinary), which is about the wonder of turning humble foodstuffs into simple but lovely meals (something that makes me happy on a daily basis).

All this is the antithesis of the worst Western eating where, starving and mindless, you sink your teeth hungrily into a fast food burger. I'm not saying we should all become Zen about food or try to apply Japanese culinary principles, but once you start cooking with more vegetables, leaves and grains there is a spirit in Japanese cooking – the attention to colour and texture – that makes you produce better food, and makes you eat it in a more mindful way. Eating is not just about sating appetite but about appreciating, with all your senses, what is put before you, and honouring the ingredients with which it is made. I know this sounds a little bit Californian for we no-nonsense and rather cynical Brits, but there is more to cooking and eating than ingredients and skill; there is an attitude that can make everything you serve, and everything you put in your mouth, taste better. And when you approach food this way, you eat less of it and you appreciate it more.

Now, if I could tap a little Japanese gong near your ear and give you a plateful of autumn chrysanthemums, I would.

teriyaki salmon with pickled vegetables and sesame seeds

I could live on this. It's so easy and yet utterly beautiful looking, I always feel better after eating it. The pickled vegetables are a great thing to know about. Make extra and keep them in the fridge for eating at lunch. You can make this dish with mackerel and chicken fillets too (chicken needs to be cooked for 20 minutes).

SERVES 4

FOR THE SALMON

4 tbsp soy sauce

1 tbsp caster sugar

2 tbsp mirin

1 tbsp dry sherry

4 x 125g (4½oz) salmon fillets

2 tsp black sesame seeds

FOR THE VEGETABLES

100ml (3½fl oz) rice vinegar

1 tbsp caster sugar

125g (4½oz) cucumber, halved and deseeded

2 small carrots, peeled

4 radishes, trimmed and cut into wafer-thin slices

100g (3½oz) mooli (daikon), peeled

½ tsp salt

1 tbsp pickled ginger (plus whatever liquid clings to it)

5g (⅙oz) microleaves

For the salmon, mix the soy sauce, sugar, mirin and sherry and stir to dissolve the sugar. Put the fish in this, turn to coat, cover and put in the fridge to marinate for 30 minutes.

To make the vegetables, heat the vinegar and stir in the sugar until it dissolves. Set aside to cool. (Or, if you are in a hurry, you can just whisk together the vinegar and sugar in a bowl until the sugar has dissolved.) Keeping them separate, cut the cucumber, carrots, radishes and mooli into matchsticks, each about 5cm (2in) long. Sprinkle the salt on the cucumber and put it into a colander for 10 minutes, Rinse and pat dry, then add all the vegetables to the vinegar mixture and toss to combine.

When you're ready to cook the fish, preheat the oven to 180°C/350°F/gas mark 4. Bake the salmon, in its marinade, for 12 minutes; it will remain moist and only just cooked in the middle. Sprinkle with the black sesame seeds. Add the pickled ginger and microleaves to the vegetables, toss and serve with the salmon. Offer rice on the side.

japanese ginger and garlic chicken with smashed cucumber

This dish has a great interplay of temperatures. The chicken is hot and spicy, the cucumber like eating shards of ice (make sure you serve it direct from the fridge). The cucumber recipe is adapted from a recipe in a wonderful American book called *Japanese Farm Food* by Nancy Singleton Hachisu. You can also make the chicken with boneless thighs and griddle them.

SERVES 4

FOR THE CHICKEN

3½ tbsp soy sauce

3 tbsp sake or dry sherry

3 tbsp soft dark brown sugar

½ tbsp brown miso

60g (2oz) root ginger, peeled and finely grated

4 garlic cloves, finely grated

1 tsp togarashi seasoning (available in Waitrose), or ½ tsp chilli powder

8 good-sized skinless bone-in chicken thighs, or other bone-in chicken pieces

FOR THE CUCUMBER

500g (1lb 2oz) cucumber

2 garlic cloves, roughly chopped

2 tsp sea salt

2 tbsp pink pickled ginger, very finely shredded

small handful of shiso leaves, if available, or mint leaves, torn (optional)

Mix everything for the chicken (except the chicken itself) to make a marinade. Pierce the chicken on the fleshy sides with a knife, put the pieces into a shallow dish and pour the marinade over. Massage it in well, turning the pieces over. Cover and put in the fridge for 30–60 minutes.

When you're ready to cook, preheat the oven to 180°C/350°F/gas mark 4. Take the pieces out of the marinade and put them in a shallow ovenproof dish in which they can sit snugly in a single layer. Pour over half the marinade. Roast in the oven for 40 minutes, basting every so often with the juices and leftover marinade (don't add any leftover marinade after 20 minutes, it needs to cook properly as it has had raw chicken in it). Check for doneness: the juices that run out of the chicken when you pierce the flesh with a knife should be clear and not at all pink.

When the chicken is halfway through cooking, peel and halve the cucumber and scoop out the seeds. Set on a board and bang the pieces gently with a pestle or rolling pin. This should break them up a little. Now break them into chunks with your hands.

Crush the garlic with a pinch of the salt and massage this – and the rest of the salt – into the cucumber. Put in a small plastic bag, squeeze out the air and put in the fridge for 10 minutes. When you're ready to eat, tip the cucumber into a sieve so the juices can drain away. Add the shredded ginger. You can add shiso leaves if you can find them (I can't, I have no Japanese shop nearby). Nothing else really tastes like it, but I sometimes add mint. Serve the chicken with brown rice or rice vermicelli (the rice vermicelli is good served cold) and the cucumber.

try this with… **edamame and sugar snap salad** Mix 2 tbsp white miso paste, 1 tbsp rice vinegar, 2 tbsp groundnut oil, 2 tbsp water, 1 tsp runny honey and 2cm (¾in) peeled, grated root ginger. Toss with 100g (3½oz) cooked edamame beans, 100g (3½oz) raw sugar snap peas, sliced lengthways, 8 sliced radishes and a handful of mizuna. Serves 4.

smoky poussins with hot pepper purée and bitter leaves

This dish depends on contrast: hot poussins, cold yogurt, sweet pepper, bitter leaves. So do try to use the right kind of salad leaves. You can also make this with eight chicken thighs instead of poussins; just cook them on a hot griddle pan until golden and cooked through.

SERVES 4

FOR THE CHICKEN

4 poussins

2 tsp cayenne pepper

3 tsp smoked paprika

juice of 1 lemon

7 tbsp olive oil

leaves from 4 sprigs of thyme

4 garlic cloves, crushed

200g Greek yogurt

1 tbsp extra virgin olive oil

FOR THE PURÉE

2 red peppers

olive oil

salt and pepper

1 red chilli, deseeded
and chopped

juice of ½ lemon

½ tbsp sherry vinegar

1 garlic clove

4 tbsp extra virgin olive oil,
plus more to serve

FOR THE SALAD

3 tbsp extra virgin olive oil

1 tbsp lemon juice

75g (2¾oz) bitter salad leaves,
such as frisee (use the lighter,
less coarse bits from the middle),
chicory, dandelions, whatever you
can get

Put the poussins in an ovenproof, non-reactive dish. Mix the spices, lemon juice, regular olive oil, thyme and three of the crushed garlic cloves, pour this over the poussins and turn to coat. Cover and put in the fridge for at least an hour.

To make the purée, preheat the oven to 190°C/375°F/gas mark 5. Cut the peppers in half and take out the seeds. Put into a roasting tin and drizzle with a little regular olive oil. Season. Roast in the oven for 40 minutes, or until completely soft and charred in places. Remove from the oven. Reduce the oven temperature to 180°C/350°F/gas mark 4. Lift the poussins out of the marinade, shaking off excess, then roast for 45–50 minutes, until cooked through (check by inserting a knife tip between leg and breast; the juices that emerge should run clear with no trace of pink).

Put the roast peppers into a food processor with their cooking juices, adding the chilli, lemon juice, sherry vinegar, garlic, extra virgin oil, salt and pepper. Whizz to a thick, coarse purée, then taste and check for seasoning. Put it into a serving bowl.

Put the yogurt into a serving bowl and add the remaining crushed garlic clove, 2 tbsp of water and the 1 tbsp of extra virgin oil.

For the salad mix the extra virgin oil, lemon juice and salt and pepper together and toss with the leaves. Serve the poussins with the salad, yogurt and pepper purée.

Eat with wholemeal flatbread or whole grains (try kamut for a change, see page 224 for more about it, and how to cook it), with chopped coriander or flat-leaf parsley leaves stirred in, dressed with extra virgin oil and lemon juice.

try adding... saffron Just heat ¼ tsp saffron stamens in the oil and lemon and mix in the other marinade ingredients. Smoked paprika and saffron are great together.

spring menu english spring, reconsidered

shaved vegetables with lemon and olive oil | salmon with baby leeks | blueberry and gin jellies

When spring comes, our eating definitely changes. We want food that feels pure and clean, such as this, a pared-back meal built around what is perhaps the quintessential British spring and summer ingredient: salmon. But salmon is often served with mayo or hollandaise, accompaniments so rich they can actually upstage it and detract from its pureness. So here is salmon, reconsidered.

shaved vegetables with lemon and olive oil

This rather bewilders people. They eat it and say 'What's in this?' When I say vegetables, olive oil and lemon they don't believe me. You see, when you keep things simple you can taste some foods as if for the first time.

SERVES 8

FOR THE DRESSING

salt and pepper

pinch of caster sugar

1 tbsp white wine vinegar

1 garlic clove, crushed

4 tbsp extra virgin olive oil

½ tbsp finely chopped chives

FOR THE VEGETABLES

6 carrots, peeled (leave the green tuft at the top if it is very fresh)

100g (3½oz) French Breakfast radishes, washed and trimmed

2 small fennel bulbs

juice of 1 lemon

1 just-ripe avocado

1 small raw beetroot, peeled

To make the dressing, put the salt, pepper, sugar, vinegar and garlic into a small jug or cup and, using a fork, whisk in the extra virgin oil in a steady stream. Stir in the chives. Halve the carrots lengthways and cut into fine slices, either using a very sharp knife or a mandoline. There will be a little wastage as you have to choose your best slices to present; the first and last slices aren't usable. Trim the top from each radish and cut off the tail. Slice them very finely lengthways so you have thin, teardrop-shaped slices.

Halve the fennel and trim off the tops (discard the slightly dried-out tips, but set aside any little fronds). Using a very sharp knife or mandoline, cut the fennel into wafer-thin slices. Squeeze on some lemon juice to keep the fennel from discolouring. Cut the avocado in half and remove the stone. Cut the flesh into thin slices, then carefully peel off the skin from each piece. Squeeze lemon juice on the avocado as well.

Cut the beetroot using a mandoline – the slices need to be very thin – and arrange the vegetables prettily on eight plates, adding any fennel fronds. Drizzle some vinaigrette over each serving. Because beetroot starts to 'bleed' its crimson colour you need to be careful when assembling and serve immediately.

warm salad of salmon, baby leeks, parsley and capers

We are pretty wedded to serving potatoes with salmon, but you can replace them with barley or spelt (see pages 223–224 for how to cook those). Just dress the grain while warm with some extra virgin olive oil and lemon, salt and pepper, then toss with chopped parsley leaves.

SERVES 8

FOR THE DRESSING

5 tbsp extra virgin olive oil

smidgen of Dijon mustard

1 small garlic clove, crushed

salt and pepper

juice of ¼–½ lemon

FOR THE SALMON

800g (1lb 12oz) baby leeks

600g (1lb 5oz) baby new potatoes

2 tbsp groundnut oil

5 fillets of salmon, about 200g (7oz) each

8 eggs

4 tbsp extra virgin olive oil

juice of ½ lemon

3 tbsp capers, rinsed and patted dry

2 tbsp roughly chopped flat-leaf parsley leaves

To make the dressing, just whisk everything together with a fork, adding the smaller amount of lemon juice to start off with. Check the seasoning and add more lemon juice to taste.

If you want to serve the salad warm, you have to cook everything at the same time. Preheat the oven to 200°C/400°F/gas mark 6. Trim the leeks at the base and the top (be careful not to cut so much off the base that they won't hold together). Cook the potatoes in boiling salted water until tender, drain and leave in the pot with the lid on to keep them warm.

Brush a baking sheet with the groundnut oil. Put the fish fillets on this – not too close together – and cook for 12 minutes.

Meanwhile, boil the eggs for seven minutes and cook the leeks in boiling, lightly salted water for three or four minutes or until just tender. When the leeks are done, drain them really well, rinse immediately in cold water and pat dry. Put into a shallow bowl. Season well and immediately drizzle with some extra virgin oil and lemon juice (I know you have dressing on the side, but these look and taste better if you dress and season them a little now).

Add enough extra virgin oil and lemon to the potatoes to give them a bit of gloss, then season. When the eggs are cool enough to handle, shell them and cut in half.

Break the salmon fillets up, leaving them quite chunky, and discard the skin. Now lay all the elements on a platter, sprinkle on the capers and parsley and drizzle on the dressing (only as much as much as you need to dress it lightly). Serve immediately.

blueberry and gin jellies

Okay, it is boozy (sugar), but this is a 'treat' dish. You will probably think there's a lot of gelatine in the jelly, but alcohol inhibits the setting properties so you need more. The Angostura bitters isn't absolutely necessary but it makes the jelly a lovely pale pink colour and foxes diners… they can never guess the secret ingredient.

SERVES 8

400ml (14fl oz) tonic water

250ml (9fl oz) gin

finely grated zest and juice of 2 lemons (zest removed with a zester)

150g (5½oz) granulated sugar

16g (generous ½oz) leaf gelatine (9 small sheets)

1 tbsp Angostura bitters

250g (9oz) blueberries

Put the tonic water, gin, lemon zest and juice and sugar in a saucepan with 150ml (5fl oz) of water and bring to just below the boil, stirring occasionally to help the sugar dissolve. Reduce the heat to very low and simmer for about five minutes.

Put the gelatine into a dish and cover with cold water. Leave to soak for about three minutes; it will soften but won't disintegrate.

Strain the boozy mixture into a clear jug and add the Angostura bitters; you should end up with a nice pale pink colour. Taste; you should get a little of the Angostura but it shouldn't overwhelm. Remove the softened gelatine, shaking off any excess liquid, and add it to the warm liquid, stirring to help it dissolve. (The liquid needs to be warm to help the gelatine melt, but you shouldn't put gelatine into boiling or very hot liquid.)

Divide one-third of the liquid between eight glasses and add one-third of the blueberries. Leave to cool. Refrigerate the jellies to allow them to set and reserve the rest of the jelly mixture.

Once the jellies have a firm-ish surface, divide another one-third of the blueberries between the glasses and gently reheat half the remaining jelly mixture if necessary to render it liquid once more (you should always be able to put your finger into it; if the liquid gets too hot it will destroy the gelatine's setting qualities). Leave to cool a little and top up the glasses evenly with this. Put in the fridge to set. Repeat, to use up the remaining berries and jelly, then leave for six hours to set firm before serving, just to be on the safe side.

madrid-style baked bream

Bream is a great fish. One makes a good-sized portion, it has gorgeous sweet flesh and they look good, too, especially when treated very simply.

SERVES 4

4 x 300g (10½oz) bream, scaled, trimmed and cleaned

6 tbsp olive oil

juice of 1 lemon, plus lemon wedges to serve

salt and pepper

4 garlic cloves, crushed

25g (1oz) breadcrumbs

small handful of flat-leaf parsley leaves, finely chopped

extra virgin olive oil, to serve

Preheat the oven to 190°C/375°F/gas mark 5.

Brush the fish inside and out with the regular olive oil, squeeze on some lemon juice and season well. Lay the fish – in a single layer but close together – in an ovenproof dish. Toss the garlic and breadcrumbs together and season. Sprinkle this all over the fish, then drizzle on the rest of the regular olive oil and lemon juice.

Bake in the hot oven for 20 minutes, throwing on the parsley after 15 minutes. The bream is cooked when the flesh near the bone is white and opaque. Drizzle with extra virgin oil and serve with lemon wedges.

another iberian idea... bream with spanish salsa verde

Cook the bream as above, but leave out the breadcrumbs. To make the salsa, blitz a small bunch of flat-leaf parsley leaves, the leaves from 10 sprigs of mint, 1 garlic clove, 1½ tbsp capers, rinsed, 1 green chilli, deseeded, the juice of ½ lemon, salt and pepper in a food processor. With the motor running, add 200ml (7fl oz) extra virgin olive oil in a steady stream. Check for seasoning. (Sometimes I add a little chilli sauce, so consider doing that if you like heat.) Put into a bowl, cover and keep in the fridge, but return to room temperature before serving. Serves 4.

farareej mashri (egyptian grilled chicken)

This Egyptian chicken is so good – herby and smoky with charring – that when I make it I wonder why I bother to cook anything more complicated. Eat the yogurt bread (see below) on the side, or the Persian spice bread on page 115, or just buy some wholemeal flatbread.

SERVES 4

12 garlic cloves, peeled and grated or crushed

sea salt and pepper

juice of 2 lemons, plus more if needed

6 tbsp olive oil, plus more if needed

2 tbsp finely chopped flat-leaf parsley leaves

8 boneless chicken thighs

extra virgin olive oil, to serve

Mix together all the ingredients except the chicken and extra virgin oil and pour this over the chicken in a shallow, non-reactive dish. Turn to coat, cover and put in the fridge for at least two hours.

Preheat the grill to its highest setting. Take the chicken out of the marinade (if you find you don't have a lot, then mix in more oil and lemon and season again). Put the chicken on the grill rack – skin side-down first if you've left the skin on – and cook for about six minutes on each side, or until the chicken is cooked through. Baste every so often with the marinade and reduce the heat if it is charring too much before the meat is cooked through.

Scatter with a little sea salt, drizzle with good extra virgin oil (a punchy one) and serve with salad, flatbread and Greek yogurt.

middle eastern yogurt bread

This is quite tangy – it's the yogurt – and very simple to make. You can incorporate chopped olives, chilli, crumbled feta or sun-dried tomatoes (not very Middle Eastern but still good) into the dough. Just work it in when you knock the bread back, before you shape it.

MAKES 1 MEDIUM ROUND LOAF

160g (5¾oz) wholemeal flour

160g (5¾oz) strong white bread flour, plus more to dust

½ tsp salt

1 tsp dried yeast

¾ tsp caster sugar

150g (5½oz) plain yogurt

3 tbsp olive oil, plus more for the top and for oiling

sesame seeds, cumin seeds, nigella seeds or rosemary leaves, to finish

Mix the flours with the salt. Stir the yeast in a bowl with the sugar and 3½ tbsp of warm water. Leave for 15 minutes. Make a well in the flours and pour in the yeast mixture, then the yogurt and oil. Mix everything to a soft, but quite wet, dough.

Knead for 10 minutes on a work top dusted with flour until smooth and shiny, then oil the dough, put in a clean bowl and cover with lightly oiled cling film. Leave for two hours; it should double in volume.

Knock the dough back, shape into a 22–25cm (9–10in) loaf and put on a baking sheet. Cover with the cling film and leave for 45 minutes. Preheat the oven to 200°C/400°F/gas mark 6. Drizzle with oil, top with seeds or rosemary and bake for 35 minutes.

chicken and fennel with honey, mustard and orange

An easy midweek dish. Bung it all in the oven and let the heat do its work.

SERVES 4

5 tbsp orange juice, plus finely grated zest of ½ orange

4 tbsp runny honey

2 tbsp wholegrain mustard

2 tbsp olive oil

8 chicken thighs, skin removed or not, as you like

sea salt and pepper

6 sprigs of thyme

3 fennel bulbs

Preheat the oven to 200°C/400°F/gas mark 6. Mix the orange juice, zest, honey, mustard and oil. Put the chicken in a shallow ovenproof dish in which both chicken and fennel can lie together in a single layer. Pour two-thirds of the orange mixture over, sprinkle with salt and scatter on the thyme. Bake for 15 minutes.

Trim the tips of the fennel bulbs, retaining any fronds, and remove the tough outer leaves. Quarter the bulbs and remove the core (don't take away too much, or the wedges will fall apart).

Take the chicken out of the oven, baste it with its juices, then tuck in the fennel and spoon the rest of the orange mixture over. Season, return to the oven and cook for 30 minutes, basting every so often. The chicken should be dark gold and cooked through and the fennel tender and glazed. Serve with the pilaf below.

black and white pilaf

I'll be honest: this is black and beige, really… but that doesn't sound as good! The watercress tastes great with the orange in the chicken recipe above. Use these basic quantities (150g/5½oz brown rice and 300ml/½ pint liquid) for any brown rice-based pilaf and ring the changes.

SERVES 6

75g (2½oz) wild rice

1 tbsp olive oil

1 onion, finely sliced

2 garlic cloves, finely chopped

4 cardamom pods, bashed (but leave the pods intact)

150g (5½oz) brown rice

300ml (½ pint) chicken or vegetable stock

salt and pepper

35g (1¼oz) watercress, leaves only

juice of ½ lemon

Put the wild rice in a saucepan and cover with water. Bring to the boil, reduce the heat to a simmer and cook for about 45 minutes. Wild rice never softens completely, but becomes a little tender.

Heat the oil in a pan and sauté the onion over a medium-high heat until really golden. Add the garlic and cardamom and cook for a minute. Add the brown rice and stir for a couple of minutes, then the stock and pepper. Bring to the boil, reduce the heat to low and cover. Cook for 25–30 minutes; the stock will be absorbed. Make sure the rice doesn't boil dry, but don't add too much liquid.

Drain the wild rice, toss with the brown rice and taste. When you cook grains in stock they become pretty well seasoned anyway, but you might need a little more. Fork through the watercress and add as much lemon as you think you need. It just 'lifts' the dish.

vietnamese beef with rice vermicelli and crispy vegetables

This is where meat plays a role, but isn't any more important than the vegetables. You don't actually need much (I've served this successfully with just 300g/10½oz of meat). Limiting the meat keeps the dish fresh. Texture is very important here and the crunch is great. The veg and noodles with the sauce make a great healthy lunch on their own (no meat required).

SERVES 4

FOR THE MARINADE

1 shallot, chopped

4 garlic cloves, chopped

2 lemon grass stalks, chopped

1 tbsp fish sauce

1 tsp soft light brown sugar

pepper

FOR THE REST

400g (14oz) sirloin steak

125g (4½oz) rice vermicelli

½ ridge cucumber, cut into fine batons (use regular cucumber if you can't find this)

50g (1¾oz) beansprouts

150g (5½oz) Iceberg lettuce, shredded

1 carrot, peeled and cut into julienne

15g (½oz) coriander leaves

leaves from 12 sprigs of mint

1 tbsp roasted peanuts, chopped

FOR THE DIPPING SAUCE

1 red chilli, chopped, or to taste

1 garlic clove, chopped

2 tbsp lime juice, or to taste

4 tbsp fish sauce

5 tsp caster sugar, or to taste

Make the marinade by pounding the shallot, garlic and lemon grass together in a mortar, then gradually adding the fish sauce, brown sugar and pepper. Rub this all over the steak, put in a bowl, cover with cling film and put in the fridge for an hour.

To make the dipping sauce, pound together the chilli and garlic and gradually add the lime juice, fish sauce and caster sugar. Taste for heat and sweet-sour balance, adjusting the levels of chilli, sugar and lime juice until it is as you like it. Add 1 tbsp of water, or as much as you want; the sauce should be strong though. Set aside.

Heat a griddle pan over a high heat until really hot and cook the steak for 1½ minutes each side. The meat should be rare for this dish. Cover with foil to allow the steak to rest briefly.

Put the noodles into a heatproof bowl and pour over boiling water. Help to separate the strands using chopsticks, then drain, run cold water through them and shake out as much water as you can.

Put the noodles into a large shallow bowl and put the vegetables and herbs on top, each one in separate little piles. (You can toss it all together but I like the vegetables arranged separately.) Cut the beef into strips and serve it on a platter alongside, with the dipping sauce in a bowl. Scatter the peanuts over the beef or the salad, whichever you prefer, then serve.

butterflied leg of lamb with sekenjabin

This might seem like a very short cooking time (especially if you want to eat the lamb pink), but that is the wonder of butterflied lamb. The meat is so spread out that the heat doesn't have far to penetrate. I leave the fat on to get a good flavour; those who don't want to eat it can cut it off.

Sekenjabin is a Persian mint syrup, but this version is less sweet and thick than they would normally have it. I like it better, to be honest; it's lighter and cuts through the meat better. In Iran, sekenjabin is taken on picnics and lettuce leaves are dipped in it. Pairing it with lamb seems like a lovely Anglo-Persian mix.

Serve with wholemeal flatbread (such as Cumin flatbread, see page 108) or a whole grain side dish (such as Spring couscous, see page 20). Broad beans are also perfect on the side, if you want another vegetable. This makes a wonderful celebratory spring or summer meal.

SERVES 8

FOR THE SEKENJABIN

150g (5½oz) granulated sugar

150ml (5fl oz) white wine vinegar

15g (½oz) mint leaves

FOR THE LAMB

2.25kg (5lb) leg of lamb, pre-boned weight, boned and butterflied

6 garlic cloves, chopped

15g (½oz) mint leaves

salt and pepper

3 tbsp olive oil, plus more to rub the meat

2 heads Romaine lettuce, leaves separated, washed and patted dry

Make the sekanjabin the day before (just to get it out of the way). Put 300ml (½ pint) of water into a saucepan with the sugar and bring gently to the boil, stirring to help the sugar dissolve. Add the vinegar, reduce the heat and simmer for 15 minutes. You should end up with a syrup (it will thicken as it cools, though even then this is not a thick syrup). Take off the heat and add one-third of the mint leaves. Leave until cold, strain the mint out and refrigerate the syrup until you want to serve it.

When you are ready to cook the lamb, preheat the oven to 220°C/425°F/gas mark 7. Pierce the lamb all over with a small sharp knife to make little slits. Put the garlic, mint, salt and pepper into a mortar and grind it, adding the oil. You should end up with a rough paste. (A mini food processor will do just as well as a mortar.) Push this paste into all the slits in the lamb. Now rub some oil over it and season well. Spread it out in a roasting tin, fatty side up. Put it into the oven and cook for 15 minutes. Reduce the oven temperature to 190°C/375°F/gas mark 5 and cook for another 15 minutes. The lamb will be pink. (If you want it more well done then increase the cooking time by five minutes.) Cover with foil, insulate and leave to rest for 15–20 minutes.

Chop the rest of the mint for the sekenjabin and add to the syrup.

Put the lettuce leaves into a broad, shallow bowl and serve them with the lamb, along with a smaller bowl containing the sekanjabin. Guests should dip the lettuce leaves in the sekanjabin and add them to their lamb. Serve the lamb's cooking juices, skimmed of excess fat, in a warm jug on the side.

chocolate and rosemary sorbet

This is a bitter, grown-up ice. I like it with slightly sweetened Greek yogurt and fresh raspberries. It's a clean combination, somewhat austere, but very good.

SERVES 6

120g (4½oz) granulated sugar

120g (4½oz) cocoa powder

small sprig of rosemary

Put the sugar, cocoa powder and 500ml (18fl oz) of water in a saucepan and heat, stirring gently to help the sugar and cocoa dissolve. Add the rosemary and bring to the boil. Boil for one minute. Take the pan off the heat and leave to cool with the rosemary still in the chocolate syrup.

Remove the rosemary and churn the liquid in an ice-cream machine. If you haven't got one, freeze the mixture in a shallow freezer-proof container, whizzing it in a food processor three or four times during the process in order to break up the crystals.

grapefruit and mint sorbet

Another fairly adult sorbet. Grapefruit are now much sweeter than they used to be – they're bred that way, especially pink and red ones – so try and get some good, tart, regular fruits. You want this to be mouth-puckering.

SERVES 6

175g (6oz) granulated sugar

finely grated zest of 1 white grapefruit (removed with a zester), plus the juice of 3

finely grated zest of 1 lemon (removed with a zester)

40g (1½oz) mint leaves

Put the sugar and 300ml (½ pint) of water into a small saucepan with both the zests. Place over a medium heat and gradually bring to the boil, stirring from time to time to help the sugar dissolve.

Boil for eight minutes, then take the pan off the heat and add the mint leaves. Cover and leave to cool completely.

Strain the syrup through a sieve into a bowl and mix it with the grapefruit juice.

Churn the liquid in an ice-cream machine. If you haven't got one, freeze the mixture in a shallow freezer-proof container, whizzing it in a food processor three or four times during the process in order to break up the crystals.

pistachio and lemon cake

A perfect cake for spring. Take the cake out of the tin before pouring on the syrup, or it sticks.

SERVES 8

200ml (7fl oz) olive oil, plus more for the tin

150g (5½oz) unsalted, shelled pistachio nuts

50g (1¾oz) stale breadcrumbs

200g (7oz) golden caster sugar

2½ tsp baking powder

finely grated zest of 1 lemon, plus the juice of 2

4 eggs, lightly beaten

60g (2oz) granulated sugar

Oil a 20–23cm (8–9in) cake tin and line the base with baking parchment. Put 115g (4oz) of the pistachios in a spice grinder or coffee blender and grind to a powder. (You can use a food processor but it won't do it as finely.) Mix with the breadcrumbs, caster sugar, baking powder and lemon zest. Mix together the oil and eggs, beating lightly with a fork, then stir this into the dry ingredients. Scrape into the prepared tin and place in a cold oven. Set the oven to 180°C/350°F/gas mark 4 and bake for 50–55 minutes. It should be coming away from the sides of the tin.

Meanwhile, put the lemon juice and granulated sugar in a pan with 100ml (3½fl oz) of water and stir over a medium heat until the sugar dissolves. Bring to the boil, then reduce the heat and simmer for about seven minutes.

Turn the cake out of the tin, peel off the paper and place on a plate, baked side-up. While it is still warm, pierce it all over with a skewer. Slowly pour on the syrup and leave it to cool and sink in.

Just before serving, chop the remaining pistachios so some are fine- and others coarse-chopped. Scatter them over the cake.

beetroot and poppy seed loaf cake

You don't have to make the candied beetroot (it does mean you increase the sugar content), but the slices are utterly beautiful. Just icing and a sprinkling of poppy seeds is good too, though.

SERVES 8

FOR THE CAKE

butter, for the tin

3 large eggs

225g (8oz) soft light brown sugar

100ml (3½fl oz) hazelnut oil

200ml (7fl oz) olive oil

½ tsp vanilla extract

150g (5½oz) regular wholemeal flour

50g (1¾oz) wholemeal spelt flour

good pinch of salt

¾ tsp baking powder

¾ tsp bicarbonate of soda

finely grated zest of 1 orange

2 tbsp poppy seeds, plus 1 tsp to serve (optional)

2 tbsp chopped toasted hazelnuts

225g (8oz) raw beetroot, peeled and coarsely grated

FOR THE CANDIED BEETROOTS (OPTIONAL)

280g (10oz) granulated sugar

½ small 'candy-stripe' beetroot, finely sliced horizontally

½ small crimson beetroot, finely sliced horizontally

FOR THE ICING

½ egg white

150g (5½oz) icing sugar, sifted

squeeze of lemon juice

Preheat the oven to 180°C/350°F/gas mark 4. Butter a 22 x 11 x 6cm (9 x 4½ x 2½in) loaf tin and line the base with baking parchment.

Beat the eggs with the sugar, using an electric whisk, until pale and light. Stir in the oils and vanilla then, with the whisk on its lowest speed, mix in the flours, salt, baking power, bicarbonate of soda and orange zest. Stir in the 2 tbsp of poppy seeds, hazelnuts and beetroot. Scrape into the prepared tin.

Bake for 40 minutes, then reduce the heat to 170°C/340°F/ gas mark 3½ and cook for 20 minutes, or until a skewer inserted into the centre comes out clean. Leave in the tin for 10 minutes, then turn out on to a wire rack and leave to cool completely.

Meanwhile, make the candied beetroots. Put the sugar in a saucepan with 200ml (7fl oz) of water and bring gradually to the boil, stirring a little to help the sugar dissolve. Boil for five minutes, then reduce the heat and cook the 'candy-stripe' beetroot slices for 15 minutes. Scoop them out, shake off the excess syrup and set them on greaseproof paper to dry a little (they will still be sticky but they'll dry out enough to use in about 30 minutes). Repeat with the crimson slices.

To make the icing, lightly beat the egg white, then gradually mix in the icing sugar, beating until smooth. Add a squeeze of lemon juice. Spoon over the top of the cake, allowing the icing to drip down the sides. Put the prettiest slices of beetroot on top or sprinkle over the 1 tsp of poppy seeds, if you like. Allow to set before serving (though the icing will stay quite soft).

summer

eating in summer

The summer appetite is fickle. Sometimes it seems completely absent. It can be so hot that all you want is for your thirst to be quenched, then suddenly you can't resist the sweetness of fruit – you want the juice of a peach to run down your arm – or the smokiness of griddled chicken. It's certainly the easiest season in which to eat 'healthily' and there doesn't have to be much cooking done at all if you don't feel like it. Tomatoes with olive oil, anchovies and parsley, broad beans with feta and mint, they're simple assembly jobs. Fruit and veg are abundant and varied, but it's also a good time to eat fish – it goes down easily – and the lighter grains. Wholemeal couscous and bulgar wheat make perfect summer eating (and are quick to prepare, too).

Don't miss out on one of the key joys in cooking. Edible flowers and petals aren't girly or fusty – they really enable you to be a painter in the kitchen – and summer herbs, such as tarragon, chervil and basil, also allow this scented quality to come to the fore.

early summer

asparagus
aubergines
beetroots
broad beans
carrots
courgettes
fennel
french beans
globe artichokes
jersey royals
lettuces
nettles
new potatoes
peas
radishes
rocket
runner beans
spinach
spring onions
tomatoes
watercress

basil
chervil
chives
dill
elderflower
mint
nasturtiums
oregano
sorrel
tarragon

apricots
blueberries
cherries
gooseberries
greengages
peaches
rhubarb
strawberries

bream
cod
crab
haddock
halibut
herring
plaice
pollack
prawns
salmon
sardines
scallops
sea trout
shrimps
squid

mid summer

chard
summer cabbages

blackcurrants
loganberries
melons

lamb
rabbit

late summer

cucumbers
peppers
sweetcorn
wild summer mushrooms

blackcurrants
figs
loganberries
nectarines
plums
raspberries
redcurrants

dover sole
grey mullet
lemon sole
mackerel
monkfish
red mullet
sea bass

nectarine, tomato and basil salad with torn mozzarella

One of the best salads in the book, this shows just how perfumed basil is. You can leave out the mozzarella if you are watching your fat intake (though first consider the discussion on fats on pages 284–285), or serve burrata instead of mozzarella (it's even better) if you're not.

This is a very simple dish, so you do need to buy good-quality ingredients.

**SERVES 6 AS A STARTER,
4 AS A MAIN COURSE**

3 nectarines

275g (9¾oz) tomatoes, mixed colours if possible

250g tub of buffalo mozzarella, drained of whey

leaves from 1 large bunch of basil

salt and pepper

1½ tbsp white balsamic vinegar

3 tbsp extra virgin olive oil

Halve and pit the nectarines and cut each half into four equal wedges. Halve the smaller tomatoes, quarter the larger ones (or cut into six or eight, depending on the size). Tear the mozzarella roughly into pieces.

Get a broad shallow bowl and layer the salad components, seasoning and sprinkling with white balsamic and extra virgin oil as you go. Serve immediately.

tons of tomatoes… tomato, melon and cucumber salad Put 1½ tbsp white wine vinegar, 2 tbsp groundnut oil, 4 tbsp olive oil, 18 mint leaves, ½ tsp Dijon mustard, salt, pepper and 1 tsp caster sugar into a blender and whizz. Check the seasoning, this is a sweet-sour dressing so you need to get the balance of vinegar and sugar right. Halve 350g (12oz) cherry tomatoes (get mixed colours if you can) and deseed 1 small melon (Galia or Ogen). Cut the melon flesh into cubes. Half-peel 1 small ridge cucumber so it ends up stripy (use a regular cucumber if you can't find a ridge type), halve along its length, scoop out the seeds with a spoon and slice the flesh. Toss the tomatoes, melon and cucumber with the dressing and season. Serve this quickly, as the components turn quite flaccid if left for longer than 45 minutes. Serves 6–8 as a side dish, though it can make more of a main course salad if you add chunks of feta. (If you do this, add more torn mint leaves to the finished dish.)

chilled tomato soup with cumin and avocado

The flavour of the tomatoes is everything here, as very little happens to them except for chopping and puréeing. The key thing is to get good ingredients and taste all the time to get the right balance of flavours (the seasoning, oil and vinegar are all very important) and textures.

SERVES 6–8

1kg (2lb 4oz) really well-flavoured tomatoes

300g (10½oz) cucumber, peeled

1 red pepper

4 spring onions, trimmed

2 fat garlic cloves

2 tsp ground cumin, plus more if needed

150ml (5fl oz) extra virgin olive oil, plus more to serve

2 tbsp sherry vinegar

2 tsp caster sugar

salt and pepper

2 avocados

juice of 2 limes

4 tbsp chopped coriander leaves

Chop the tomatoes, cucumber, pepper, spring onions and garlic roughly (discard the seeds, pithy ribs and stem of the pepper) and put into a blender – in batches – with the cumin, extra virgin oil, vinegar, sugar and seasoning. Whizz.

Push the puréed mixture through a nylon sieve into a large bowl. Before you blend the last batch, taste the purée to see whether you are getting the cumin flavour through. It should be subtle but clear; add a little more if you need it. When it's all been pushed through the sieve, taste for seasoning, cover and chill.

To serve, halve and pit the avocados. Peel and cut the flesh into slivers or cubes (depending on the size of the bowls you are going to serve the soup in). Squeeze the lime over them and season well. Serve the soup cold, with a drizzle of extra virgin oil, the avocado and coriander.

burmese melon and ginger salad

Fresh and thirst-quenching, make sure you serve this really cold. I sometimes add cubed deseeded cucumber as well (it's lovely with melon). Some recipes include shredded cabbage, or try Romaine lettuce instead. This is great with fish or pork, or as part of a mixture of salads. (Try it with Burmese-style chicken salad, see page 216.) You don't have to add coconut, but as you can now buy packets of fresh coconut chunks in supermarkets, it's far more convenient to include it if you want.

SERVES 4

500g (1lb 2oz) melon flesh, deseeded and cubed (a mixture of types is best: watermelon, Ogen, Galia, whatever you can find)

2 tbsp groundnut oil

2 shallots, finely sliced

3cm (1¼in) root ginger, peeled and cut into julienne

3 garlic cloves, very finely sliced

1 tbsp fish sauce

½ tbsp caster sugar

juice of 2 limes

2 tbsp torn mint leaves

2 tbsp chopped coriander leaves

2 tbsp torn basil leaves

1 tbsp toasted sesame seeds

2 tbsp fresh coconut shavings (optional)

1 tbsp roasted peanuts, chopped

Put the melon into a serving bowl. Heat the oil in a frying pan and sauté the shallots gently until they are beginning to soften. Add the ginger and cook for a minute, then the garlic and cook for another minute. Leave to cool.

Mix together the fish sauce, caster sugar and lime juice and pour it over the melon in the bowl. Gently toss in the shallot mixture, then chill briefly. If you leave it for longer than about an hour the melon gets too soft and the dish loses its freshness.

Gently mix in all the herbs, the sesame seeds, coconut (if using) and peanuts. Serve immediately.

and also... kachumber (indian cucumber salad)

This is ubiquitous in India, and deliciously cooling. It's great with spicy chicken, but I also eat it just with grains and other salads. (It's lovely with Crazy salad, see page 230, even though they come from different parts of the world.)

Chop 6 really well-flavoured plum tomatoes and 200g (7oz) peeled, deseeded cucumber into small chunks. Mix in 4 radishes, cut into matchsticks, ¼ red onion, very finely chopped, the torn leaves from 8 sprigs of mint, 15g (½oz) coriander leaves, roughly chopped, 1½ tbsp extra virgin olive oil, 2 tbsp lemon or lime juice and 1 small green chilli, deseeded and finely chopped. Season well. Put 1 tsp cumin seeds into a dry frying pan and toast for about a minute, or until you can smell the cumin. Toss this into the salad, too. Mix everything together, taste for seasoning and serve immediately. (I sometimes drizzle plain yogurt – the really sour stuff, not a Greek one – over the top as well.) Serves 4.

summer menu lunch in sicily

sicilian artichoke and broad bean salad with saffron dressing | espresso granita

A lunch that is light but full of contrasting flavours; perfect for hot weather.
If you want starch alongside the beans, try Barley tabbouleh (see page 135)
or Summer fregola (see page 142).

sicilian artichoke and broad bean salad with saffron dressing

You can add other classic Sicilian flavours, such as chopped anchovies or capers, and I sometimes include peas, tomatoes or roast peppers as well. It might seem paltry to serve just this as a main course, but Sicilian flavours are big and satisfying. Roast red mullet, seared tuna, roast peppers or tomatoes would be good if you wanted to extend the meal, though. Slipping the skins off the broad beans is a bit laborious, but it's worth it for the emerald green colour.

Artichoke hearts in oil are expensive, so I often buy them canned. Once they have marinated in oil for a while they're really great. In fact it's good to do this and have them to hand in the fridge.

SERVES 4 AS A LIGHT LUNCH

30g (1oz) raisins

1½ tbsp lemon juice

½ tbsp white balsamic vinegar

good pinch of saffron stamens

1 tsp runny honey

salt and pepper

5 tbsp extra virgin olive oil

175g (6oz) canned artichoke
hearts, drained

450g (1lb) podded broad beans

½ tbsp olive oil

4 shallots, finely sliced

2 garlic cloves, finely chopped

¼–½ tsp chilli flakes, to taste

2 tbsp pine nuts, toasted

leaves from 1 small bunch
of mint, torn

Put the raisins to soak in boiling water for 30 minutes, then drain. Make the dressing by mixing the lemon juice, white balsamic and saffron in a very small saucepan and gently heating: the saffron will colour and flavour the liquid as it heats. Leave to cool, then whisk in the honey, salt and pepper and extra virgin oil. Slice the artichoke hearts, put them in a serving dish, pour on the dressing and gently turn to coat. It really helps the artichokes if they can sit in this for a while (an hour is great).

Put the broad beans in a saucepan with boiling water and cook until they are tender (about three minutes). Drain, run them under cold water and then slip off the skins. Set aside.

Heat the regular olive oil and gently sauté the shallots until soft and pale gold, then add the garlic and chilli and sauté for another minute. Scrape these into the dish with the artichokes. Add all the other ingredients to the dish and gently toss together. Taste for seasoning and sweet-savoury balance, then serve.

espresso granita

Dark and bitter-sweet, this is one of the classic Italian granitas. In Sicily it is eaten with thick cream – you can decide whether that's on the menu or not – but it really doesn't need it.

SERVES 4
50g (1¾oz) coffee beans
115g (4oz) granulated sugar
2 strips of lemon zest and a
squeeze of lemon juice

Grind the coffee beans and put them in a saucepan with 675ml (1 pint 3fl oz) of water, the sugar and lemon zest. Bring to the boil, stirring to help the sugar dissolve, then take off the heat and leave to stand until lukewarm. Strain through coffee filter paper. Add the lemon juice and leave to cool, then chill in the fridge.

Pour the mixture into a shallow freezer-proof container and put in the freezer. Roughly fork through the crystals to break them up three or four times during the freezing process, to get a lovely mixture of glassy shards. Spoon the granita into glasses and serve.

an alternative… **lemon and basil granita** We don't know for sure whether ices were invented in Sicily, or even Naples, but the Arabs who invaded certainly introduced the habit of using snow from Etna to cool their fruit juices. From that it is only a small step to granitas, which Sicilians adore. Make this if you don't fancy the espresso granita. Mix 200g (7oz) granulated sugar and 350ml (12fl oz) of water in a small saucepan and add the finely grated zest of 3 lemons (removed with a zester). Heat gently, stirring every so often to help the sugar dissolve. Bring to the boil and cook for four minutes. Take off the heat and add 6 good-sized sprigs of basil. Leave to infuse for about 45 minutes. Remove the basil, strain the syrup and add 500ml (18fl oz) lemon juice (that's the juice of about 7 large juicy lemons). Stir and pour the mixture into a shallow freezer-proof container. Freeze, forking through the mixture roughly three or four times during the freezing process. Serve in frosted glasses with a little sprig of basil on top. Serves 8 (but halve the quantities if you want).

cucumber and yogurt soup with walnuts and rose petals

I always love the look – and the idea – of Middle Eastern cucumber soups, but have never tasted one that actually has enough depth of flavour (not for me, anyway). So this isn't purely Middle Eastern as I've used some stock, which they wouldn't do, but it has the right spirit: light, healthy and 'green' tasting. I actually prefer it without the dried fruit garnish, but that is traditional.

SERVES 8

FOR THE SOUP

600g (1lb 5oz) cucumber, peeled and chopped, plus matchsticks of cucumber to serve

100g (3½oz) walnuts, plus more chopped walnuts to serve

4 garlic cloves, chopped

6 spring onions, chopped

3 tbsp chopped mint leaves

3 tbsp chopped dill fronds, plus more to serve

good pinch of chilli flakes

leaves from 5 sprigs of tarragon

50g (1¾oz) stale coarse white country bread, crusts removed, torn

250ml (9fl oz) strong chicken stock

200g (7oz) Turkish yogurt (or Greek, Turkish is thinner)

150ml (5fl oz) extra virgin olive oil, or to taste

juice of ½ lemon, or to taste

2 tbsp white balsamic vinegar, or to taste

salt and pepper

TO SERVE

handful of raisins (optional)

pink or red rose petals

If you will be serving the soup with raisins, put them in a small bowl and cover with just-boiled water. Leave for 30 minutes to plump them up, then drain.

Put all the ingredients for the soup into a blender, in batches if necessary, and blitz. You will have to stop every so often and move the ingredients around so that all of them get to be near the blade. Taste for seasoning: this soup needs really careful adjusting. You may find you need a drop more lemon juice or white balsamic or extra virgin oil, rather than salt or pepper.

Chill well, then serve in small bowls, with the raisins (if using), chopped walnuts, cucumber matchsticks, dill and rose petals.

try a heartier version Cucumber soup is wonderfully adapatable and can be dressed in all sorts of ways. Instead of rose petals and walnuts, top this with spoonfuls of Salmon tartare (see page 53) or flaked hot-smoked salmon, or even with chopped, still-warm hard-boiled egg and sautéed prawns. You could also try replacing the dill in the recipe with basil, and the walnuts with almonds, to make a more Italian soup. Top with finely chopped tomatoes and torn basil leaves mixed into a vinaigrette, or Almond and basil gremolata (see page 98).

hot-smoked salmon, rye, beetroot and radish salad

Scandi fare. If you've never tried rye grains before, this is a good introduction. It won't surprise your palate, as we are already used to the rye bread-smoked salmon combo.

SERVES 4 AS A MAIN COURSE

FOR THE SALAD

200g (7oz) rye grains

4 small raw beetroots

a little olive oil

salt and pepper

12 radishes, preferably French Breakfast variety

5 tbsp extra virgin olive oil (fruity rather than grassy)

juice of 1 small lemon

50g (1¾oz) salad leaves (a mixture including crimson-veined leaves looks lovely)

680g (1lb 8oz) hot-smoked salmon (fillets or slices)

FOR THE DRESSING

75ml (2½fl oz) buttermilk

2 tbsp extra virgin olive oil

½ garlic clove, crushed

2 tbsp chopped dill fronds

Soak the rye grains overnight, then rinse well. Put in a pan with plenty of water to cover, then bring to the boil. Reduce the heat a little and cook until tender (50–60 minutes). Check during this time to make sure there's plenty of water in the pan, adding boiling water if you need to.

Preheat the oven to 190°C/375°F/gas mark 5. Trim the beetroots but don't peel them. Set them on a large piece of foil in a baking dish. Drizzle with a little regular olive oil and season. Scrunch the foil up round the beetroots to make a parcel. Roast them for 30–40 minutes. To check whether they are ready, open the parcel and pierce them with the tip of a knife; they should be tender. Leave to cool, then peel – the skins should just slip off – and cut them into matchsticks. Top and tail the radishes and cut them into thin slices lengthways.

When the rye is cooked it should be plump and tender, but will remain chewy. Drain and rinse with boiling water. While it is still warm, dress it with 4 tbsp of the extra virgin oil and the lemon juice and season.

When the grain is at room temperature, gently toss it with the beetroots, leaves, radishes and the remaining 1 tbsp of extra virgin oil (or arrange them on a plate without tossing them together). Quickly mix the ingredients for the dressing. Put the salmon on top of the rye and beetroot. Drizzle on some buttermilk dressing and serve the rest in a jug.

warm salad of pink grapefruit, prawns and toasted coconut

Some supermarkets now do little packs of fresh, shelled coconut flesh in small chunks so you don't need to go to through all the palaver of smashing coconuts on the front door step (my usual trick).

SERVES 4 AS A LIGHT MAIN COURSE

FOR THE DRESSING

2 tbsp lime juice

2 tbsp fish sauce

1 tbsp soft light brown sugar (or palm sugar if you can get it)

1½ tbsp groundnut oil

FOR THE SALAD

2 pink grapefruits

30g (1oz) fresh coconut flesh

1 tbsp groundnut oil

400g (14oz) raw king prawns, shelled and deveined (ideally organic)

2 red chillies, deseeded and finely chopped

salt and pepper

good squeeze of lime juice

2 Baby Gem lettuces, leaves separated and torn

about 30 mint leaves, torn

2 tbsp chopped roasted peanuts

1 tbsp white sesame seeds

To make the dressing, just mix all the ingredients together.

Cut the grapefruits into segments: cut a slice off the bottom and top of each fruit so they have a flat base on which to sit. Using a very sharp knife, cut the peel and pith off each grapefruit, working around the fruit and cutting the peel away in broad strips from top to bottom. Working over a bowl, slip a sharp fine-bladed knife in between the membrane on either side of each segment and ease the segment out.

Either shave – it's only really possible to do this if you have a chunk of coconut – or cut the coconut into fine slices using a very sharp knife. Toast it in a dry frying pan until golden; be careful as this happens very quickly. Tip out on to a plate.

Heat the oil in a frying pan and quickly sauté the prawns over a medium heat, cooking them until they turn from grey to pink (it will only take about three minutes). When there's one minute to go, throw in the chillies. Season and add a squeeze of lime juice. Immediately toss the prawns with the lettuce leaves, grapefruit, mint and dressing. Scatter with the peanuts, coconut and sesame seeds and serve immediately.

try a crab version Mix 1 chopped and deseeded red chilli, 1 tbsp fish sauce, 1 tbsp light soy sauce, 3 tbsp rice vinegar, 1 small shallot, finely chopped, 3 tbsp warm water and 1½ tbsp caster sugar, whisking to make sure the sugar dissolves. Segment 2 grapefruits (see above). Arrange 115g (4oz) salad leaves, 15g (½oz) basil leaves and 15g (½oz) mint leaves on four plates, top with the grapefruit and 400g (14oz) white crab meat and spoon on the dressing. Serve immediately with lime wedges. Serves 4.

goat's cheese and cherry salad with almond and basil gremolata

There's nothing new about the combination of goat's cheese and cherries, but this takes it to a new level; the macerated cherries are a dream. The gremolata is also very good made with mint instead of the basil used here.

SERVES 6

FOR THE CHERRIES

400g (14oz) cherries

1 tbsp brandy or grappa (optional)

2 tsp white balsamic vinegar

4 tbsp extra virgin olive oil

1 tbsp lemon juice

FOR THE GREMOLATA

40g (1½oz) blanched almonds

finely grated zest of 1 lemon

1 garlic clove, very finely chopped

about 12 basil leaves

FOR THE SALAD

150g (5½oz) goat's cheese, crumbled into chunks

125g (4½oz) lamb's lettuce, or baby spinach, or a mixture

1 tbsp white balsamic vinegar

3 tbsp extra virgin olive oil (fruity rather than grassy)

salt and pepper

Prepare the cherries so that they can macerate. Pit them: I just pull them apart with my fingers as it produces lovely shapes, but use a knife if you prefer. Put into a bowl with all the other ingredients for the cherries, stir and leave for anything from 30 minutes to two hours.

To make the gremolata, toast the almonds in a dry frying pan until they are golden (be careful as this happens very quickly). Tip on to a chopping board and leave to cool. Add the zest, garlic and basil and chop finely with a sharp knife.

For the salad, toss the goat's cheese with the leaves, white balsamic, extra virgin oil and seasoning. Arrange on a platter or divide between plates. Scatter the cherries over with their macerating juices, then the gremolata. Serve immediately.

turkish spoon salad with haydari

Turkish pepper paste has a very bright, front-of-the-mouth chilli flavour (there is a recipe for it in my book *Salt Sugar Smoke*). If you can't find it, use another chilli paste. This is a dish for a special occasion. It's delicious and healthy, but such fine chopping takes time.

**SERVES 8 AS A STARTER,
4 AS A LIGHT LUNCH**

FOR THE HAYDARI

400g (14oz) Greek yogurt

¼ tsp salt

2 garlic cloves, crushed

1 green chilli, deseeded and finely chopped

6 tbsp chopped dill fronds

FOR THE SALAD

4 ripe, really well-flavoured plum tomatoes

2 Romano peppers, deseeded and finely chopped

2 red chillies, deseeded and finely chopped

2 small cucumbers, about 225g (8oz) each, peeled, deseeded and finely chopped

2 shallots, finely chopped

3 tbsp finely chopped flat-leaf parsley leaves

2 tbsp finely chopped mint leaves

2 tsp Turkish pepper paste or harissa

1 tbsp pomegranate molasses

2 tsp white wine vinegar

100ml (3½fl oz) extra virgin olive oil, plus more to serve

salt and pepper

seeds from ½ pomegranate (optional)

TO SERVE

paprika or sumac

warm flatbread

To make the haydari, put the yogurt into a new J-cloth or a piece of muslin. Gather the cloth up into a bag and gently squeeze it into the sink to help some of the excess moisture to run out. Put it in a sieve over a bowl and place in the fridge for 24 hours. More moisture will run out during that time, to leave quite a firm mixture. Tip it from the muslin into a bowl and mix in all the other ingredients for the haydari.

Plunge the tomatoes into boiling water for 10 seconds, remove and immediately run cold water over them. Remove the skin. Halve and deseed them (chuck away the seeds) and finely chop the flesh.

Put the tomato flesh into a bowl with the peppers, red chillies, cucumbers and shallots. Add the herbs, pepper paste, pomegranate molasses, wine vinegar and 2 tbsp of the extra virgin oil. Season and gently stir. Leave for 30 minutes to allow the flavours to meld.

The mixture will be a little watery after 30 minutes, so gently drain some of this away by putting the mixture into a large nylon sieve. You don't want a dry mixture, but you don't want a watery one either. Put into a bowl and add the rest of the extra virgin oil. Taste for seasoning and scatter on the pomegranate seeds (if using).

Sprinkle the haydari with paprika or sumac and drizzle with some extra virgin oil. Serve with the spoon salad and warm flatbread.

you can never have too many salads

The salad, over the last twenty years, hasn't just grown up, it has become a complex dish, multi-faceted and capable of surprising. Time was when 'salad' was a collection of limp leaves, woolly tomatoes, hard-boiled eggs and salad cream (and the inevitable globe of bleeding – in both usages of the word – pickled beetroot). Or, when we were dieting, that hard-to-love combination of undressed leaves and cottage cheese. Then a few 'foreign' salads crept in, namely salade Niçoise and caesar salad. But the dish that really changed our attitude towards salads was the (now much-traduced) goat's cheese salad. Once we'd eaten well-dressed leaves with rounds of grilled, tangy cheese, we became open to the idea of different temperatures and textures as part of a salad.

Eventually, the salad stopped being only a starter or a side dish and moved into pole position as the main course. It wasn't just ladies who lunched who embraced them either, we all succumbed. Now salads are infinitely variable: they can contain sesame-crusted chicken and sautéed shiitakes, warm smoked haddock and eggs, hot roast tomatoes, cold yogurt and pomegranate seeds. They're no longer just gentle, they can also be peppery, minerally, assertive, bitingly spicy. They can encompass opposites, in fact contrast is one of their chief joys – hot and cold, subtle and strong, crisp and soft – and they feel vital. Sometimes, as I carry a platter of salad to the table, edges splashed with vinegar and oil, leaves practically tumbling over the sides, it seems like an almost living thing: big, sprawling and beautiful.

When my eating started to change (to become – inadvertently – more 'healthy'), I realized that my idea of salads had broadened even more. Salads now reflect the latest shifts in our eating habits and have become increasingly inventive. Our growing familiarity with 'unusual' ingredients – preserved lemons, Japanese pickled plums, fish sauce, unusual grains – means that salads can be inspired by the food of the Middle East, Asia and beyond. A salad can be a plateful of crisp raw vegetables – carrots, radishes, mooli, cucumber – sitting in little piles alongside fistfuls of mint and basil leaves, waiting to be doused in a spicy Vietnamese dressing. Our growing love of vegetables has led to all sorts of roots and leaves – from pumpkins to pea shoots – turning up in them. And they're not just for summer, we can eat a salad every day of the year.

Of course a salad doesn't have to be complicated. We can go back to basics: eat a bowl of dressed watercress at every meal and we're giving our bodies the very best food there is. Eat salad with your main course – cool leaves wilting in the heat of warm chicken is not going to make you feel deprived – or have it, as the French do, after the main course. It's a good – and delicious – habit to get into.

Why am I telling you all this? Think of what salads, predominantly, are: vegetables. There can be grains and meat too but there's always vegetables, the only thing nutritionists and experts don't argue about: they are universally agreed to be good for you (see pages 252–253 for more about this). Eating more salads – even just incorporating a simply dressed green salad into every meal – means eating more vegetables. And that's a no-brainer.

dressing it up

These will dress about four portions… but it depends whether you are dressing leaves, which need less dressing, or starches, which need more. There are loads of other dressings throughout the book.

asian hot, sour, salty and sweet

FOR ASIAN HOT, SOUR, SALTY
AND SWEET

3½ tsp caster sugar, or to taste

juice of ½ lime

1 small garlic clove, grated

½ tsp grated root ginger

¾ tbsp fish sauce, or to taste

1 red chilli, deseeded and very
finely chopped

4 tbsp groundnut oil

One of the most useful and versatile dressings I make. Toss it with simple batons of carrot and mooli / daikon (add basil, mint or coriander leaves, too), or use it for Eastern salads of duck breast, green beans and leaves, or seared tuna, herbs and glass noodles. Use half the chilli if you don't want the heat.

Whisk the sugar with the lime juice to help the sugar dissolve. Add the garlic, ginger, fish sauce and chilli, then whisk in the oil. Taste for sweet-salty balance, adding sugar or fish sauce if you want.

rose and raspberry

FOR ROSE AND RASPBERRY

1 tbsp raspberry vinegar
(one containing raspberry pulp)

pinch of caster sugar

salt and pepper

3½ tbsp extra virgin olive oil
(fruity rather than grassy)

1¼ tsp rose water, or to taste

Fragrant and summery. Use it on a salad of griddled chicken (that you've marinated in pomegranate molasses and spices), or on a salad of chicken, cherries, watercress and almonds. It's a great dressing for leaves to serve with Moroccan or Persian food.

You need vinegar which contains raspberry pulp for this, or use 1 tbsp of regular raspberry vinegar mixed with two crushed raspberries (pushed through a nylon sieve to get rid of the seeds).

Put the raspberry vinegar into a small cup. Add the sugar and seasoning (only a pinch of salt), then whisk in the extra virgin oil. Add the rose water little by little; it varies in strength quite a bit so taste as you go. You may even want a little more than suggested.

anchovy, olive and caper

FOR ANCHOVY, OLIVE AND CAPER

1½ tbsp white wine vinegar

1 garlic clove, grated

salt and pepper

4½ tbsp extra virgin olive oil

½ tbsp finely chopped flat-leaf
parsley leaves

½ tbsp capers, rinsed and
chopped

4 anchovies, drained or rinsed
and chopped

5 black olives, pitted and
finely chopped

This is quite a chunky dressing. It's good on tomatoes, sliced radishes, warm waxy potatoes (with green beans or chopped shallots), white beans, roast peppers and warm hard-boiled eggs.

Simply mix everything together, then taste. Adjust the seasoning according to what you are going to dress; hard-boiled eggs and potatoes can take a well-seasoned dressing (you may even want to add a squeeze of lemon). If you are using this to dress tomatoes, it shouldn't be quite as sharp, so use less vinegar.

sweet saffron roast tomatoes with labneh

Saffron and hot spices, sweet tomato flesh, clean acidic yogurt, there is an irresistible interplay of flavours here. Try to make sure you get some of the saffron juices to smear the labneh; the golden streaks on creamy white yogurt look beautiful.

Make this a complete main course by serving couscous on the side, or try kamut flavoured with preserved lemons (see page 307). You can scatter either pistachios or almonds on top.

SERVES 8

FOR THE LABNEH

400g (14oz) Greek yogurt

2 garlic cloves, crushed

3 tbsp finely chopped coriander, mint or parsley leaves

pinch of salt

pepper

FOR THE TOMATOES

18 plum tomatoes

4 tbsp olive oil

2 tsp harissa

good pinch of saffron stamens, plus more to serve

½ tbsp golden caster sugar (unless you have great sweet tomatoes)

TO SERVE

Arab flatbread

15g (½oz) flaked almonds, lightly toasted

juice of ½ lemon

4 tbsp extra virgin olive oil

2 tbsp chopped coriander leaves

Make the labneh the day before you want to serve the dish. Line a sieve with a piece of muslin or a brand new J-cloth and set it over a bowl. Mix the yogurt with the garlic, herbs, salt and pepper. Tip into the cloth, tie it up and refrigerate. The yogurt will lose moisture over the next 24 hours, leaving a firmer, 'cheese-like' substance. Help it along by giving it a squeeze every so often.

Preheat the oven to 190°C/375°F/gas mark 5. Halve the tomatoes and lay them in a single layer in a large roasting tin (or two small tins). Mix the regular olive oil, harissa and saffron and pour over the tomatoes. Turn the tomatoes over in the oil to make sure they are well coated, ending with them cut side up. Sprinkle with the sugar and season. Roast in the oven for about 45 minutes, or until caramelized and slightly shrunken. Leave to cool a little.

Take the labneh out of its cloth.

Carefully move the tomatoes (they are quite fragile and can fall apart easily) to a serving platter, dotting nuggets of the labneh among them as you go. You can also toast the flatbread, break it up, and arrange it among the tomatoes as well (or serve it on the side). Pour on any cooking juices which have collected in the tomato roasting tin, being sure to douse the flatbread if you have included it within the dish.

Scatter the almonds over the top, then heat another good pinch of saffron stamens with the lemon juice in a small saucepan. Add the extra virgin oil and mix with a spoon. Spoon over the dish; the golden dressing looks beautiful against the white labneh. Scatter with the coriander and serve warm, or at room temperature.

bulgarian griddled courgettes and aubergines with tarator

Tarator – a nut-based sauce – appears in different guises in Bulgaria, Turkey and Greece. It can be made with hazelnuts, walnuts, almonds or pine nuts and is just as good with a salad of raw cucumber, leaves, herbs and tomatoes as it is with cooked vegetables. It also keeps well in the fridge for a day or so, just take it out and let it come to room temperature before serving, otherwise it gets a bit solid.

SERVES 8 AS A STARTER

FOR THE TARATOR

1 slice of coarse country bread

2 garlic cloves

100g (3½oz) walnuts, plus more to serve

100ml (3½fl oz) extra virgin olive oil, plus more to serve

juice of ½ lemon

salt and pepper

150g (5½oz) Greek yogurt

2 tbsp chopped dill fronds, plus more to serve

FOR THE GRIDDLED VEGETABLES

1.2kg (2lb 10oz) mixed green and yellow courgettes

1.2kg (2lb 10oz) aubergines

olive oil

Tear the bread into pieces and put it into a food processor with the garlic and walnuts. Purée while adding the extra virgin oil and lemon juice. Add the seasoning and the yogurt with 50ml (2fl oz) of water and purée again. Stir in the dill, taste and adjust the seasoning. Put into a bowl and set aside until you're ready to serve (or cover and put in the fridge).

Trim each end from the courgettes and slice lengthways about 3mm (⅛in) thick. Remove the stalks from the aubergines and cut them widthways into slices of the same thickness as the courgettes. Brush all the sliced vegetables on both sides with regular olive oil.

Heat a griddle pan and cook the slices of courgette on both sides until golden and quite soft. You will need to do this in batches. Do the same with the aubergines, making sure they get a good colour on each side, then reduce the heat until the slices are soft and cooked through. Season the vegetables as you cook them.

Put the vegetables on to a serving plate, drizzling with a little extra virgin oil. Spoon some of the tarator over (offer the rest in a bowl) and scatter with more walnuts and dill.

macedonian grilled vegetable salad

This is not like an Italian roast vegetable salad, instead it is so soft it's almost a purée. It has a brilliant smoky flavour which you can only achieve by grilling the vegetables until they are scorched, so do it. It is not possible to make this if you don't have a naked flame on which to cook the aubergines (a gas hob or a barbecue). The smoky flavour just isn't there otherwise, roasting or grilling don't come anywhere near. If you can't cook the aubergines over a flame, I'd make something else instead.

SERVES 8 AS A STARTER (WITH OTHER MEZZE) OR AS A SIDE DISH

4 peppers, all red, or a mixture of red and yellow

olive oil

4 plum tomatoes, halved

salt and pepper

2 aubergines

4 garlic cloves, crushed

¼ tsp chilli flakes

2 tbsp extra virgin olive oil (preferably a gutsy Greek one), or to taste

juice of ½ lemon

1½ tbsp red wine vinegar

Preheat the grill to its highest setting.

Halve, core and deseed the peppers and brush all over with regular olive oil. Line the grill pan with foil (it helps collect the cooking juices and saves on washing-up later) and set the peppers on this, cut side down. Add the tomatoes, cut side up, and drizzle them with oil. Season. Put under the hot grill and cook until the skins of the peppers are soft and both vegetables are scorched in places. Reduce the heat – or move the grill rack away from the heat source – and cook until both the peppers and the tomatoes are completely tender. You will need to remove the tomatoes before the peppers.

Pierce the aubergines all over so they won't burst, then hold each one over a naked flame on a gas hob (you can do two at a time if you are careful and have a couple of long forks or tongs). Cook all over. The skins should be scorched and the aubergines completely tender. It takes a while, and you do have to keep adjusting the flame, but be patient. Leave to cool a bit, then remove the skin. Cut the flesh into small cubes.

Peel the skins from the peppers – this should be easy if they got well scorched – and chop or slice the flesh. Chop the tomatoes. Mix all the vegetables together in a bowl and add all the other ingredients. Check to see whether you need more oil or seasoning. You can serve this warm or at room temperature. It tends to improve in flavour as it sits and is often even more delicious the following day.

broad bean purée with feta relish and cumin flatbread

One of those bits-and-pieces dishes that can be a good starter, or a complete main course with kebabs (try it with the lamb kebabs on page 141). Of course you don't have to make the bread. You can just buy Arab flatbread and warm it up instead. Peppery French Breakfast radishes look – and taste – lovely alongside. Add hard-boiled eggs (hen's or quail's) for a great lunch dish.

SERVES 6 AS A STARTER, OR MORE WITH OTHER MEZZE

FOR THE BREAD

100g (3½oz) wholemeal flour

75g (2¾oz) plain flour

¼ tsp salt

½ tsp dried yeast

¼ tsp caster sugar

150ml (5½fl oz) warm water

1 tbsp olive oil, plus more to oil

½ tbsp extra virgin olive oil

4 shallots, finely sliced

2 red chillies, deseeded and finely sliced

1 tsp black cumin seeds

FOR THE BROAD BEAN PURÉE

500g (1lb 2oz) broad beans, podded

½ tbsp olive oil

1 small onion, finely chopped

3 garlic cloves, finely chopped

¼ tsp dried chilli flakes

juice of 1 lemon, or to taste

3½ tbsp extra virgin olive oil

2 tbsp light chicken stock or water

FOR THE FETA RELISH

75g (2¾oz) feta

75g (2¾oz) good black olives, pitted and coarsely chopped

2½ tbsp extra virgin olive oil

½ garlic clove, very finely chopped

1 tbsp chopped dill fronds, or flat-leaf parsley or torn mint leaves

To make the bread, put the flours and salt into a bowl. Mix the yeast in another bowl with the sugar and half the water. Leave this somewhere warm for 15 minutes. Pour the yeast mixture into a well made in the flours, then mix in. Add the oil, then use enough of the remaining water to make a dough. Knead for 10 minutes until soft, shiny and elastic. Oil lightly, then put into a bowl, cover with cling film and leave for two hours. It should double in size.

For the purée, cook the beans for three minutes in boiling water. Drain and rinse in cold water. Slip the skin off each bean. It's a bit of a pain at first, but quite soothing when you get into the rhythm.

Heat the regular olive oil in a large frying pan and sauté the onion until it is soft but not coloured. Add the garlic and chilli and cook for another three minutes. Add the beans to help them meld with the other flavours and warm through for three minutes. Season.

Tip the contents of the pan into a food processor and add the lemon juice, extra virgin oil and stock or water. Pulse-blend to a rough purée. Taste for seasoning; you may also want to add more oil or lemon. Scrape into a broad shallow dish.

Crumble the feta into a small bowl and toss in the olives. Pour on the extra virgin oil, sprinkle on the garlic and herbs. Grind on some pepper, carefully mix and scatter over the top of the purée.

Meanwhile, set your oven to its highest setting and put some unglazed quarry tiles or a large pizza stone into it. Knock back the bread then divide it into six. Put on to a lightly floured tray, cover lightly with cling film and leave for 10 minutes. Roll each piece into a circle about 15cm (6in) across. Heat the extra virgin oil in a pan and cook the shallots until golden, then add the chilli and cook for two minutes. Set this aside until the breads are cooked.

Slap the breads on to the tiles or pizza stones and cook for two to three minutes, or until puffed up and blistered in patches. Wrap in a tea towel until all are ready. Spread the shallot and chilli mixture over each and sprinkle with cumin seeds. Serve with the purée.

salad of smoked anchovies, green beans and egg

I've eaten a lot of salade Niçoise in my time, usually when 'on a diet' (and while trying to convince myself that the spuds in it were okay…). Here is something a bit different, but – I think – better. And not a potato in sight. (See page 328 for where to buy the totally addictive smoked anchovies.)

SERVES 4 AS A STARTER

FOR THE DRESSING

¾ tbsp white balsamic vinegar

½ tsp Dijon mustard

4 tbsp extra virgin olive oil (fruity French or Sicilian rather than bitter, grassy Tuscan)

juice of ¼ lemon, or to taste

salt and pepper

FOR THE SALAD

200g (7oz) green beans, topped but not tailed

small bunch of radishes (preferably French Breakfast radishes), leaves removed, tops and tails trimmed

4 large eggs

2 shallots, very finely sliced

50g (1¾oz) watercress, coarse stalks removed

175g (6oz) cherry tomatoes or baby plum tomatoes, halved

handful of flat-leaf parsley leaves

150g (5½oz) smoked anchovies, drained of oil

Make the dressing by whisking all the ingredients together. Check for seasoning.

Steam or boil the green beans until only just tender, then run cold water through them to set the colour and cool them. Cut the radishes lengthways into thin slices.

Boil the eggs for seven minutes. They should be hard-boiled, but with a yolk that is still a little soft right in the centre.

Toss all the vegetables and herbs together with most of the dressing and divide between plates or put into a broad shallow bowl. Shell the eggs, carefully halve and put these on the salad, then dot the smoked anchovies among the leaves. Grind some black pepper on top and drizzle on the rest of the dressing. Serve immediately.

broad bean, leek, tomato and dill pilaf

This is based on a Persian dish where it is served with a fried egg on top – that makes a good supper – but it would equally be very good with Butterflied leg of lamb with sekenjabin (see page 76) or with roasted fish.

SERVES 4 AS A MAIN COURSE
(WITH EMBELLISHMENTS),
OR 8 AS A SIDE DISH

2 leeks

2 tbsp olive oil

2 garlic cloves, finely chopped

3 plum tomatoes, peeled, deseeded and chopped (see page 101)

¾ tsp ground cumin

250g (9oz) brown basmati rice

½ cinnamon stick

500ml (18fl oz) vegetable stock, light chicken stock or water

400g (14oz) broad beans (podded weight)

juice of ½ lemon

4 tbsp chopped dill fronds

1½ tbsp extra virgin olive oil

salt and pepper

Remove the tough outer leaves from the leeks and trim the tops. Cut into thin rounds and wash thoroughly in running water.

Heat the regular olive oil in a heavy-based saucepan and sauté the leeks over a medium heat until they are beginning to soften but still hold their shape (about six minutes). Add the garlic and tomatoes and cook for another two minutes, then add the cumin and cook for another 30 seconds. Add the rice, cinnamon and stock. Bring to the boil and boil fiercely until the surface of the rice looks pitted (as if there are little holes in the top). Reduce the heat to as low as possible, cover and leave to cook for about 25 minutes. The liquid should be absorbed as the rice cooks, but take a peek to make sure the dish hasn't boiled dry before the rice is ready (it should be tender, but each grain will retain a nutty bite).

Meanwhile, boil the broad beans until tender (about three minutes). Rinse with cold water, then slip the skins off (laborious but worth it for the colour of the beans). Reheat by running boiling water through them, then carefully fork into the rice with the lemon juice, dill and extra virgin oil. Taste for seasoning.

serve with any of the following

a fried egg on top

a good dollop of Greek yogurt, crumbled feta and a drizzle of extra virgin olive oil

a bowl of yogurt and Hot pepper purée (see page 64)

omit the tomato in the pilaf and serve with Roast tomatoes (see page 104)

Feta relish (see page 108)

summer menu unexpected flavours

white beans with roast peppers, eggs and hilbeh | persian spice bread | berry and hibiscus sorbet

It's good to throw a curve ball when you're thinking about meals for friends. They'll like it and will look at some ingredients in a completely new way, while it's a thrill for the cook to put unusual flavours together, especially in summer when the same dishes crop up again and again. This menu is not what anyone would expect.

white beans with roast peppers, eggs and hilbeh

A sprawling feast, but easy to put together. I actually got the idea from the Egyptian breakfast of beans, eggs, onion, preserved lemons and flatbread; it has always seemed such a lovely meal to me. This has elements you don't need to cook at all. Add other simple things such as roast or raw tomatoes, cucumbers with a minty dressing, pickled chillies or feta cheese. Hilbeh is the red version of the Yemeni relish, zhoug. You'll need to soak the fenugreek seeds overnight.

SERVES 6

FOR THE HILBEH

2 tbsp fenugreek seeds

1½ tbsp olive oil

1 onion, chopped

4 garlic cloves, chopped

4 red chillies, deseeded and chopped

2 large tomatoes, deseeded and chopped

½ tbsp tomato purée

juice of 1 lemon

½ tsp ground cumin

½ tsp ground coriander

leaves from 1 small bunch of coriander

salt and pepper

FOR THE REST

3 red peppers, halved

3 tbsp olive oil

6 eggs

2 x 400g cans cannellini or haricot beans, drained and rinsed

1 small red onion, peeled and very finely sliced (the slices should be almost transparent)

The night before, put the fenugreek seeds in cold water to cover.

Next day, when ready to cook, drain the fenugreek and preheat the oven to 190°C/375°F/gas mark 5.

To make the hilbeh, heat the olive oil in a frying pan and sauté the onion until it is soft and pale gold, about seven minutes. Add the garlic, chillies and drained fenugreek and cook for another two minutes, then add the tomatoes and cook for another minute, followed by the tomato purée and lemon juice. Put the mixture into the bowl of a food processor.

Toast the cumin and coriander in a dry frying pan and add them to the food processor too, with the coriander leaves and some salt. Pulse-blend for about 30 seconds – it should be like a relish, not like a purée – then scrape into a bowl. This can be served warm or at room temperature.

For the rest, brush the peppers with some of the olive oil and put into a small roasting tin. Season. Roast in the oven for 40 minutes, or until completely tender and slightly charred. Cut them into strips about ½cm (¼in) in width.

Cook the eggs in boiling water for seven minutes. The yolk should still be a little soft right in the middle.

Put the beans into a frying pan with 1 tbsp of olive oil and sauté and toss until they are warmed through. Put them into a bowl with the strips of pepper and some of the very finely sliced onion on top (provide the rest on the side). Serve with the eggs – allowing each person to peel their egg and put it on top of their beans – the hilbeh and bread; try the Persian spice bread (see right).

persian spice bread

This is unusual; you don't think of turmeric flavouring bread. You can use any dried fruit: dates, figs and cherries are all good. It is based on a recipe in Greg Malouf's inspiring book on modern Middle Eastern food, *Malouf*. You could also serve home-made or bought wholemeal Arab flatbread with this menu, if you prefer.

MAKES 8 ROLLS

1¼ tsp dried yeast

15g (½oz) soft light brown sugar

175ml (6fl oz) warm water

1 egg, lightly beaten, plus 1 egg yolk, to glaze

1 tbsp olive oil, plus more to oil

170g (6oz) plain flour, plus more to dust

170g (6oz) granary flour

½ tsp salt

½ tsp turmeric

45g (1¾oz) dates, chopped

35g (1¼oz) butter

½ tbsp cumin seeds, very lightly crushed

Put the yeast into a bowl with ¼ tsp of the sugar and 3½ tbsp of the water and leave somewhere warm to froth (it will take about 15 minutes). Mix half the beaten egg (retain the other half) with the 1 tbsp of olive oil.

Mix the flours, salt, remaining sugar and the turmeric together in a bowl. Make a well in the centre and pour in the frothy yeast followed by the egg and oil mixture. Add the remaining water. Gradually bring the dry ingredients into the middle using a knife, then start working the mixture with your hands.

Knead for 10 minutes, or until the dough is shiny and feels elastic. Very lightly oil the ball of dough with your hands, then put it into a bowl and cover with lightly oiled cling film. Leave in a warm place to prove for an hour (it should double in size). Knock the dough back, then return it to the bowl and leave, covered with the cling film, for another hour.

Divide the dough into eight equal balls. Roll each out on a lightly floured surface into a circle about 12cm (5in) across. Divide the dates between these, putting them in the centre, and put a little knob of butter on top of the dates. Pull the dough up over the dates and butter, pinch it, then smooth it over and turn what is now a ball of dough over so that the seam is underneath. Set these on a non-stick baking sheet, cover loosely with lightly oiled cling film and leave for 15 minutes. Meanwhile, preheat the oven to 200°C/400°F/gas mark 6.

Mix the reserved half egg with the egg yolk. Brush the tops of each roll with this and sprinkle with the cumin seeds. Bake in the oven for 15 minutes, by which time the rolls should be golden and cooked through. Leave to rest for about 10 minutes before serving.

berry and hibiscus sorbet

Hibiscus flowers are very citrussy, so they add an extra mouth-puckering element to the sorbet. (See pages 328–329 for where to buy the dried hibiscus flowers.)

SERVES 6

4 tbsp dried hibiscus flowers

230g (8oz) granulated sugar

450g (1lb) mixed berries (blackberries, raspberries, loganberries, tayberries)

Put 230ml (8fl oz) of water and the hibiscus flowers in a saucepan and bring to the boil. Pull the pan off the heat and leave for about 30 minutes so the flowers can flavour the water. Strain. The liquid should taste very citrussy. Return the liquid to the saucepan.

Add the sugar and heat gradually to help the sugar dissolve. Add the berries and poach gently for about three minutes. Leave to get completely cool.

Whizz the mixture in a food processor, not a blender which would break down the seeds and make the sorbet bitter. Push the puréed fruit and syrup through a nylon sieve.

Churn the mixture in an ice-cream machine following the manufacturer's instructions. If you don't have a machine, pour into a shallow, freezer-proof broad container and put into the freezer. Take the mixture out of the freezer three or four times during the freezing process and whizz in the food processor. This breaks down the ice crystals and incorporates air to give a smooth sorbet.

scandi salmon burger with dill and tomato sauce

I've been very taken with salmon burgers while travelling in Scandinavia. For some reason I always feel over-full and as if I've eaten badly when I have a beef burger (however 'good' it is). This has quite a different effect. If you can't find rye bread, use a good wholemeal bread instead. Or, of course, eat it without bread.

SERVES 4

FOR THE BURGERS

500g (1lb 2oz) skinless salmon fillet

25g (1oz) butter

½ onion, very finely chopped

2 tbsp finely chopped chives

2 tbsp mayonnaise

1 tbsp crème fraîche

salt and pepper

groundnut oil

FOR THE SAUCE

150g (5½oz) Greek yogurt

1 tbsp mayonnaise

1 tbsp finely chopped dill fronds, plus sprigs of dill to serve

½ small garlic clove, crushed

75g (2¾oz) really well-flavoured tomatoes

TO SERVE

4 slices of rye bread

baby salad leaves

sliced cucumber

Chop the salmon flesh very finely indeed – about 3mm (⅛in) square – though you don't have to be pedantic about the shape. Melt the butter in a frying or sauté pan and sauté the onion over a very gentle heat until soft but not coloured. Add this to the salmon with the chives, mayonnaise, crème fraîche, salt and pepper. Mix, cover and put into the fridge for 30 minutes. Form the salmon into four burger shapes. Set these on a tray or plate, cover and refrigerate for another 30 minutes.

For the sauce, stir the yogurt with the mayonnaise and add the dill and garlic. Cover and put in the fridge so the flavours can meld.

About 30 minutes before you want to serve the dish, deseed the tomatoes and chop them finely (no need to skin them). Set aside ready to add to the mayonnaise at the last minute. (Even without the seeds the tomatoes make the sauce sloppy if they're in it too long, and the flesh of the tomatoes softens too.)

Preheat the grill to its highest setting and place the oven shelf 5cm (2in) below the grill. Brush a piece of foil with a little oil and set the salmon burgers on top. Grill them for about two minutes, then reduce the grill heat to medium (or move the burgers further away from it, if you can't reduce the heat) until cooked through, about another two minutes. You don't need to turn them over – they are pretty fragile – they will cook through anyway.

Add the tomatoes to the yogurt mixture and spread some on each slice of rye bread (toasted or not, as you like). Add leaves and cucumber and put a salmon burger on each slice of bread. Top with more of the sauce, a sprig of dill and serve.

salmon on the plate

This is clean tasting but rich at the same time. I love the utter plainness of it. You need good salmon for something this simple, though. Wild stocks are suffering, but you can get very good organic farmed salmon (which is also better for the environment). It's surprising what you can do with raw salmon, especially for those of us brought up in a culture that always serves it cooked. Apart from these two recipes and the one overleaf, you can use it for a Japanese rice bowl; Sashimi; or an Avocado, raw salmon and brown rice salad (see pages 43, 210 and 306).

SERVES 8 AS A STARTER

700g (1lb 9oz) skinless salmon fillet (wild or organically farmed)

8 tbsp light, fruity extra virgin olive oil

flaked sea salt and freshly ground black pepper

2 tbsp roughly chopped dill fronds

juice of ½ large lemon

With a very sharp knife, slice the salmon finely, as if you were slicing smoked salmon. Arrange the slices on individual plates, in such a way that they are not overlapping.

Brush with the extra virgin oil, then sprinkle on salt, pepper and dill. Squeeze lemon juice over and serve immediately.

eastern salmon carpaccio

This packs a punch and is very satisfying. To stretch it and make it less intense, serve it on lightly dressed leaves with thinly sliced avocado. You could treat tuna or mackerel in the same way. When I need a healthy, quick lunch, I eat the fish on grated carrot and mooli tossed with herbs and watercress, with the sauce spooned over. (Keep a jar of it in the fridge.) Filling and sinus-clearing.

SERVES 6 AS A STARTER

600g (1lb 5oz) spanking-fresh skinless salmon fillet

10g (¼oz) coriander leaves

6 basil leaves

about 12 mint leaves

100g (3½oz) Japanese carrot and mooli salad (see page 273), very finely chopped

½ small red onion, very finely sliced (almost shaved)

3 tbsp Vietnamese dipping sauce (see page 75)

lime wedges, to serve

Using a very sharp knife, slice the salmon finely, as if you were slicing smoked salmon. Put it on to a platter or individual plates.

Tear and scatter the herb leaves over the top. Spoon on the carrot and mooli salad and scatter with red onion.

Spoon the dipping sauce on top and serve with lime wedges.

citrus-marinated salmon with fennel and apple salad

This is the kind of dish I could eat at every meal: clean tasting, with bright flavours. If you want bread with this, rye is the obvious choice. Or try Rye crackers (see page 53).

SERVES 6

FOR THE SALAD

4 tbsp caster sugar

6 tbsp rice vinegar

1 tsp wholegrain mustard

1 fennel bulb

juice of ½ lemon

½ red onion, very finely sliced

1 large, tart green apple
(such as Granny Smith)

1 small beetroot, cooked, skin
slipped off (see page 36)

2 tbsp very roughly chopped
dill fronds

FOR THE SALMON

500g (1lb 2oz) very fresh salmon
fillet (tail end is good for this)

4 tbsp light, fruity extra virgin
olive oil

sea salt flakes

freshly ground black pepper

juice of 1 lemon

Make the dressing for the salad by mixing the sugar with the vinegar and stirring until dissolved. Whisk in the mustard until well combined.

Don't make the salad too far in advance as it becomes flaccid if it sits around. Try to do it no more than 30 minutes before serving.

Quarter the fennel, trim the tops and remove any coarse outer leaves. Core each quarter. Using a very sharp knife or a mandoline, cut the fennel into wafer-thin slices. Put the fennel into a bowl and toss with the lemon juice. Add the onion. Halve and core the apple and cut the flesh into matchsticks. Add the apple to the fennel and lemon with the dressing. Toss. Cut the beetroot into matchsticks or very thin slices. (Hold on to the beetroot; it needs to be added at the last minute or will stain everything.)

Using a very sharp knife, slice the salmon finely, as if you were slicing smoked salmon (leave the skin behind). Arrange the slices on individual plates (or a platter), not overlapping. Brush the slices with the extra virgin oil, then sprinkle on salt and pepper. Squeeze lemon juice over and leave for two or three minutes before serving. Add the beetroot and dill to the salad and serve with the salmon.

another rare bite… **japanese seared tuna and radish salad** Sprinkle freshly ground black pepper all over 400g (14oz) tuna loin. Heat 1 tbsp groundnut oil in a frying pan until hot. Add the tuna and cook very briefly on all sides, just until the tuna turns white. Set aside and pour 1 tbsp rice vinegar over it. Make a dressing by whisking together ½ tbsp wholegrain mustard, 2 tsp juices from a jar of pickled ginger, 2 tsp grated root ginger, 1 tbsp soy sauce, 1 tbsp rice vinegar, salt, pepper, 2 tbsp groundnut oil and 2 tbsp light, fruity extra virgin olive oil. Cut the tuna into very thin slices (about the thickness of smoked salmon slices) and divide between four plates. Arrange 60g (2oz) mizuna, 12 radishes, cut into matchsticks, and ¼ finely sliced small red onion alongside. Spoon the dressing over both salad and fish and serve. Serves 4.

salmon barbecued in newspaper with dill and cucumber sauce

This recipe seems strange, I know, and it's only for the summer months when barbecuing is an option… but it is a great way to cook salmon. The results are so moist. It's also a bit of 'event' cooking (mainly because nobody believes it will work). Once the salmon is cooked it is very well behaved and can be left – wrapped in the paper – for a good half hour before you serve it.

Directions to use a broadsheet newspaper are because of size, not the content of the newspaper. (Though it does look lovely in the FT: good colour palette!)

SERVES 10

FOR THE SALMON

1.8kg (4lb) whole salmon, scaled and cleaned

olive oil

salt and pepper

4 handfuls of soft herbs (coriander, chervil, parsley)

bunch of spring onions (about 8), trimmed and roughly chopped

2 lemons, sliced

8 layers of broadsheet newspaper

FOR THE SAUCE

2 tbsp extra virgin olive oil

3 shallots, finely chopped

1 small ridge cucumber, peeled, halved, deseeded and finely chopped, or ½ a regular cucumber

2 tbsp chopped dill fronds

1½ tbsp drained, rinsed and chopped capers

1½ tbsp drained chopped gherkins

300g (10½oz) Greek yogurt

squeeze of lemon juice

Heat the barbecue to a good hot smoulder.

Rub the salmon all over with olive oil, including the inside. Season all over too and in the cavity. Stuff with half the herbs, half the spring onions and some of the lemon slices.

Open out the newspaper – you should be faced with double pages – and put your salmon in the middle. Put the rest of the herbs, spring onions and lemon slices on top and underneath the fish. Wrap the paper round the salmon – use all the paper – and tie it up with kitchen string. Put this parcel under the tap and soak it thoroughly, then lay it on the barbecue.

Cook for 20 minutes on each side (depending on the heat of your coals). Your fire should be warm, but not so hot that the newspaper catches light. You can unwrap the fish and check it carefully for doneness, rewrapping in a couple of layers of foil and cooking for a little longer if it needs it, but there is something great about presenting it in the newspaper.

Meanwhile, make the sauce by mixing all the ingredients for it together with a fork. Taste for seasoning. Cover and keep in the fridge until you want to serve it.

You can either take the salmon to the table in its newspaper or unwrap it behind the scenes and present it on a platter (though why bother with the latter?). As you unwrap the newspaper it will bring most of the salmon skin with it. Serve pieces of the warm salmon with the sauce.

roast sea bass with spiced aubergine, lemon and honey relish

A very special dish. This looks and feels very impressive and luxurious and, to be honest, it isn't cheap to make, but you don't cook this kind of thing every day.

SERVES 8

FOR THE RELISH

2 aubergines

3 tbsp olive oil, plus more if needed

1 large or 2 small onions, chopped

2 plum tomatoes, finely chopped

2 garlic cloves, finely chopped

1 red chilli, deseeded and chopped

2 tsp ground cumin

2 tsp cayenne pepper

salt and pepper

2 tbsp juice from the preserved lemon jar

2 tbsp runny honey, or to taste

1 small preserved lemon (if shop-bought, or ½ home-made one)

4 tbsp chopped coriander leaves

FOR THE FISH

6 tbsp olive oil, plus more to oil

1 sea bass, about 2.5kg (5lb 8oz), scaled and cleaned

2 dried chillies, crumbled

2 heads garlic, cloves separated but not peeled

75ml (2½fl oz) dry white wine

Slice the stalks from the aubergines, then cut the flesh into chunks. Heat 2 tbsp of the oil and sauté the aubergines in a heavy-based pan over a medium heat until gold. You will need to do this in batches. As the aubergines are ready, set them aside. (You may have to use more oil.) Now add another 1 tbsp of oil to the pan and cook the onions until soft and golden, about 10 minutes. Add the tomatoes and cook for another five minutes. Add the garlic, chilli, cumin and cayenne and cook for another two minutes, then return the aubergines. Pour on 100ml (3½fl oz) of water, season, then add the preserved lemon juice and the honey and bring to the boil. Immediately reduce the heat and simmer gently for 10 minutes. The mixture should have the consistency of a thick sauce.

Shred the zest of the preserved lemon – discard the insides – and add half of it to the relish. Taste and see whether you would like to add the rest or not; the relish should be quite assertive. You also need to judge the seasoning and the sweet-tart balance. Now stir in the coriander. Leave to cool to room temperature (you can keep it in the fridge but return to room temperature before serving).

For the fish, preheat the oven to 200°C/400°F/gas mark 6. Lay a large piece of foil in a roasting tin or on a baking sheet (it should be big enough to come up in a 'tent' round the fish) and lightly oil the centre. Put the sea bass on top and season it inside and out. Scatter the chillies over. Throw the garlic cloves around it and drizzle the olive oil over the top. Pull the foil up round the fish and pour on the wine. Pull the sides of the foil together and scrunch the edges together to make a tent around the fish (the fish needs space to steam, it must not be tightly 'wrapped' in the foil). Cook in the hot oven for 30 minutes. Check for doneness after 25 minutes: the flesh near the bone in the thickest part of the fish should be completely white, not at all glassy, and coming away from the bone. Either serve the fish in the foil in which it was cooked, or carefully lift it on to a serving platter. Serve with the aubergine relish. Couscous, bulgar wheat or brown rice is good on the side.

smoked paprika sardines with white beans and roast tomatoes

Make the roast tomatoes in advance (I often have a load of them, and there are quite a few in this book, because they're so useful and good for you) and you can put this dish together very quickly. The oily sardines and the smoky paprika are gorgeous against the earthy beans. You don't need any additional starch. Substitute the white beans with chickpeas if you prefer, or serve the fish and tomatoes with lentils instead of beans (use the recipe on page 164, omitting the coriander). This is just as good with mackerel, serve one per person and grill for three to five minutes on each side.

SERVES 6

FOR THE ROAST TOMATOES

9 large plum tomatoes

3 tbsp olive oil

¾ tbsp balsamic vinegar

2 tsp harissa (optional)

½ tsp caster sugar (if your tomatoes aren't sweet)

salt and pepper

FOR THE SARDINES AND BEANS

3 tbsp olive oil

1 red onion, very finely sliced

2 garlic cloves, finely chopped

2 x 400g cans cannellini beans

2 good squeezes of lemon juice, plus lemon wedges to serve

1 tbsp very finely chopped flat-leaf parsley leaves

12–18 sardines (depending on size), scaled and cleaned

1 tsp smoked paprika

2 fistfuls – literally – of baby spinach leaves or rocket

extra virgin olive oil, to serve

Start by roasting the tomatoes. Preheat the oven to 190°C/375°F/ gas mark 5. Halve the tomatoes and lay them in a single layer in a small roasting tin or ovenproof dish. Mix the regular olive oil, balsamic and harissa (if using) together and pour over the tomatoes. Turn the tomatoes over in the oil to make sure they are well coated, ending with them cut side up. Sprinkle with the sugar (if using) and season. Roast in the hot oven for 45 minutes, or until the tomatoes are caramelized and slightly shrunken.

Heat 1 tbsp of the regular olive oil in a large frying pan and sauté the onion gently until soft but not coloured. Add the garlic and cook for another two minutes. Add the beans and another 1 tbsp of the oil. Season and let them heat through and become imbued with the cooking juices. Add a good squeeze of lemon juice and the parsley. Taste; beans need plenty of seasoning.

For the sardines, preheat the grill to its highest setting. If the sardines haven't been scaled, use your fingers to remove the scales under a cold running tap. Make sure to remove any traces of blood from the inside, too. Dry. If your sardines are medium-large in size, cut two slashes in the flesh on each side (without cutting right down to the bone). These will help the heat penetrate.

Mix the smoked paprika and the last 1 tbsp of oil together. Line a grill tray with foil and lay the sardines on this. Brush the fish with the paprika oil and season on both sides. Place under the very hot grill and cook for two or three minutes each side, or until completely cooked through.

Meanwhile, quickly reheat the beans – tossing them in the pan rather than stirring, so you don't crush them – and toss in the spinach or rocket. It will wilt slightly. Add some more lemon juice and check the seasoning. Drizzle with extra virgin oil. Serve the sardines with the beans, roast tomatoes and lemon wedges.

squid with couscous, chilli, mint and lemon

It's hard not to love food like this: big flavours; easy preparation. The couscous doesn't have to be hot, so you can get it ready in advance, just add the herbs and cook and add the green beans at the last minute (it's never a good idea to have green beans waiting around, they become limp). The only thing you might have to adjust if you make the couscous in advance is its seasoning and the amount of olive oil, as it does soak up dressing as it sits. Then fry the squid – it takes just over a minute – and you're good to go.

SERVES 4–6

FOR THE SQUID

800g (1lb 12oz) squid, cleaned

3 tbsp olive oil

juice of ½ lemon

FOR THE COUSCOUS

300g (10½oz) wholemeal couscous

6 tbsp extra virgin olive oil

salt and pepper

150g (5½oz) French beans, topped but not tailed

2 tbsp olive oil

6 shallots, sliced

3 garlic cloves, finely sliced

2 red chillies, deseeded and finely chopped

6 spring onions, trimmed and sliced on the diagonal

leaves from 12 sprigs of mint, torn

leaves from 10g (¼oz) flat-leaf parsley, left whole

1½ tbsp capers, rinsed

finely grated zest and juice of 1 lemon (zest removed with a zester)

Cut the little wings from the main body of the squid. If the squid are big, slice these wings into three or four strips. Slice the whole body into rings, about 1cm (½in) thick. Wash the squid, making sure that you have removed any remaining whitish gunge from inside the bodies. Drain, cover and keep in the fridge until needed.

Put the couscous into a bowl and add 2 tbsp of the extra virgin oil, 500ml (18fl oz) of boiling water and seasoning. Cover with cling film and leave to plump up for 15 minutes.

Steam the green beans until they are tender but still al dente, then run cold water through them and drain.

Heat the 2 tbsp of regular olive oil in a frying pan and sauté the shallots until they are just soft and still pale, then add the garlic, chillies and spring onions and cook for another two minutes or so.

Fork through the warm couscous to fluff it up, then add the green beans, all the stuff in the frying pan and the herbs, capers and lemon zest and juice and, finally, the remaining 4 tbsp of extra virgin oil. Taste; you might want to add a little more seasoning. Put into a broad shallow bowl.

Pat the squid dry with kitchen paper. (If the squid is damp it won't fry well.) Heat the 3 tbsp of olive oil in a large frying pan or wok until really hot. Stir-fry the squid for 40 seconds, then reduce the heat and cook for 30 seconds. Squeeze on the lemon and season. Scatter the squid on top of the couscous and serve immediately.

summer menu let's start with white peaches

grilled summer herb mackerel | poached white peaches with rosé wine jelly

It's good to plan a menu round a specific ingredient, or a particular feel. I began here with the dessert. White peaches are so elegant, so beautiful, that you don't need to embellish them. From there I worked backwards to greenery and silver scales. Nothing here is difficult to cook, yet it's probably the loveliest menu in the book.

grilled summer herb mackerel, summer mushrooms and green veg

This is one of those dishes that doesn't actually require much skill, just a bit of juggling, but is wonderful to pull off. (Make life easier for yourself by making the purée in advance and then reheating it.) It's the mix that's so impressive and satisfying, the layers of flavours and textures. Rich contrasts with fresh, sweet with savoury. You don't really need anything starchy with it, but you could offer bulgar wheat dressed with a little olive oil, lemon zest and juice.

SERVES 6

FOR THE VEGETABLES

600g (1lb 5oz) peas, fresh or frozen

90ml (3fl oz) strong chicken stock

3 tbsp lemon juice

1½ tbsp extra virgin olive oil

sea salt and pepper

225g (8oz) podded broad beans

1½ tbsp olive oil

175g (6oz) wild summer or shiitake mushrooms

200g (7oz) asparagus, trimmed

FOR THE MACKEREL

6 whole mackerel, scaled, trimmed and cleaned

leaves from a bunch of mint, torn

bunch of dill, roughly chopped, plus more fronds to serve

olive oil

Make the pea purée first. Cook the peas in boiling water until tender, then drain. Put in a blender with the stock, lemon juice, extra virgin oil and seasoning. Purée until smooth. Cook the beans in boiling water for three minutes. Drain, then slip off the skins.

Now for the mackerel. Wash the fish and remove any blood inside (it can be bitter). Dry with kitchen paper, then make three deep slashes in both sides of each. Stuff the herbs inside each cavity. Rub the fish with oil and lay on a grill tray lined with foil (saves washing up). Pat sea salt all over the fish, including in the slashes.

You need to back-time the cooking so all the vegetables and fish are ready together. Preheat a grill to its highest setting. Heat the regular olive oil in a frying pan and quickly fry the mushrooms until they are golden. Season and toss in the broad beans to heat them through. Gently warm the pea purée. Steam the asparagus for about four minutes, or until only just tender.

Grill the mackerel for three to five minutes each side, depending on size. They should be crisp and charred. Serve with the purée and the beans, asparagus and mushrooms, scattered with dill.

poached white peaches with rosé wine jelly

A beautiful dessert. If you find perfectly ripe white peaches, you can dispense with a formal pudding entirely for this menu. Just serve the peaches as they are (though the jelly does accentuate what is good about them: their colour).

SERVES 6

FOR THE JELLIES

groundnut or other flavourless oil, for the moulds

16g (generous ½oz) leaf gelatine (9 small sheets)

175g (6oz) granulated sugar

475ml (17fl oz) rosé wine

FOR THE PEACHES

750ml bottle of white wine

175g (6oz) granulated sugar

2 strips of lemon zest, plus juice of ½ lemon

6 white peaches

Lightly oil six 150ml (5fl oz) pudding moulds.

Cover the gelatine with some cold water and let it soak until it is completely soft. Gently heat the sugar in 200ml (7fl oz) of water until it has dissolved. Take off the heat. Wait until the syrup is hand-hot, then lift the gelatine out of its water and squeeze out the excess liquid. Add to the syrup mixture and stir until the gelatine has completely melted, then pour in the rosé wine. Divide the jelly between the moulds, cover and refrigerate until set.

For the peaches, put the white wine, sugar and lemon zest and juice in a saucepan broad enough to hold the peaches in a single layer. Bring gently to the boil, stirring to help the sugar dissolve.

If the peaches are quite ripe and not too big, poach them whole, otherwise halve them. Add them to the wine and poach gently, turning every so often, until just tender. Remove the peaches and boil the poaching liquid until reduced and slightly syrupy. Leave to cool – the liquid will thicken – then remove the zest. While the peaches are still warm, gently slip off their skins.

To unmould the jellies, dip the moulds very briefly – for only about four seconds – in very hot water. Invert each on to a plate and give it a good shake; the jelly should slide out.

Gently place a whole peach, or two peach halves (with a little syrup) beside each jelly and serve.

seared tuna with chilli and peanut dressing

This is, like all seared tuna dishes, really quick to cook. You can serve it with the rice vermicelli and vegetables that form part of the Vietnamese beef recipe (see page 75), or simply with brown rice.

(see page 75)

SERVES 4

FOR THE DRESSING

2½ tbsp groundnut oil

4 shallots, finely chopped

3 red chillies, deseeded and finely chopped

2 garlic cloves, finely chopped or grated

2.5cm (1in) root ginger, peeled and grated

4 tsp soft light brown sugar, or to taste

1 tbsp fish sauce, or to taste

juice of 2 limes, or to taste

40g (1½oz) raw peanuts

2 tbsp chopped coriander leaves

FOR THE TUNA

2 tbsp groundnut oil

8 tbsp soy sauce

1 tbsp soft light brown sugar

4 tuna steaks, 175g (6oz) each

salt and pepper

juice of 1 lime

For the dressing, heat 1 tbsp of the groundnut oil in a frying pan and cook the shallots over a medium-high heat until golden. Add the chillies, garlic and ginger and cook for another two minutes, then add the sugar. Cook until the sugar slightly caramelizes, then add the fish sauce and lime juice.

Toast the peanuts in a dry frying pan, then roughly chop them. Stir them into the mixture in the frying pan with the rest of the oil, the coriander leaves and 1½ tbsp of water. Taste for a balance of sweet, sour and salty flavours and add more sugar, lime or fish sauce as needed. Set aside while you cook the tuna.

For the tuna, place a griddle pan over a high heat, or get a barbecue up to cooking temperature. Mix the oil with the soy sauce and sugar then put the tuna in this, turning the steaks over so they get well coated, and season well. Cook the tuna on the preheated barbecue or griddle pan for about 1½ minutes on each side (this gives you a moist, slightly raw interior), basting with the marinade. Squeeze some lime juice over each steak and serve with the peanut dressing. A salad of baby spinach and sugar snap peas sprinkled with sesame seeds is lovely on the side.

baked stuffed red mullet

Sitting down to a plateful of red mullet lifts your spirits – that pinky-gold skin immediately makes you think of olive groves and blue sea – and its flesh is so pure you know you are doing yourself good as you eat it. The skin is almost pearlized, iridescent… move it into a patch of light and you can see little streaks of rainbow shimmering in it. And red mullet delivers in the mouth as well. The flakes are smaller than those of haddock, but bigger than those of sole, and almost oily. It's classified as a round white fish but there is a kind of butteriness to it, a rich sweetness which you normally only find in shellfish. The taste is both delicate and robust.

Red mullet is also the most amenable fish, requiring – if you want to be purist – only the simplest treatment. Lay whole red mullet in a gratin dish, drizzle with olive oil, season, bake and serve with lemon wedges. But if you want to do something more, a stuffing is a good way to go.

SERVES 4

salt and pepper

4 fat red mullet, scaled, trimmed and cleaned

olive oil

½ onion, very finely chopped

200g (7oz) tomatoes, finely chopped

3 garlic cloves, finely chopped

leaves from 3 sprigs of thyme, plus sprigs of thyme to cook

200g (7oz) spinach, coarse stalks removed

75g (2¾oz) wholemeal breadcrumbs

juice of 1 lemon

Preheat the oven to 190°C/375°F/gas mark 5.

Season the mullet inside and out and rub olive oil all over them.

Heat 1 tbsp olive oil in a frying pan and sauté the onion over a medium heat until it is soft and pale golden. Add the tomatoes and garlic and cook until the tomatoes are really soft. Sprinkle on the leaves from the three sprigs of thyme, season and cook for another few minutes. Chop the spinach, add it to the pan and allow it to wilt, stirring a little to help incorporate it into the tomatoes. It will throw out some water, but that's okay as you are going to add bread. Mix in the breadcrumbs and add a little more oil if you don't now have a moist stuffing. Check for seasoning too.

Divide the stuffing between each fish cavity, then put them in an ovenproof dish where they can lie in a single layer. Scatter thyme sprigs over and around the fish and drizzle with olive oil. Bake in the hot oven for 20 minutes, then check for doneness. The flesh should be white, not at all glassy, and coming away from the bone. Squeeze the lemon juice on top and serve.

also try… a sweet-sour sicilian-inspired stuffing. Sauté 2 chopped shallots and 1 chopped garlic clove in 1 tbsp olive oil until soft (but still pale). Add 15g (½oz) pitted and chopped black or green olives, 50g (1¾oz) toasted pine nuts, 2 tbsp raisins or currants, the juice and finely grated zest of 1 lemon, 2 tbsp chopped flat-leaf parsley or torn mint leaves and 2½ tsp rinsed capers. Heat through so the flavours meld. Chuck in 75g (2¾oz) breadcrumbs, season and mix. Stuff the fish as above and cook in the same way.

roast red mullet with tahini dressing and barley tabbouleh

Red mullet are low-effort, big impact fish. They roast quickly, their flesh is pearlescent and their skin shimmering. You can use any other grain instead of barley (farro or wheat berries would be good, see pages 223–224 for how to cook them). In winter you can make a grain tabbouleh such as this using pomegranates, green olives and chopped walnuts in place of the tomatoes and olives.

SERVES 4

FOR THE TABBOULEH

150g (5½oz) pearl barley

3 tbsp extra virgin olive oil, or to taste

1 tbsp lemon juice, or to taste

1 tbsp white balsamic vinegar

salt and pepper

1 tbsp olive oil

1 small red onion, very finely chopped

2 garlic cloves, finely chopped

2 tsp ground cumin

1 red chilli, deseeded and finely shredded

big handful of mint leaves, torn

6 tbsp finely chopped flat-leaf parsley leaves

5 really well-flavoured plum tomatoes, peeled, deseeded and finely chopped (see page 101)

1 ridge cucumber, peeled, deseeded and finely chopped, or use a regular cucumber

FOR THE TAHINI DRESSING

2 tbsp tahini

juice of ½ lemon, or to taste

2 tbsp extra virgin olive oil

1 garlic clove, crushed

FOR THE FISH

4 large red mullet, about 225g (8oz) each, cleaned and scaled

4 tbsp olive oil

juice of 1 lemon

a little sumac

Put the barley into a saucepan and cover with plenty of cold water. Bring to the boil, then reduce the heat and cook for 30 minutes, or until tender. Drain, rinse with boiling water, shake dry, and immediately mix with the extra virgin oil, lemon juice, vinegar and seasoning. Leave to cool to room temperature.

Heat the regular olive oil in a saucepan and sauté the onion until it is soft but not coloured. Add the garlic, cumin and chilli and cook for another couple of minutes. Leave to cool. Stir this into the barley along with the herbs, tomatoes and cucumber. Check for seasoning. You may also want to add a little more extra virgin oil or lemon juice.

To make the tahini dressing, beat the tahini (just use a fork), then add 75ml (2½fl oz) of water, the lemon juice, extra virgin oil and garlic. (Make sure you add the water before the lemon juice, or the tahini suddenly thickens.) Taste and season. You may also want to add a little more water or lemon juice; different brands of tahini have varying consistencies, so add water and seasonings accordingly. Your finished mixture should have the consistency of double cream.

When ready to cook the fish, preheat the oven to 180°C/350°F/gas mark 4. Season the mullet in their cavities and put them in an ovenproof dish where they can lie in a single layer. Mix the regular olive oil with the lemon juice and pour all over the fish. Season the outside. Bake for 15 minutes. Drizzle the fish with some of the tahini dressing (serve the rest on the side) and sprinkle both dressing and fish with sumac. Serve with the barley tabbouleh.

israeli chicken with moghrabieh, harissa-griddled peaches and mint

The chicken here is based on a recipe in Paula Wolfert's excellent book, *Mediterranean Cooking*. (If you don't own anything by Paula Wolfert, seek her out. Her books are full of dishes that are 'accidentally' healthy.)

Moghrabieh (Middle Eastern giant couscous) is difficult to find in wholemeal form, but Merchant Gourmet sell it (see page 328). You could also use matfoul, a bulgar wheat product, and cook it in the same way. Either can be used as a salad base.

SERVES 4

FOR THE CHICKEN AND
MOGHRABIEH

5 tbsp hot mustard (I use
English mustard)

8 skinless bone-in chicken thighs
(or other chicken joints)

3 tbsp soft dark brown sugar

salt and pepper

3 tbsp olive oil

150ml (5fl oz) orange juice

200g (7oz) wholemeal moghrabieh

1 tbsp extra virgin olive oil

good squeeze of lemon juice

FOR THE PEACHES

3 just-ripe peaches, halved
and pitted

2 tbsp olive oil

3 tbsp harissa, or to taste (reduce
the amount if you want it less hot)

juice of ½ lemon

leaves from 1 small bunch of
mint, torn

Preheat the oven to 190°C/375°F/gas mark 5.

Spread the mustard on both sides of the chicken thighs and put them into a small roasting tin or gratin dish in which they will fit snugly. Sprinkle with half the sugar and season. Drizzle on 2 tbsp of the regular olive oil and all the orange juice. Roast in the oven for 20 minutes. Take the pan out, turn the chicken over, baste it and sprinkle with the rest of the sugar. Season and return to the oven for another 15 minutes. The chicken should be dark gold.

When the chicken has about 15 minutes of cooking time left, sort out the moghrabieh. Heat the final 1 tbsp of regular oil in a saucepan, add the moghrabieh and stir over a medium heat until golden; after about four minutes, you should be able to smell it getting toasted. Cover with boiling water, season and simmer gently for about 10 minutes, until the moghrabieh is tender. Drain, toss with the extra virgin oil and the lemon and season.

Meanwhile, cut the peach halves into wedges and toss in a bowl with the 2 tbsp of regular olive oil and the harissa. Heat a griddle pan until it is really hot. Lift the peach slices out of the harissa mixture, shaking off the excess, and cook on both sides until tender. Remove from the griddle and squeeze lemon juice on top. Once the moghrabieh is ready, toss it with the peaches and mint. Serve with the chicken.

skewered chicken with lime, chilli and mint salad and china rose sprouts

A child-friendly dish (my kids love it and they're pretty fussy). The salad is fabulous (hot and fresh) and goes with any spicy griddled or roasted meat dish. China rose radish sprouts are beautiful but hard to find. It is very easy to grow them, honestly. (See page 329 for where to buy seeds.)

SERVES 6

FOR THE CHICKEN

12 skinless boneless chicken thighs

1½ tbsp groundnut oil

juice of 1 lime, plus lime wedges

FOR THE MARINADE

finely grated zest of 4 limes and juice of 6

2 red chillies, deseeded and shredded

3 tbsp soy sauce

½ tbsp fish sauce

6 garlic cloves, crushed

2 tbsp chopped mint leaves

freshly ground black pepper

FOR THE DRESSING

2 tbsp rice vinegar

1 tbsp caster sugar

½ tbsp fish sauce

juice of 1 lime

2 tsp ginger syrup

1 tbsp chopped peanuts (optional)

2 tbsp groundnut oil

salt and pepper

FOR THE SALAD

10 radishes, cut into matchsticks

5 Chinese leaves, shredded

1 carrot, cut into matchsticks

15g (½oz) coriander leaves, torn

leaves from 4 sprigs of mint, torn

70g (2½oz) mizuna, or watercress

35g (1¼oz) China rose radish sprouts

Soak six bamboo skewers in water for 30 minutes; this stops them burning when the chicken is cooking.

Cut the chicken into cubes. Mix all the ingredients for the marinade together. Put the chicken into this, turning it to make sure it is all coated, cover with cling film and put in the fridge. Leave for one to four hours.

To make the dressing, whisk all the ingredients, except the oil, together. The sugar should dissolve in the lime juice. Now whisk in the oil and taste for seasoning.

Have everything for the salad prepared and ready to mix.

Thread the chicken on to the skewers and heat the oil in a large frying pan (it needs to be big enough to accommodate the length of the skewers and allow the chicken to touch the base of the pan). You can also griddle the chicken, in which case just heat a griddle pan and brush each of the skewers with oil rather than putting the oil in the pan. Shake the marinade off the chicken.

Cook on all sides, starting on a high heat to get a good colour all over, then reducing the heat so the chicken can cook right through. The whole process takes about 10 minutes. Add salt and pepper and squeeze lime juice over them.

Toss all the salad ingredients with the dressing and serve the skewers on the salad. Serve extra wedges of lime on the side and offer brown rice.

pollo alla diavola with green beans and sicilian breadcrumbs

This chilli-hot Italian chicken is usually cooked on the barbecue or grilled, but roasting works well too and requires much less attention. Go as hot with the chilli as you dare.

The Sicilian breadcrumbs are good with other vegetables too and feel free to improvise with them, adding chilli, capers or grated lemon zest when serving them with other vegetable dishes.

Opinions vary on how many poussins one should serve (I have seen some people recoil in horror at the thought of eating a whole one, others get stuck right in). Some guests may only want half. So you can either cut the amount you cook (if you know your diners), or expect some leftovers.

If you prefer to make this with chicken thighs (skin on or off, as you prefer), use only 6 tbsp of olive oil in the marinade and cook the joints for 40–45 minutes at 180°C/350°F/gas mark 4.

SERVES 8

FOR THE POUSSINS

leaves from 4 sprigs of rosemary, chopped

2 tbsp dried oregano

8 tbsp olive oil

freshly ground black pepper

juice of 1 large lemon

1–1½ tbsp chilli flakes (use your discretion, it depends how hot you like it)

8 poussins

flaked sea salt

FOR THE BEANS WITH CRUMBS

3 tbsp olive oil

125g (4½oz) coarse country bread, crusts removed, torn into small pieces

35g (1¼oz) raisins

35g (1¼oz) pine nuts

4 garlic cloves, finely sliced

4 cured anchovies, drained of oil and finely chopped

700g (1lb 9oz) green beans, topped but not tailed

juice of ½ lemon

about 2 tbsp extra virgin olive oil

pepper

leaves from about 8 sprigs of mint, torn

For the poussins, mix the herbs, olive oil, pepper, lemon and chilli flakes together. Pour this all over the poussins in a non-reactive dish or dishes and use your hands to rub it in, inside and out. Cover with cling film and leave in the fridge to marinate. A couple of hours is all they need, but turn them over every so often. When ready to cook, preheat the oven to 190°C/375°F/gas mark 5 and lift the poussins out of the marinade. Season the birds with sea salt and roast for 50 minutes. Check that they are completely cooked: if you pierce a thigh, the juices that run out should be clear with no trace of pink. Cover with foil, insulate with towels (reserved for this purpose) and leave to rest for 15 minutes.

For the beans, heat 2 tbsp of the olive oil a frying pan and sauté the bread until it is golden on all sides. Add another 1 tbsp of oil and add the raisins, pine nuts, garlic and anchovies. Allow the pine nuts to get toasted (this happens pretty quickly so beware) and press the anchovies with a wooden spoon to break them up. Take off the heat and keep warm while you are cooking the beans.

Cook the beans in boiling salted water until tender (but al dente). Drain them, toss in a serving bowl with the lemon juice, extra virgin oil and seasoning and stir in the breadcrumbs and mint.

Serve the poussins with the beans. You don't need starch (though Summer fregola is good, see overleaf), but roast peppers (which you can make in advance) are good on the side.

lamb kebabs with georgian adzhika

This sauce is hot, though my version is actually less spicy than it would be eaten in Georgia. As chillies vary, I would add half the amount suggested here, taste, then add more if you want.

MAKES 6

FOR THE KEBABS

600g (1lb 5oz) cubed leg of lamb

4 tbsp olive oil

1½ tsp ground cinnamon

1 tsp ground allspice

2 tsp cayenne pepper

2 garlic cloves, crushed

FOR THE ADZHIKA

4 garlic cloves, roughly chopped

1 celery stick, roughly chopped

4 red chillies, chopped

1 red pepper, chopped

25g (1oz) dill fronds

25g (1oz) coriander leaves

3½ tbsp red wine vinegar

4 tbsp extra virgin olive oil

Trim the lamb of any fat or sinew. Mix all the other ingredients for the kebabs in a bowl and put the lamb in it. Turn the meat over in this, cover with cling film and put in the fridge to marinate for anything from two to 24 hours. Turn the meat over every so often. Soak six bamboo skewers in water for at least 30 minutes so they won't burn on the barbecue or griddle.

To make the adzhika, put the garlic in a food processor and blitz. Add the celery, chillies (deseeded if you like) and pepper and pulse-blend to a salsa-like mixture. Add the herbs and pulse about three times; you don't want a purée, just a rough, lumpy mix. Scrape into a bowl and add salt, the vinegar and extra virgin oil.

Thread the lamb cubes on to the skewers and season with salt. Cook on a hot griddle pan, or a barbecue, until golden brown all over, turning them regularly. It's best if they are still rare in the middle, so these only need about seven minutes in total. Serve with the adzhika, or either of the sauces below.

more sauces… **raisin, chilli and pine nut salsa** Hot, sweet and with a streak of minty freshness, this is Sicilian in influence. Put 2 small garlic cloves in a mortar and crush with a little sea salt. Add 60g (2oz) pine nuts and crush very roughly. Now add 2 tbsp raisins, 1 red and 1 green chilli, deseeded and finely chopped, the torn leaves from about 12 sprigs of mint, 2 finely chopped spring onions, 2 tbsp white balsamic vinegar, the juice of ½ lemon, black pepper and 8 tbsp extra virgin oil. Give a brief bash to start to bring the flavours out. Taste, adjust the seasoning and serve. Serves 6.

mint and almond pesto Put 60g (2oz) toasted almonds in a food processor with 4 garlic cloves, 80g (2¾oz) mint leaves, 40g (1½oz) flat-leaf parsley leaves, 3 tsp runny honey, the juice of 1 lemon and salt and pepper. Purée while adding 300ml (½ pint) extra virgin oil in a steady stream. Taste for seasoning. Pour a layer of olive oil on top to protect it and cover with cling film until ready to serve. Serves 6.

lamb scottadito with summer fregola

Literally lamb that 'burns your fingers', this is a great casual supper or weekend lunch dish. It does need to be cooked at the last minute, but it's very easy. It's best to cook it with the fat on; if you or your guests don't want to eat it, just cut it off.

Fregola is really a type of large couscous from Sardinia. If you can't get it, use a grain such as farro (see page 223 for how to cook that).

SERVES 6

FOR THE LAMB

18 best end lamb cutlets, well scraped (get your butcher to do it)

3 tbsp olive oil

juice of 1 lemon, plus lemon wedges to serve

1½ tbsp chopped oregano leaves

8 tsp chilli flakes (or even more for extra heat)

FOR THE FREGOLA

400g (14oz) fregola

4 tbsp extra virgin olive oil

1½ tbsp lemon juice

salt and pepper

1 tbsp olive oil

4 shallots, finely chopped

150g (5½oz) cherry tomatoes, quartered or chopped

leaves from 1 small bunch of basil, torn, or 3 tbsp roughly chopped flat-leaf parsley leaves

Put the cutlets into a large, shallow, non-reactive bowl. Add the regular olive oil, lemon juice, oregano and chilli flakes. Turn everything over with your hands, cover, put in the fridge and leave to marinate for a couple of hours. Turn the meat over every so often if you can.

Cook the fregola in boiling water for 10 minutes, then drain and immediately add the extra virgin oil, lemon juice, salt and pepper. Fork this through.

Meanwhile, heat the 1 tbsp of regular olive oil in a small frying pan and cook the shallots until they are soft but not golden. Add to the fregola with the tomatoes and herbs.

Heat a griddle pan over a high heat. Lift the lamb out of the marinade, shaking off the excess liquid (there shouldn't be much). Season the meat well. When the pan is really hot, cook the chops on each side until well coloured. Press the meaty part of the chops down on the griddle with the back of a wooden spoon as you are cooking. They should still be pink in the middle, so about 1½ minutes on each side is enough. Insert a sharp knife into one of them to see how well the meat is done, but make sure you serve the chop the other way up so people can't see the slit.

Put the cutlets on a platter with the lemon wedges and serve immediately with the fregola. Make sure you supply napkins. Your guests will almost certainly want to clean every last morsel of meat from the chops, so fingers will definitely be in use.

japanese beef with country-style ponzu and wasabi

Sometimes you want a burst of protein. I don't eat red meat that often but I do sometimes get a craving for it (and so does my teenage son). This is an occasional – and expensive – treat, and I love its cleanness. It's very filling, too. You can serve Japanese pickled vegetables alongside (see page 60) if you want to extend it.

The ponzu dressing is from an inspiring book, *Japanese Farm Food*, by Nancy Singleton Hachisu, and is much simpler to make than regular ponzu.

SERVES 6

FOR THE PONZU

125ml (4fl oz) Japanese soy sauce

125ml (4fl oz) bitter orange juice (such as from Seville oranges), or a mixture of lime and orange juice

1 tbsp chopped chives

FOR THE BEEF

sea salt

450g (1lb) top-quality fillet of beef, all visible fat removed

wasabi (preferably fresh, then grated, see page 329 for stockists), to serve

shreds of zest from 2 lemons, plus lemon wedges to serve

2 small red chillies, deseeded and finely sliced

To make the ponzu just mix all the ingredients together. Cover and put in the fridge.

Sprinkle sea salt all over the beef. Sear it all over either on a very hot griddle pan, or on a barbecue. Immediately wrap in kitchen paper and put in the fridge for one hour to cool.

Cut into slices across the grain and lay them out, overlapping, on each serving plate. Give everyone a little wasabi on the side of the plate and sprinkle the beef with the lemon zest and chillies. Put a little dipping bowl of the ponzu on each plate. Offer wedges of lemon in a bowl as well.

tagliata

A quick Italian steak salad that is a real treat. Cherry tomatoes, dressed with some lemon juice and extra virgin olive oil, are lovely alongside.

SERVES 8

4 sirloin steaks, about 300g (10½oz) each, fat removed

4 garlic cloves, unpeeled

200g (7oz) mixed watercress and rocket leaves

olive oil

salt and pepper

125ml (4fl oz) extra virgin olive oil

4 sprigs of rosemary

2 strips of lemon zest, plus the juice of 1 lemon

25–50g (1–1¾oz) Parmesan, shaved

You need to work fast for this recipe. Get your steaks to room temperature. Bash the garlic cloves with the side of a knife and put the salad leaves in a broad, shallow bowl.

Heat a heavy-based frying pan until really hot, add a thin film of regular olive oil and heat until the oil is just beginning to smoke. Season the steaks all over and fry them for 2½ minutes in total, turning every 20 seconds so they get cooked evenly. Put the steaks on a warm plate, cover with foil and leave to rest.

There won't be much oil in the pan but whatever there is, throw it out. Don't wipe the pan, though: there's flavour in it. Add the extra virgin oil to the pan and set it over a medium heat. Throw in the garlic, rosemary and lemon zest. Allow the flavourings to infuse the oil for three minutes, then add the lemon juice.

Cut the steaks into slices about ½cm (¼in) thick. Strain half the dressing in the pan through a sieve on to the leaves in the bowl. Scatter the steak and Parmesan on the leaves as well, then strain on the rest of the dressing. Sprinkle more salt over the whole thing with a good grinding of pepper and serve immediately.

how many diets can you fit into a life?

During my life I've followed the Mayo Clinic, Scarsdale, F-plan, Atkins, Cabbage Soup, Cambridge, Lighter Life, South Beach and Dukan diets. I have spent so much energy angsting about them I could weep. Friends, especially women (many of them slim), have done the same thing. (If there is a more effective way to keep women down, insecure and wasting time I have yet to find it.)

Analysts Mintel found one in four adults in the UK are trying to lose weight 'most of the time'. That's thirteen million people on a permanent diet. Everyone has an opinion on the best or fastest way. You'll be told you're wasting your time, or that you should be on a different regime. Smug skinny people will say you lack willpower, or don't move enough.

If you're reading this page, you've probably dieted, too. If you've bought this book, you probably love food passionately and find it hard to diet. I'm in exactly the same position. Unfortunately, once you start dieting it's difficult to stop, because you're on the whole deprivation <-> rebellion, eating too little <-> overindulging roller coaster.

I believe that, without our collective neurosis about appearance, we would each hit an acceptable weight that suited us (we might be rounded, we might be skinny, but it would be right). But we don't live in that kind of society. Further, we live in a culture that is so full of fattening food – refined carbs, especially sugar – that eating in a balanced way is harder than it was. My children want a 'treat' (a sweet one) on the way home from school every day, because everyone else has one. When I was little, sweet treats were for the weekend. So we're judged more severely on how we look, yet there's more temptation to eat things that will make us unhealthy and put on weight. Not ideal for a sane, balanced approach to food.

I don't advocate being skinny; I gave up that option years ago. In my twenties I managed to stay at seven and a half stone (I'm five feet four inches tall) by being extremely strict for five days and eating what I wanted at the weekend. It was a grim existence – though it 'worked' for my appearance – and it certainly wasn't healthy. But it's not 'healthy' to be overweight either and, while this book isn't about losing weight, we need to look at it. Dieting – even if it just means cutting down for a few days – is okay from time to time. (After Christmas or a week's holiday in Paris you're going to have put on a few pounds.) But constant dieting is not a good way to live. It's unhealthy and it's miserable.

Diets do work – some spectacularly – but only while you're on them. I can hear you groaning as I say this (as I've groaned when people have said it to me), but you need to get to a weight you're comfortable with *and then you need to change the way you eat*. I have spent years not listening to this. In fact I could have punched people who said it to me. So I am not *instructing* you; it's your battle. But the food in this book (bar the cakes and sorbets, which are for weekends) and the information in it should help you stay at a decent weight without feeling deprived. I adore food. But I got sick of dieting. And this is the most satisfying food I have ever eaten.

ricotta with summer berries and honey

No cooking required. Just good, pure ingredients. Go to a deli and buy fresh ricotta rather than the UHT stuff you find in tubs in supermarkets. There's a world of difference.

SERVES 4–6

300g (10½oz) fresh ricotta

a little icing sugar (optional)

400g (14oz) raspberries, loganberries, redcurrants or blackberries

lovely scented runny honey (orange blossom or thyme are good here)

Line a sieve with muslin or a brand new J-cloth. Set this over a bowl and tip the ricotta into it. Pull the cloth round it and set a plate on top. Put into the fridge and leave for a couple of hours.

Pull the cloth off and taste the ricotta. If you feel it needs to be sweeter, mash a little icing sugar into it. Divide the ricotta between serving plates, or put it on to one large plate.

Scatter some berries alongside each serving and drizzle with honey.

other fruity ways with ricotta... You can serve ricotta like this with other fruits. Good ripe figs are delicious (in which case use a good lavender honey, it's perfect with figs) and whitecurrants look wonderful (their almost pearlized skin is gorgeous against the creamy ricotta). Poached peaches or apricots are lovely, too (see page 130, but add less sugar to their poaching liquor as you will be drizzling them with honey). If you're using golden stone fruits, scatter them with pistachios before serving. Another idea is to slightly sweeten the ricotta with icing sugar and serve it in a mound with fresh cherries scattered all round it.

gooseberry, almond and spelt cake

Sweet-tart and moist. There's sugar in this, of course, making it an occasional treat. But it's made partly with wholemeal spelt flour, which is both better for you than white flour and also brings a nutty tone. You can replace it with wholemeal wheat flour, if you prefer.

SERVES 8

125g (4½oz) unsalted butter, plus more for the tin

125g (4½oz) soft light brown sugar

3 large eggs, lightly beaten

50g (1¾oz) wholemeal spelt flour, sifted

25g (1oz) plain flour, sifted

75g (2½oz) ground almonds (preferably freshly ground)

¾ tsp baking powder

350g (12oz) dessert gooseberries (red or green), topped and tailed

4 tbsp golden caster sugar

30g (1oz) flaked almonds

icing sugar, to dust

Preheat the oven to 190°C/375°F/gas mark 5. Butter a 20cm (8in) springform cake tin.

Beat the butter and soft light brown sugar until light and fluffy. Add the eggs a little at a time, beating well after each addition. If the mixture starts to curdle, add 1 tbsp of the spelt flour. Fold in the rest of the flours, the almonds and baking powder using a large metal spoon, then scrape into the prepared tin.

Toss the gooseberries with the golden caster sugar and spread them over the top of the cake. Bake for 20 minutes. Sprinkle on the flaked almonds and return to the oven for 10 minutes. The cake is ready when a skewer inserted into the centre comes out clean.

Leave to cool in the tin, then carefully remove the ring and base of the tin. Dust with icing sugar before serving.

a cherry version… This is just as good made with cherries. Just pit 500g (1lb 2oz) of them and throw them on to the cake just before it goes into the oven. They'll be soft in the time that it takes the cake batter to cook. This makes a lovely squidgy cake.

raspberries with basil and buttermilk sherbet

A sherbet is an unusual thing. It is made with milk and sugar syrup and feels, in the mouth, more like sorbet than ice cream. This buttermilk version is mouth-puckeringly refreshing.

In order to cut down on sugar, the syrup for the raspberries contains less than is normal. Once you get rid of the notion that fruits have to be in a thick syrup, it is rather liberating. They taste better. But you do need to adjust your expectations when it comes to texture.

SERVES 6

FOR THE SHERBET

125g (4½oz) granulated sugar

225ml (8fl oz) buttermilk

juice of 2 lemons

FOR THE RASPBERRIES

75g (2¾oz) granulated sugar

3 strips of lemon zest, plus the juice of 1 lemon

3 sprigs of basil, plus a few more small sprigs or leaves to serve (optional)

325g (11½oz) raspberries

For the sherbet, heat 75ml (2½fl oz) of water and the sugar together until the sugar has completely dissolved, then leave to cool. Stir in the buttermilk and lemon juice and either churn in an ice-cream machine according to the manufacturer's instructions, or freeze in a shallow, wide freezer-proof container, removing it three or four times during the freezing process and blitzing it in a food processor, or mashing it (vigorously) with a fork.

To prepare the raspberries, put the sugar and lemon zest into a saucepan with 300ml (½ pint) of water and gently heat, stirring a little to help the sugar dissolve. Boil for two minutes, then remove from the heat, add the lemon juice and basil and leave to cool. The basil will infuse the syrup. Put the raspberries into a serving bowl and strain the cold syrup over them. (The berries become flaccid if they are left too long in the syrup, so don't leave these for longer than 15 minutes before you want to serve them.)

Serve the raspberries, with a few basil leaves or sprigs (if using), along with the buttermilk sherbet.

figs and melon with ginger and star anise

Figs and melons are great 'almost autumn' fruits, so they're good at the end of summer. Melons are kind of musky, figs rich and sexy, while the warm spices anticipate the season to come.

SERVES 6

125g (4½oz) granulated sugar

2cm (¾in) root ginger, peeled and sliced

1 star anise

juice of 5 juicy limes, plus 2 broad strips of lime zest

6 large figs (not too ripe), stalk trimmed, halved

400g (14oz) sweet ripe melon flesh, deseeded (that's the amount of flesh in 1 Ogen or Galia melon)

Put the sugar into a saucepan – one large enough to hold the figs in a single layer – with 300ml (½ pint) of water. Add the ginger, star anise, half the lime juice and both strips of zest. Heat the pan, stirring to help the sugar dissolve. Bring to the boil and boil for four minutes. Reduce the heat.

Add the figs and poach them gently for three to four minutes; you just want them to be there long enough to flavour the syrup a little and also take in some of the flavourings in the pan. You don't want them in there so long they fall apart, though. Lift the figs out with a slotted spoon and put them into a bowl.

Discard the zest and the star anise from the syrup. Reduce the poaching liquid by about one-quarter by boiling it, then add the rest of the lime juice and leave to cool. Add the melon to the figs and pour over the cold syrup.

Leave the fruit to macerate in the syrup for at least 30 minutes (though no more than three hours as the melon gets too soft). This is good with Greek yogurt and a drizzle of honey.

loving breakfast

The breakfast I ate as a teenager now horrifies me: a slice of white toast with Dairylea and a cup of sweet tea, or maybe a bowl of Frosties. No wonder I was nodding off in Spanish class by eleven o'clock. As an adult I didn't fare much better. I like nothing better than a French breakfast. Baskets of brioche, croissants, tartines… my autobiography could be called 'Viennoiserie were my downfall'. I haven't banned these (I couldn't, so I leave them for the weekend) but they put weight on and, more importantly, leave you hungry. Breakfast is the most important meal we eat – it's when we 'break the fast' – and as such needs to give us energy that will last. (Many experts are convinced that people who skip breakfast in order to lose weight eat more at the other meals during the day, and snack more, too.) Yet the most popular breakfast foods in Western culture are refined carbohydrates. Processed cereals, muffins, croissants and white bread are just about the worst things you can eat (not just at breakfast but at any time of day). Even the glass of fruit juice we down is basically sugar, it may contain vitamins but it's much better to eat whole fruit (as you then get fibre as well) than drink the juice. No breakfast, or a breakfast that doesn't fill you up, means the hormone, ghrelin, which sends you the signal telling you you're hungry, isn't suppressed and you'll overeat at lunch time (or hit the biscuit tin mid-morning). So breakfast is important.

I didn't start eating better breakfasts because somebody told me I should. It happened out of curiosity and a love of food. I grew more interested in it as a meal when I saw what people in other countries ate first thing. Breakfast in a guest house in Mexico was sliced avocado, salty fresh cheese, warm black beans and mangoes with lime. There wasn't a box of cereal in sight. In Germany I had 'eggs in a glass' every morning: two soft-boiled eggs that are ingeniously shelled and put into a tumbler (which kind of makes them special), with the sort of bread that requires a lot of chewing (and luckily I love). In Greece it's tomatoes, cucumber, feta cheese, olives, yogurt and fruit. But it was the Scandinavian breakfast that really got me going. Breakfast in a hotel in Helsinki a few summers ago offered home-made muesli, porridge, fruit compote, cheeses, hard-boiled eggs, tomatoes, cucumber and sliced peppers, cured herring, gravlax, ham and five types of dense whole grain bread. Every morning I approached breakfast as I do a good dinner.

I didn't eat everything on offer, but getting protein first thing (fish, eggs and cheese) really makes you feel full, while the complex carbs (porridge and solid whole grain bread) kept me going too. I breakfasted the Finnish way for two weeks – it was my favourite meal of the day – and was rarely hungry before three in the afternoon. Returning home I was terrified to get on the scales. I had, as the advice goes, breakfasted like a king. I knew this was supposed to be good for you, but I was sure I'd pay for it. However, my bathroom scales showed that I hadn't put on a single pound. And I'd had boundless energy every day.

We're all short of time in the morning. That is partly why cereal manufacturers convinced us that a bowl of processed grains is adequate (we wanted to believe it). For all the boring reasons you've ever heard – they have added sugar, added salt – they aren't good enough.

Make your own cereal with whole grains, nuts and seeds or, if you want to buy muesli, check the sugar and salt content on the packet. You'll find, though, that home-made muesli is cheaper as well as more delicious. And you know exactly what's in it, as you've made it.

I've given 'best case scenario' recipes for some breakfasts (proper slow-cooked porridge, for example), but there's nothing wrong with the quick-cook type; it certainly beats packaged cereal hands down. I love a bowl of porridge oats that has simmered – with the occasional stir – on the hob for five minutes while I've been trying to find my youngest's school shoes. We live in the real world. But you'll probably find, if you start to eat porridge regularly, that you'll look forward to it way more than you did the bowl of cold cereal you used to down. And you might make more time for it.

The main thing to be is open-minded. I like thinking about breakfast as a meal, like any other, with all the pleasures that entails, rather than something that you wolf down before leaving the house. Don't let one of your three meals a day be dictated by breakfast cereal manufacturers. Think savoury, too. Think creatively. It might not be your bag, but cured herrings make a great breakfast (very filling), or try some smoked fish every so often. Or omelettes – filled with grated cheese, shredded spinach or watercress – in fact eggs done any way are great (they're full of protein and keep you going until lunch time). Then there's kedgeree (made with brown rice and lentils), or toasted sourdough with avocado or labneh and roast tomatoes, or mushrooms sautéed and splashed with soy sauce… Hungry yet?

A breakfast high in protein has proved the best for me. It keeps me full for longer and I find that even 'good carbs' like porridge – if I eat it every day – keep weight on. Your experience of your own body will tell you what will work best for you.

Nobody's going to deprive you of your glass of freshly squeezed, but try to eat fruit rather than drink it (or do both). Stewed apples – I try to add very little sugar – are cheap and allow you to get the first of your five a day in at breakfast, and even out of season I make red fruit compote with big bags of frozen berries: add enough sugar to sweeten, throw in fresh blueberries and eat with yogurt. (I go for full-fat which tastes better and keeps you feeling full for longer than low-fat versions. Many low-fat yogurts are very high in sugar or sweeteners, so check the label. And read more about fats on pages 284–285.)

Breakfast – even midweek – can be as enjoyable as dinner. And if you're into food, that's another lovely meal to think about. Breakfast can be varied, even exotic, filling enough to keep you away from hitting the chocolate digestives at 11 o'clock and – this is the real plus – bloody delicious. Even when they're a croissant-free zone.

turkish poached eggs with spinach and yogurt

The Turks are very good with eggs. You wouldn't think that poached eggs could become an exotic feast, but here they do. A lovely simple breakfast, lunch or supper for two.

SERVES 2

100g (3½oz) Greek yogurt

1 garlic clove, crushed

1–2 flatbreads

2–4 eggs

50g (1¾oz) butter

½ tsp cumin seeds

½ tsp chilli flakes

100g (3½oz) spinach leaves, tough stalks removed, washed

1 tbsp olive oil

salt and pepper

Mix the yogurt with the crushed garlic. Warm or toast the flatbread and put a piece on each of two plates. Top each piece with some of the yogurt, spreading it out.

Meanwhile, poach the eggs, either one or two per person depending on appetite. At the same time, heat the butter until it is foaming, then add the spices and cook for a minute. Put the spinach in a frying pan with the olive oil and quickly heat it, allowing the spinach to wilt. Season. Try to have all these components ready at the same time.

Put some spinach on top of the yogurt, top with the eggs and pour the warm spiced butter on top. Season and serve.

roopa's indian scrambled eggs

A Punjabi dish from my great friend Roopa Gulati. You can get rid of the seeds in the chillies if you want to (you lightweight…). This makes a brilliant breakfast (especially at the weekend) or lunch. Never was Indian food on the table so quickly. Roopa recommends eating this with fresh carrot chutney. I'd suggest either of the carrot salads on pages 273 and 277.

SERVES 3–4

1 tsp cumin seeds

2 tbsp sunflower oil

2 large red onions, finely chopped

2 green chillies, chopped (with their seeds)

½ tsp coarsely ground black peppercorns

3 tomatoes, finely chopped

6 eggs, lightly beaten and seasoned with salt

2 tbsp chopped coriander leaves

Heat the cumin seeds in a dry frying pan for a minute or two, until you can smell their aroma. Tip into a mortar and crush to a powder. Heat the oil in the frying pan and cook the onions over a medium heat until golden. Add the chillies and black pepper and continue frying for another two minutes.

Stir in the tomatoes and cook until they get soft and any excess liquid has cooked off; it will take at least five minutes.

Reduce the heat slightly and add the eggs. Don't stir them for about two or three minutes, then gently lift and turn them over in the pan. Continue cooking until set. Just before serving, toss in the cumin and finish with the coriander leaves.

shaken currants with yogurt and rye crumbs

A Scandinavian breakfast that is great in the summer when there are lots of berries around (you can make this with any kind of berry, though it's not brilliant with strawberries as they get too soft). The berries' tartness as they burst against the deep, almost coffee-flavoured rye breadcrumbs is a good morning wake-up call for the taste buds. Have some pickled herring alongside (read about it on page 155, you might be persuaded) and imagine you are starting the day in Helsinki…

SERVES 4

300g (10½oz) currants, any colour, or a mixture

75g (2½oz) caster sugar

100g (3½oz) dry dark rye bread

2 tbsp soft dark brown sugar

plain yogurt, or Greek yogurt, to serve

Wash the currants but don't dry them. Spread them out on a large tray or roasting tin and sprinkle them with the caster sugar. Leave them there for a couple of hours, shaking from time to time, then transfer them to a jar and keep in the fridge.

For the crumbs, preheat the oven to 100°C/210°F/gas mark ¼. Break the bread up into little chunks with your hands (you don't want something as small as breadcrumbs you produce in the food processor). Scatter them on a baking sheet (no need to grease it), put into the oven and toast for 15 minutes. Leave them to cool, then mix them with the soft dark brown sugar.

Serve the currants with the yogurt and rye crumbs.

more fruity breakfasts… I cook all sorts of fruit in the summer for breakfast, even using bags of frozen berries (they're cheaper than fresh, even at the height of the berry season). Just put them in a pan, heat gently, add enough sugar to sweeten slightly and leave to cool. You can also bake apricots, nectarines or peaches. Preheat the oven to 180°C/350°F/gas mark 4. Use 16 apricots or 8 nectarines or peaches. Pit the fruits. Halve the apricots, or cut the nectarines or peaches into 8 wedges each. Lay them in a gratin dish. Add 225ml (8fl oz) of water, the juice of 1 orange and 2 tsp vanilla extract, then sprinkle with 50g (1¾oz) soft light brown sugar. Bake for 20–25 minutes, or until the fruit is tender. Serves 4–6.

autumn

eating in autumn

Autumn is the best season for the cook. It spans both warm and cool months and the slide towards the latter is kindly, almost imperceptible. After a summer of wavering appetite (it can be too hot to cook, too hot to eat), I love the pull towards the kitchen that cooler weather engenders. September is almost embarrassingly fulsome as summer and autumn merge, bringing a collision of pumpkins and apples, raspberries and courgettes. Many of the ingredients we used to see as summery have a longer season now: late raspberries are around in October; mounds of aubergines, griddled to meltingness, make perfect autumnal eating; tomatoes go on and on (though once summer has gone, they're better roasted). Then coolness really comes. You need a jumper and you want to eat the sweet, starchy flesh of pumpkin.

Don't forget that some of the best autumnal eating can be found at the back of your kitchen cupboard. I fall again for lentils – Puy, black and workaday brown – and am glad to get back to the heartier grains, too.

early autumn

aubergines
beetroots
broccoli
carrots
celeriac
celery
chard
cobnuts
courgettes
cucumbers
fennel
french beans
hazelnuts
horseradish
kale
leeks
lettuces
peppers
potatoes
radishes
rocket
runner beans
spring onions
sweetcorn
tomatoes
turnips
watercress
walnuts
wild mushrooms

apples
blackberries
damsons
figs
grapes
melons
nectarines
peaches
pears
plums
raspberries
redcurrants

mid autumn

chestnuts
jerusalem artichokes
pumpkins
squashes

late autumn

fennel

cranberries
pomegranates
quinces

roast tomatoes and lentils with dukka-crumbed eggs

You will end up with more dukka than you need for this dish, but it seems silly to make a smaller amount. Put it into an airtight container and keep it for sprinkling on braised beans, bean purées, or for eating with hard-boiled eggs and radishes. You can use pumpkin seeds instead of sunflower seeds, if you prefer.

**SERVES 6 FOR LUNCH
OR A LIGHT MAIN COURSE**

FOR THE DUKKA

75g (2½oz) hazelnuts (skins on)

50g (1¾oz) sesame seeds

1 tsp nigella seeds

1 tbsp sunflower seeds

3 tbsp coriander seeds

1 tbsp white peppercorns

1½ tbsp cumin seeds

1 tsp ground paprika

½ tbsp sea salt flakes

FOR THE TOMATOES AND EGGS

12 large plum tomatoes, halved

3 tbsp olive oil

2 tsp harissa

½ tbsp caster sugar

salt and pepper

6 large eggs

FOR THE LENTILS

1 tbsp olive oil

½ onion, very finely chopped

1 celery stick, very finely chopped

1 garlic clove, finely chopped

250g (9oz) Puy lentils

1 sprig of thyme

1 bay leaf

juice of ½ lemon

1 tbsp sherry vinegar

3½ tbsp extra virgin olive oil

2 tbsp chopped coriander leaves

To make the dukka, put the hazelnuts in a dry frying pan and toast over a high heat until they smell roasted. Be careful not to go too far, they burn very easily. Tip them on to a plate to cool a little, then crush them in a mortar to a coarsely ground mixture.

Put the sesame seeds into the dry frying pan with the nigella and toast until the sesame seeds are golden. Follow with the sunflower seeds. Roughly crush all the toasted seeds and add to the nuts. Toast the coriander seeds until they smell toasted, then grind them very roughly. Do the same with the peppercorns, then the cumin seeds. Combine the nuts, seeds and toasted spices with the paprika and salt. Store in a jar or other airtight container until you need it.

For the tomatoes, preheat the oven to 190°C/375°F/gas mark 5. Lay the tomatoes in a single layer in a roasting tin. Mix the olive oil and harissa together and pour over. Turn to coat, ending cut side up, then sprinkle with sugar and season. Roast in the oven for 45 minutes, or until caramelized in parts and slightly shrunken.

Meanwhile, cook the lentils. Heat the oil in a saucepan and gently sauté the onion, celery and garlic until soft but not coloured. Add the lentils and turn them over in the oil. Chuck in the thyme and bay leaf. Pour on 700ml (1 pint 3½fl oz) of water, season lightly, bring to the boil, reduce the heat and simmer, uncovered, until the lentils are just tender. This could take 15–25 minutes depending on their age, so watch them; they can turn to mush quickly. When they are cooked, they should have absorbed all the liquid (simply drain them if they haven't). Remove the thyme and bay leaf. Add the lemon juice. Mix the vinegar and extra virgin oil together and stir it into the lentils with the coriander. Taste for seasoning.

Cook the eggs in boiling water for six minutes. They should still be a little runny in the middle. Rinse them in cold water and, once cool enough to handle, quickly peel. Roll them lightly in the dukka and set each on top of a serving of lentils and tomatoes, or if you prefer to see the yolk, break the egg in half and sprinkle some dukka on top. Serve immediately.

eastern broth with shallots, lime and coriander

This is quite a basic recipe. You can add tofu, slices of shiitake mushrooms, beansprouts, cooked chicken or raw prawns. It's lovely, though – and totally head-clearing – just as it is. The sugar (it's only a small amount) is there to achieve that wonderful hot, sour, salty, sweet balance that is characteristic of South East Asian food, but leave it out if you really want to stay away from sugar.

SERVES 4

12 shallots, peeled

1 litre (1¾ pints) well-flavoured chicken stock

4cm (1½in) root ginger, peeled and sliced

2 lime leaves (if you have them)

1 red chilli (or ½ chilli, depending on how hot you want it), finely sliced

juice of 1 lime, or to taste

small bunch of coriander, chopped or not, as you prefer

1½ tsp fish sauce, or to taste

1 tsp caster sugar, or to taste

2 spring onions, cut into very fine julienne strips

Halve the shallots and cut them into slices lengthways.

Put the stock into a saucepan and bring to the boil. Reduce the heat and add the ginger, lime leaves and shallots. Simmer gently for about 15 minutes, then add the chilli and simmer for another couple of minutes. Add all the other ingredients and taste for seasoning. Aim for a good balance of chilli, lime, fish sauce and sugar (hot, sour, salty, sweet).

You don't have to remove the ginger, but warn people it's there.

or in the japanese style… **miso broth with greens** A good quick lunch if you have some stock in the fridge. You can add spinach instead of bok choi, if that's what you have. Bring 500ml (18fl oz) well-flavoured chicken stock to the boil in a saucepan and stir in 4 tbsp sweet white miso paste. Reduce the heat to a simmer. Put ½ green chilli, chopped, 2 spring onions, chopped, 2 tbsp roughly chopped coriander or mint leaves, 1 garlic clove, chopped and 1cm (½in) root ginger, peeled and chopped, into a mortar and pound to a paste. Stir this into the broth, then add the juice of ½ lime (or more to taste) and 75g (2¾oz) bok choi, each head cut in four lengthways. Cook for a few minutes to wilt the greens, taste for seasoning and serve. Serves 2.

miraculous broth

Despite all the food trends that come and go, some dishes never change. Like soup. Ancient recipes for soups and broths are very similar to those in modern cookbooks – it's always a liquid, usually stock, plus vegetables or grains – and the way you turn to them when you feel under the weather shows sound survival instincts. Doctors were recommending chicken broth to combat colds as early as the twelfth century and, according to American food historian Ken Albala, this is because they are anti-inflammatory and easy to digest. They don't just appear to soothe you as you carefully sip another spoonful, they actually do you good. If you're in the habit of eating chicken soup when you're ill, you'll know that it's miraculously restorative.

There are lots of soup recipes in this book – and they're great for increasing your vegetable intake – but I want to talk about broth, because you don't even need a recipe for that. 'Broth' sounds like something your granny made, but I just mean a pot of stock – usually chicken in my house – that you can transform depending on how you feel and what's in your veg drawer. You do need to start with decent stock. I sometimes use bought stuff, but it's usually not strong enough. Make your own if you can.

Broths don't need to be puréed and they can be made in an ad hoc way. If you have a pot of stock you're already halfway there. Want something chunky? Add chopped pumpkin, canned white beans, sliced garlic and a tablespoon of tomato purée. Cook until the pumpkin is tender, add shredded spinach and herbs (basil or flat-leaf parsley leaves) and Parmesan shavings and you're good to go. In the summer use courgette, French beans and chopped tomatoes. Fancy something from northern climes? Then cook some spelt or barley in the broth before adding salmon (fresh or hot-smoked) and dill and spoon some soured cream or buttermilk on top. If you need a jolt of spice, make an Eastern-style hot-and-sour soup by adding chilli, slices of ginger, tamarind paste or lime juice and maybe a dash of fish sauce. Craving that sweet-sour thing? Throw in a little soft brown sugar, too. You can add chopped leftover chicken, prawns, bok choi, beansprouts and sliced mushrooms. You just need to simmer your soup for as long as it takes to cook (or, if you're using leftovers, to warm through) the various components. Whether you're concerned about your intake of carbs or just keeping an eye on how many vegetables you're eating, a brothy soup is a great thing to eat, filling and satisfying.

It's lunch time, it's raining and my boiler has once again given up the ghost. Thank God there's a pot of stock in the fridge. By the time it boils I'll have chopped some veg, decided how I want to flavour the soup (miso today, I think) and soon I'll be eating a bowlful of lip-smacking nourishment. You have to agree it beats a ready meal.

carrot and ginger soup with cucumber raita

Indian heat, intensely carrot flavour. If you don't want to use carrot juice – and this tastes best if you use some you've juiced yourself – then replace it with stock or water.

SERVES 4

FOR THE SOUP

2 tbsp olive oil

1 onion, finely chopped

1 celery stick, finely chopped

10 carrots, finely chopped

2 garlic cloves, very finely chopped

2.5cm (1in) root ginger, peeled and very finely chopped

2 tsp ground cumin

500ml (18fl oz) chicken stock

500ml (18fl oz) carrot juice

salt and pepper

FOR THE RAITA

¼ cucumber

125ml (4fl oz) plain yogurt (regular, not Greek)

1 garlic clove, crushed

about 1 tbsp torn mint leaves

Heat the oil in a saucepan. Cook the onion over a medium heat with the celery and carrots, stirring them around and getting a bit of colour on them. Now add the garlic, ginger and cumin and cook for another couple of minutes. Add the chicken stock and carrot juice, season and bring to the boil.

Reduce the heat to a simmer and cook until the carrots are completely tender, about 20 minutes. Leave to cool a little while you make the raita.

Halve the cucumber lengthways and use a teaspoon to scoop out the seeds. Chop the remaining flesh and mix it with the yogurt, garlic and mint.

Purée the soup in a food processor or with a hand-held blender. Reheat, check for seasoning and serve with some raita spooned on top of each bowl.

a caribbean version… **I-tal carrot and sweet potato soup** Made for me by a friend who follows some Rastafarian dietary guidelines. They believe food should enhance your 'levity' (life energy). I couldn't believe something that tasted this good could also be, well, so utterly simple. Put 1 litre (1¾ pints) of fresh carrot juice into a pan and add 2 chopped leeks, 2 peeled and chopped sweet potatoes, 3½ tbsp creamed coconut, 1 crushed garlic clove, 1 deseeded and chopped red chilli, 2cm (¾in) root ginger, peeled and finely chopped and the leaves from 2 sprigs of thyme. Season, bring to a simmer and cook for 10 minutes or until the sweet potato is tender. Now leave it as it is or purée the soup. Return to the heat and add 50g (1¾oz) baby spinach leaves and a drained 400g can of chickpeas (optional). Allow the spinach to wilt and add lots of chopped coriander. Serves 6.

red mullet and saffron broth with corfu garlic sauce

This is very rich, so it makes a main course rather than a starter. You can serve the broth without the garlic sauce, it's still very good. The sauce has many other uses, too; serve it with other meaty fish, or with lamb, pork or chicken as well as with roast or raw vegetables.

SERVES 4

FOR THE FISH

8 red mullet fillets

juice of ½ orange

10 crushed black peppercorns

4 tbsp extra virgin olive oil

2 tbsp olive oil

FOR THE SAUCE

25g (1oz) coarse country bread, without crusts

50g (1¾oz) walnuts

3 garlic cloves

¼ tsp salt, or more to taste

100ml (3½fl oz) extra virgin olive oil

1–2 tbsp red wine vinegar

pepper

FOR THE BROTH

2 slim leeks

3 small fennel bulbs

8 waxy baby potatoes, peeled and halved

2 tbsp olive oil

6 shallots, sliced

1 small dried chilli, crumbled (optional)

generous pinch of saffron stamens

600ml (1 pint) well-flavoured fish stock

Put the red mullet into a dish with the orange juice, pepper and extra virgin oil. Turn the fish over in this and cover with cling film. Put in the fridge and leave to marinate for three to four hours.

For the sauce, put the bread in a bowl. Sprinkle with 3–4 tbsp of water. Leave to soak until the bread feels softish. Cook the walnuts in a dry pan until they smell toasty, then remove from the pan. Put the garlic and salt into a mortar and crush the garlic. Squeeze the water from the bread and grind this in as well, then add the nuts and pulverize them. Add the extra virgin oil, pounding, then the vinegar to taste, more salt if you need it and some pepper. You can do this in a food processor, but it doesn't produce such a good texture. If it seems too thick, mix in hot water until you have the texture you want, then adjust the seasoning. Set aside.

Trim the base and top of the leeks and remove the outer leaves. Cut into 3cm (generous 1in) lengths. Wash carefully, getting any grit out without breaking up the pieces. Trim off the fennel tips, reserving feathery bits, and remove any tough outer leaves. Quarter the bulbs lengthways and carefully trim the base of each, but don't cut too much off or the fennel will fall apart.

Cook the potatoes in boiling salted water for 12–15 minutes, or until tender, then drain. Meanwhile, heat the olive oil in a sauté pan and gently sauté the shallots, leeks and fennel for five minutes, until slightly soft. Add the chilli (if using), saffron and stock and bring to the boil. Reduce to a simmer and cook, uncovered, for 15 minutes, adding the potatoes a few minutes before the end. The liquid should reduce a little. Add any reserved fennel fronds.

Take the mullet fillets out of their marinade and place two frying pans over a medium heat. Heat 1 tbsp of the regular oil in each and divide the mullet skin-side down between them, cooking for one minute; it's nice to get a slight gold colour on the skin. Turn carefully, reduce the heat to low and cook for a further minute.

Ladle the broth and vegetables into bowls and place two fish fillets on each. Serve with a dollop of sauce and offer the rest in a bowl.

beluga lentil, roast grape and red chicory salad

Whoever thought of calling black lentils 'beluga' was a marketing genius. Of course it's a bit of nonsense – they don't taste any better than Puy lentils – but the moniker makes them seem luxurious (yes, lentils now have that much cachet…) and their colour is fantastic. It makes you think up all sorts of painterly platefuls on the black and crimson theme. You can add crumbled goat's cheese or a blue cheese to this, and chopped toasted walnuts work well, too.

SERVES 4 AS A LIGHT MEAL

2 tbsp olive oil

½ red onion, finely chopped

½ celery stick, finely chopped

1 garlic clove, finely chopped

250g (9oz) black lentils

4 tbsp extra virgin olive oil, plus more for the chicory

1 tbsp white balsamic vinegar

good squeeze of lemon juice, plus more for the chicory

salt and pepper

2 tbsp roughly chopped flat-leaf parsley leaves

300g (10½oz) seedless red grapes, broken up into sprigs (not too small, as they shrink on cooking)

½ tbsp balsamic vinegar

2 small chicons of red chicory

Heat 1 tbsp of the regular olive oil in a saucepan and add the onion and celery. Sauté until the vegetables are soft but not coloured. Add the garlic and cook for another two minutes, then add the lentils and enough water to cover by about 5cm (2in). Bring to the boil, then reduce the heat and simmer until the lentils are tender (check after 15 minutes; lentils need different cooking times depending on their age). Drain and add the extra virgin oil, white balsamic vinegar, lemon juice, salt and pepper and parsley. The lentils should be moist but not swimming in oil. Leave to cool to room temperature.

For the grapes, preheat the oven to 200°C/400°F/gas mark 6. Put the grapes on a baking sheet and drizzle with the remaining 1 tbsp of regular olive oil and the regular balsamic vinegar. Bake in the hot oven for 15–20 minutes.

Break the chicory into leaves. Arrange these on plates, drizzle with extra virgin oil and squeeze on some lemon. Spoon on the lentils and top with grapes.

celeriac, radicchio, fennel and apple salad with hazelnuts

This was inspired by rémoulade, but I didn't want to make it with just mayonnaise (I find that a bit cloying). It's good as a side salad, particularly with hot-smoked salmon or smoked mackerel (in which case do use the horseradish, in fact if it is to accompany smoked fish you can use both dill and horseradish). It's good, too, to cut through the richness of both roast pork and cheese.

SERVES 4 AS A SIDE DISH

FOR THE SALAD

juice of ½ lemon

125g (4½oz) celeriac

1 small fennel bulb

2 small tart apples, preferably tawny- or red-skinned

¼ head radicchio, shredded

1 tbsp chopped dill fronds or freshly grated horseradish

50g (1¾oz) toasted hazelnuts, roughly chopped

2 tsp poppy seeds (optional)

FOR THE DRESSING

1½ tbsp Greek yogurt

2 tbsp mayonnaise

½ tsp Dijon mustard, or to taste

¼ tbsp cider vinegar

2 tbsp olive oil

¼ tsp runny honey

salt and pepper

Put the lemon juice into a mixing bowl. Peel the celeriac and cut the flesh into matchsticks, tossing them into the bowl containing the lemon juice as you go to stop the celeriac discolouring.

Quarter the fennel, trim the tops and remove any coarse outer leaves. Core each quarter. Using a very sharp knife or a mandoline, cut the fennel into wafer-thin slices. Toss the fennel into the bowl with the celeriac.

Halve and core the apples and cut into matchsticks, immediately adding to the bowl and tossing in the lemon.

To make the dressing, put the yogurt into a bowl and, using a fork, mix in the other ingredients with 1 tbsp of water. At some stages it might seem that the mixture won't come together into a smooth amalgam, but just keep whisking. Taste for seasoning and balance.

Add the dressing, radicchio, dill or horseradish and hazelnuts to the celeriac bowl and stir everything together. Taste for seasoning, you may want a little more mustard as well as salt or pepper. Transfer to a serving bowl and sprinkle with poppy seeds (if using).

carrot, cabbage and apple salad with caraway

A big, sprawling, healthy salad with plenty of crunch and Scandi flavourings. If you have young kale, you can add it raw (just remove and discard the firm central ribs and shred the leaves). Add whatever seeds you fancy (pumpkin, sunflower, sesame or flaxseed).

SERVES 6 AS A SIDE DISH

FOR THE DRESSING

1 tsp caraway seeds

1½ tbsp runny honey

2 tsp wholegrain mustard

juice of 1 lemon

salt and pepper

4 tbsp rapeseed oil

FOR THE SALAD

¼ red cabbage

¼ Savoy cabbage

1 tart, firm apple

1 large carrot, peeled

10 radishes

To make the dressing, bruise the caraway seeds in a mortar and pestle to release their fragrance. Put the honey, mustard and half the lemon juice into a cup or small jug. Add the salt, pepper and caraway. Now add the rapeseed oil gradually, whisking with a fork as you do so. Taste for seasoning.

Remove the tough core from each cabbage quarter and discard. Pull off any slightly soft or discoloured outer leaves, then shred the cabbages finely. Halve and core the apple (no need to peel it) and cut it into matchsticks. Immediately toss in the remaining lemon juice to stop the apple discolouring. Trim the carrot and cut it into matchsticks, too. Top and tail the radishes and cut them very finely (use a mandoline if you have one).

Toss all the vegetables and the apple in a bowl with the dressing. Taste for seasoning, then serve.

another fruity salad... farro, hazelnuts, grapes and figs

Lovely. And very autumnal. Add cheese to make a more substantial main course dish (goat's cheese or a blue would be good). Put 1 tbsp white balsamic vinegar, 4 tbsp hazelnut or walnut oil, 2 tbsp fruity extra virgin olive oil and ½ tsp runny honey into a small bowl, season, and whisk with a fork to make a dressing. Put 150g (5½oz) semi-pearled farro in a pan, cover with water and bring to the boil. Reduce the heat to a simmer and cook for 20–25 minutes; it should be soft but still have a little bite. Drain, season and add the juice of ½ lemon and 1 tbsp olive oil. Leave to cool to room temperature. Taste for seasoning; farro can take quite a bit. Add the leaves from 1 chicon of red chicory, 75g (2¾oz) watercress, coarse stalks removed, 8 ripe figs, stalks snipped off, halved, 25g (1oz) seedless black grapes, halved, and 15g (½oz) toasted hazelnuts, very roughly chopped. Gently toss with the vinaigrette. Serve immediately. Serves 4–6 as a side dish.

the question of lunch

Proper weekday lunches are a thing of the past. We are all, apparently, too busy. Sometimes I watch old French and Italian movies just to see what a civilized lunch culture was like. Antipasti *and* a main course? Wow, those were the days.

I'm guilty of demoting lunch myself. I eat it at my desk, but at least that also happens to be the kitchen table (the laptop remains open, mind you). This isn't a great way to live, but it's not my job to call for a change in modern working habits. I want to help you reclaim lunch, even if you eat it while surfing the net and barking orders (or taking them).

If you eat lunch at work it needs to be portable; if you eat it at home it needs to be quick. The easy thing – and what I, a carb lover, am always tempted to do – is to make a cheese sandwich. Okay, it's not a bag of Doritos and a bucket of Gatorade, but it's not ideal. There's no veg. It's built on carbs (bad for blood sugar spikes and laying down fat, though better if you are eating proper whole grain bread). With a sandwich I am usually hungry again by four o'clock. I tried to work out – apart from laziness – what made me choose it so often. I concluded that I didn't think I 'ought' to have anything more elaborate. In our workaholic culture it's hard to think we 'deserve' to stop and eat a considered meal. But it's the second chance in every twenty four hours for some food pleasure, and the meal that needs to keep us going until supper. It's also a chance to eat food that is really *good* for you.

I had to work hard, but I've managed to change my lunch habits. If you aren't worried about carb intake then a sandwich (on whole grain bread) is fine, but look at incorporating vegetables. There are loads of things in this book that can work inside two slices of bread (houmous, carrot salads, Thai chicken salad and roast tomatoes and avocado for starters). If you are watching your carb intake, you can halve the bread quotient by having a tartine (use a slice of toasted sourdough) or smørrebrød (a slice of rye) instead. And for some reason – perhaps its visual nature – the open sandwich lends itself more to creativity.

If we journey beyond bread there are masses of healthy dishes to make and keep in the fridge, or seal in a box and take to work. You can incorporate these into daily cooking, preparing extra to create a stash of good things. Griddled aubergines, raw vegetables with punchy Asian dressings, lentils, beans and whole grains are perfect (and grains and pulses really fill you up), and there are salads for every season in this book that you can make ahead. Keep dressings (there's plenty of options on page 103, and throughout the book) in jars in the fridge to anoint leaves (and get more greens under your belt) at the last minute.

Then there are things you don't even need a recipe for, but that will do you the world of good: watercress and orange salad; a salad of chicken, blueberries and brown rice; avocado vinaigrette; sliced tomatoes with olive oil, garlic and chopped anchovies. Some of the dishes I suggest for breakfast are worth considering, too. Stick a list of options on the fridge door. Life really is too short to eat a cheese sandwich every day. *Le déjeuner, il pranzo* – call it what you will – lunch can open the door to a world of possibilities... You may even become the subject of lunch box envy.

lunches for work or home

more lunches for home

autumn menu the first meal with pumpkin

roast veg with agresto | cavolo pilaf with figs | watercress salad | blackberry-apple rye galette

I love this kind of meal. There's no meat in sight yet it is rich, satisfying and deep. And imagine what all these vegetables will do for you. The pudding isn't healthy – there's quite a bit of sugar in it – but the pastry is made of rye flour and of course there's plenty of fruit. I've suggested other options, if you do want to serve something sweet that is better for you.

roast pumpkin and jerusalem artichokes with agresto

Full of autumnal flavours, sweet with roasted vegetables and nuts. Agresto is an Italian sauce, good with meaty fish and chicken as well as with vegetables. Don't leave out the bitter red chicory leaves, they are very much needed to contrast with the sweet artichokes and pumpkin.

SERVES 6 AS A MAIN COURSE WITH
ANOTHER DISH, OR 8 AS A SIDE

FOR THE VEGETABLES

900g (2lb) Jerusalem artichokes

juice of 1½ lemons

1.5kg (3lb 5oz) pumpkin or squash

salt and pepper

3 tbsp olive oil

3 large or 4 small chicons of
red chicory

1½ tbsp extra virgin olive oil

FOR THE AGRESTO

3 garlic cloves

good pinch of sea salt flakes

150g (5½oz) walnuts, chopped

75g (2¾oz) blanched hazelnuts,
roughly chopped

240ml (8½fl oz) extra virgin olive oil

240ml (8½fl oz) verjuice

leaves from 1 large bunch of
flat-leaf parsley, chopped

Preheat the oven to 180°C/350°F/gas mark 4. Scrub the Jerusalem artichokes thoroughly and cut off any tufty bits. You don't need to peel them (too much bother, and besides their skins look lovely and give texture). Halve them lengthways and put them into a bowl of water mixed with the juice of 1 lemon, to stop them discolouring. Halve the pumpkin and scoop out the seeds and fibres. Cut the flesh into wedges, about 3cm (generous 1in) thick at the thickest part. Peel each slice.

Drain the Jerusalem artichokes and put them and the pumpkin in a roasting tin in which they can lie in a single layer. Season and add the regular olive oil. Toss everything around, put into the oven and cook for 40 minutes, until the vegetables are tender and the pumpkin slightly charred at the edges.

Meanwhile, put the garlic into a large mortar with the salt and grind to a paste. Add the nuts and pound these. Add the extra virgin oil gradually, pounding, then the verjuice. Stir in the parsley and pound; you want a rough purée. Add pepper and taste for salt.

Separate the leaves of chicory and put them in a serving bowl with the rest of the lemon juice and the extra virgin oil. Season and toss. Push the leaves to the outside of the dish, spoon the roasted vegetables into the centre and serve with the agresto.

cavolo nero and bulgar pilaf with glazed figs

Bulgar is nutty but also soft, so it's one of the most usable grains. If you can't get cavolo nero then use kale instead (just cook it the same way). Add chunks of labneh (see page 104), crumbled feta or goat's cheese and toasted hazelnuts to make this more substantial. Ideally the figs should be ready at the same time as the bulgar, so back-time the cooking (though they can wait happily at room temperature if you'd rather do them in advance).

SERVES 6

FOR THE PILAF

1 fennel bulb

1 red onion, cut into crescent moon-shaped slices

1½ tbsp olive oil

2 garlic cloves, crushed

pinch of dried chilli flakes (optional)

5 juniper berries, crushed

175g (6oz) bulgar wheat

350ml (12fl oz) chicken or vegetable stock

2 strips of orange zest

salt and pepper

400g (14oz) cavolo nero

1½ tbsp extra virgin olive oil

good squeeze of orange juice

FOR THE GLAZED FIGS

8 plump, firm figs

3 tbsp runny honey

2 tbsp balsamic vinegar

Preheat the oven to 200°C/400°F/gas mark 6.

Trim the tips from the fennel (reserve any little fronds) then quarter the bulbs and remove any tough or discoloured outer leaves. Carefully cut out the core at the base of each (don't cut off so much that the fennel falls apart). Sauté the onion and fennel in the regular olive oil in a heavy-based pan. When the vegetables are tinged with gold in patches, add the garlic, chilli (if using) and juniper and cook for a further couple of minutes. Tip the bulgar into the pan, pour on the stock, add the orange zest and season. Bring to the boil, then reduce the heat to its lowest, cover and cook for about 15 minutes. The stock will be absorbed. Let the bulgar sit off the heat, still covered, for a further 15 minutes.

Meanwhile, snip the stem from each fig, then halve the fruits lengthways. Put them in a gratin dish where they can sit snugly in a single layer. (If there is too much space around, the moisture evaporates and they burn.) Drizzle the honey and vinegar over and season. Roast in the hot oven for 20 minutes, spooning the juices over a couple of times during the cooking. The figs should be dark, rich looking and tender, but should not have collapsed.

At the same time, remove and discard the tough central ribs from the cavolo nero. Wash the leaves and chop them (not too small). Put them into a saucepan of boiling water and cook for four minutes. Drain really well, season and stir in the extra virgin oil.

Remove the orange zest from the bulgar and fork it through to fluff it up. Now fork the cavolo nero into the bulgar and check the seasoning. Put into a warm, broad, shallow serving bowl and put the figs on top, drizzling the cooking juices from the figs over as well. Squeeze the orange juice over the whole thing and serve with the roast vegetables and agresto (see page 178).

watercress and carrot salad

I try to get watercress in at least once a day and it's not hard if you make a simple salad to eat after or with your main course (or make it the basis of a main course salad). Its health properties are simply undeniable (you can read more about it on page 253).

Watercress is slightly peppery, but not so assertive that you can't blend it with lots of other ingredients. It goes with fresh-tasting foods – fennel, cucumber, dill and mint – and contrasts well with sweet, rich or meaty ingredients such as roast peppers and pumpkins, apples and pears, cherries and wild mushrooms. It's good tossed into warm dishes (such as pilafs) where it wilts a little, but not so much that it slumps.

It's available all year round, though interestingly was traditionally harvested and available when there was an 'r' in the month, so it used to be a leafy green for the colder months of the year. Don't just keep it for spring and summer.

SERVES 6–8

FOR THE SALAD

150g (5½oz) carrots

100g (3½oz) watercress, coarse stalks removed

½ tbsp mixed seeds (optional)

2 tsp poppy seeds

FOR THE DRESSING

½ tbsp sherry vinegar

1 tbsp orange juice

1 tsp Dijon mustard

1 tsp runny honey

salt and pepper

4 tbsp extra virgin olive oil

If you have slim carrots you can cut them lengthways into quarters. For bigger carrots, either cut them into matchsticks (time-consuming) or ribbons. To make ribbons (which is easier with bigger carrots), halve them lengthways then, using a potato peeler, create ribbons by pushing the peeler along the carrot. You always end up with bits that can't be used this way, so just keep them for soup (or eat them).

To make the dressing, put everything except the extra virgin oil into a cup and whisk with a fork. Now add the oil gradually, whisking as you go. Check for seasoning. This is quite a strong dressing, but you're dressing fairly robust ingredients. Toss with the carrots, watercress and mixed seeds (if using). Sprinkle on the poppy seeds (they look great against the carrot) and serve.

blackberry and apple rye galette

This only just gets inclusion in a healthy book, I'm not going to pretend that pastry is actually 'good' for you. But it does use rye flour and there's plenty of fruit here. You could serve a no-pastry fruity pudding instead: baked apples, or stewed apples and blackberries with yogurt and a little maple syrup would be lovely. But this is the only pastry in the whole book and is so gorgeously autumnal – it's the nutty rye flour in it – that I couldn't resist.

SERVES 6

FOR THE PASTRY

125g (4½oz) rye flour

125g (4½oz) plain flour, plus more to dust

pinch of salt

150g (5½oz) cold butter, cut into cubes

2 tbsp soft light brown sugar

1 egg yolk

FOR THE FILLING

250g (9oz) eating apples (about 2)

juice of ½ lemon

finely grated zest of 1 orange

4 tbsp soft light brown sugar

200g (7oz) blackberries

85g (3oz) hazelnuts

FOR THE GLAZE

1 egg, lightly beaten

4 tbsp granulated sugar

Sift the flours together then tip the grains caught in the sieve back into the mixture. Add the salt and rub in the butter with your fingers until you have small pea-sized lumps. Rub in the sugar too, then add the egg yolk and ½ tbsp of very cold water, a little at a time, until you can bring the mixture together into a ball. Press this into a disc, wrap in cling film and chill for an hour.

Unwrap the pastry and roll it out on a lightly floured surface to a circle of about 32cm (13in), trying to roll it evenly. Move this on to a baking sheet lined with baking parchment. Don't worry if the pastry is crumbly, just patch it up. This is a very forgiving tart because it is freeform.

Peel, core and slice the apples then put them in a bowl with the lemon juice, orange zest and half the brown sugar. Add the blackberries and toss around with your hands.

Whizz the hazelnuts coarsely in a food processor – you should end up with a mixture that is partly ground, partly chunky – and add the rest of the brown sugar.

Sprinkle the nut mixture on the pastry, leaving a width of about 5cm (2in) all the way round. Put the fruit on top of this, then carefully lift up the edges of the pastry to enclose the fruit all the way round. Again, just patch the pastry together if it breaks, nobody will ever know. Put the galette into the coldest part of the fridge for 30 minutes (or your freezer, if it's big enough, for 10 minutes or so). Preheat the oven to 170°C/340°F/gas mark 3½.

For the glaze, mix the egg with 2 tbsp of the granulated sugar and brush it over the pastry. Sprinkle the remaining 2 tbsp granulated sugar over the whole tart. Bake in the hot oven for 50–60 minutes. The pastry should be golden and crusted with sugar, and the fruit should be tender.

persimmon, pomegranate and red chicory salad with goat's cheese and toasted hazelnuts

There are some combinations I can't get away from, and fruit with cheese and nuts is one of them. The loveliness of persimmons eludes some people, but it's often because they eat them when they are unripe. The fruits for this can't be too ripe – once persimmons are soft it is very hard to cut them without them falling apart – but leave those you've bought in a bowl in the kitchen and keep checking them (pushing the flesh gently) to gauge how ripe they are. You get to know, with experience, when it's the right time to eat them.

SERVES 4

½ tsp white balsamic vinegar

salt and pepper

scant ¼ tsp Dijon mustard

1¼ tbsp extra virgin olive oil (don't use anything too strong, and fruity rather than grassy is best)

1¼ tbsp hazelnut oil

2 chicons of red chicory

125g (4½oz) watercress

2 persimmons

1 pomegranate

25g (1oz) unblanched hazelnuts, halved

150g (5½oz) creamy goat's cheese, broken into chunks

Make the dressing so it's ready to go. Just put the white balsamic, seasoning and Dijon mustard into a cup and whisk in the extra virgin and hazelnut oils with a fork. Check for seasoning.

Separate the leaves of the chicory (don't use the bases) and remove and discard the coarse stalks from the watercress. Put all the leaves into a broad, shallow bowl.

Remove the calyx from each persimmon and slice them as finely as you can: use either a very thin knife, such as a fish filleting knife, or a mandoline.

Halve the pomegranates and try to dislodge the seeds by hitting the fruit with a wooden spoon while holding it over a bowl, cut side down; if the fruit is very ripe the seeds should just tumble out. If this doesn't work (it doesn't always) then gouge out the seeds with a spoon. You do have to go through the laborious task of removing the white membrane around the seeds.

Put the nuts into a dry frying pan over a medium heat and toast them, this can take as little as 30 seconds so keep watching or they will burn. Tip the nuts into a bowl to cool.

Add the persimmons and nuts to the leaves with three-quarters of the dressing and toss. Now add the goat's cheese and scatter the pomegranate seeds on top. Drizzle on the rest of the dressing and serve immediately.

griddled aubergines with date, walnut and yogurt salad

A good midweek supper. Dates are very high in sugar, that's why they were eaten by desert nomads; it was said you could survive on dates and camel's milk. You can use less sweet dried fruits (such as cranberries or dried sour cherries), but dates have a wonderful affinity with aubergines.

SERVES 4

125g (4½oz) Greek yogurt

75g (2½oz) dates, pitted and roughly chopped

50g (1¾oz) walnuts, toasted and roughly chopped

6 tbsp olive oil

2 garlic cloves, crushed

4 aubergines

salt and pepper

juice of 1 lemon

To make the salad, stir the yogurt to loosen it, then add the dates, walnuts, 1 tbsp of the olive oil and the garlic.

Remove the stalks from the aubergines, then cut lengthways into slices 1cm (½in) thick. Brush on both sides with some of the remaining oil, season them and heat a griddle pan (or just use a frying pan). Cook on both sides until slightly charred and soft. You'll need to do this in batches and keep adjusting the heat: first you need to colour the aubergines on each side, then reduce the heat to cook them through. As the slices are ready, squeeze lemon juice over them, season again and layer up in a serving dish.

Serve the aubergines with the date salad and Kisir (see below).

kisir

An autumnal tabbouleh, best when the tomatoes are still good and the pomegranates are arriving.

SERVES 4

1 tbsp olive oil

1 small red onion, finely chopped

2 garlic cloves, finely chopped

2½ tsp ground cumin

1 red chilli, deseeded, shredded

1½ tbsp tomato purée

200g (7oz) bulgar wheat

4 well-flavoured plum tomatoes, peeled, deseeded and chopped

handful of mint leaves, torn

35g (1¼oz) finely chopped parsley

juice of 1 lemon, or to taste

75ml (2½fl oz) extra virgin olive oil

1½ tbsp pomegranate molasses

seeds from 1 pomegranate

Heat the regular oil in a saucepan and sauté the onion and garlic for two minutes. Add the cumin and chilli and cook for a minute. Stir in the tomato purée and add 150ml (5fl oz) of boiling water. Mix in the bulgar, remove from the heat, cover and leave for 15 minutes. Fork through the grains gently to separate them. You will be worried the mixture seems dry and that some of the grains are 'nutty': don't worry. You are about to add wet ingredients that will make all the difference, so resist the temptation to add more water.

Fork in the tomatoes and herbs. Mix the lemon juice, extra virgin oil and pomegranate molasses in a cup. The bulgar shouldn't be too dry but it shouldn't be soaked, so add three-quarters of the dressing, then judge to see whether you need more. (You can add more oil or lemon if you want to, but don't make it soggy.) Toss in the pomegranate seeds. Taste for seasoning; this needs a generous amount. The kisir will sit until you want to serve it. You can keep it in the fridge, covered, but return to room temperature to serve.

japanese aubergines with miso

The first time I tasted this dish I couldn't quite believe it: the salty-sweet miso topping soaks into the aubergine flesh, completely flavouring it. It makes the best of the aubergine's sponge-like texture. I like it made with a mixture of sweet and salty miso, but you can use white miso alone (the sweet one) if you prefer. (It's white by name, but yellow in colour, just to confuse things.) See pages 328–329 for where you can get it online. Togarashi, a Japanese spice blend containing chilli, orange peel, sesame seeds and ginger, is available from Waitrose.

SERVES 4 AS A SIDE DISH

6 long slim aubergines

2 tbsp groundnut oil

2 tbsp white miso paste

2 tbsp brown miso paste

2 tsp soft light brown sugar

3 tbsp mirin

1 tbsp sake or dry sherry

¼ tsp (or less, it's powerful) of togarashi, or chilli powder

3 tsp toasted white sesame seeds

Preheat the oven to 180°C/350°F/gas mark 4.

Halve the aubergines and cut a lattice pattern on the flesh side without cutting right through to the skin. Brush with the oil and put into an ovenproof dish. Bake in the hot oven for 40 minutes, or until completely tender, covering with foil halfway through.

Meanwhile, mix together the miso pastes, sugar, mirin and sake in a small saucepan and heat gently. Remove from the heat and add the togarashi.

Spread the miso mixture on top of each aubergine and return to the oven. Cook until golden, about another five minutes. The tops of the aubergine halves should be moist and shimmering, not at all dry. Sprinkle with the toasted sesame seeds and serve.

middle eastern-spiced squash and white beans with lemon and mint

I use cannellini beans here, but you can use haricot, borlotti or chickpeas (though chickpeas produce a less thickly textured dish). If you prefer to cook dried beans from scratch, use 130g (4¾oz). Soak them overnight, then rinse, cover with fresh water and cook for about an hour, or until only just tender. Don't add any salt until they're cooked.

You don't have to use fresh mint, but do what they do in parts of the Middle East and fry some dried mint in a couple of tablespoons of olive oil and pour it over the top. It might sound odd but it's good: slightly musty (in a good way). You can of course use chopped coriander or flat-leaf parsley leaves instead of (or as well as) the mint.

SERVES 6

2 tbsp olive oil

1 large onion, finely chopped

1 large carrot, finely chopped

4 garlic cloves, finely chopped

2 red chillies, deseeded
and chopped

5 plum tomatoes, chopped

3 tsp ground cumin

1 tbsp tomato purée

1kg (2lb 4oz) sweet pumpkin or
squash, peeled, deseeded and
cut into chunks

500ml (18fl oz) vegetable stock
or water

salt and pepper

400g can cannellini beans, drained
and rinsed

juice of ½ lemon, plus finely grated
zest of 1 lemon (removed with
a zester)

leaves from 6 sprigs of mint, torn

Heat half the olive oil in a heavy-based casserole and add the onion and carrot. Cook until the onion is slightly softened and pale gold in colour. Add the garlic, chillies and tomatoes and cook for another five minutes or so. Now add the cumin, cook for a minute, then stir in the tomato purée.

Heat the rest of the olive oil in a large frying pan and sauté the squash (you'll probably have to do this in batches) until it is golden all over and beginning to soften.

Add the squash to the onion with the stock or water and season. Bring to the boil, then reduce the heat, cover and cook gently for 40 minutes. After 30 minutes, remove the lid and add the beans.

The dish is ready when the squash is completely tender and the texture is quite thick. Add the lemon juice and half the zest and check the seasoning. Scatter with the mint and the rest of the zest. Serve with bulgar wheat (or bulgar mixed with lentils is lovely with this) and a green vegetable.

play with this... To make it Italian, add 2 bay leaves and a sprig of rosemary to the pumpkin. Chop 1 garlic clove, the finely grated zest of 1 lemon and 1 tbsp of rosemary leaves and scatter on top. To go Moroccan, add 1 tsp ground ginger, ½ cinnamon stick and ½ tbsp harissa. Green olives are good, too. Finish off with preserved lemon shreds, coriander leaves and toasted flaked almonds. For a Spanish feel, add 2 tsp smoked paprika and finish with coriander and parsley as well.

home-style punjabi lentils (tarka dal)

In a book full of big flavours, this is an oddity. It's muted, plain, some might even describe it as bland. But there are days when it's just what you want. We tend to dress lentils up; here they are cooked with spices, but still very much themselves. From time to time I try different dals – sweet and sour recipes, chilli-hot bowls – but I come back to this. It is kind of the Indian equivalent of our chicken soup. It's grounding and soothing. It's also the perfect central dish on which to hang other brighter flavours if that's what you want; a brilliant plain canvas. Try Kachumber (see page 89) or Ginger and mango relish (see page 220), or just enjoy its total plainness.

SERVES 4

FOR THE DAL

200g (7oz) chana dal, or yellow split peas (chana dal keep their shape better)

½ tsp turmeric

3cm (1¼in) root ginger, peeled

salt and pepper

FOR THE TEMPERING

2 tbsp sunflower oil

1½ tsp cumin seeds

1 tsp chilli flakes

1 small red onion, finely sliced

3cm (1¼in) root ginger, peeled and finely chopped

2 garlic cloves, chopped

1 large plum tomato, chopped

½ tsp garam masala

2 tbsp roughly chopped coriander leaves (optional)

Put the lentils into a heavy-based pan. Add 500ml (18fl oz) of water, the turmeric and the chunk of peeled ginger. Don't add any salt as it toughens the lentils. Bring to the boil, then reduce the heat and simmer until the lentils are soft and falling apart. Scoop out the ginger and leave the lentils to cool slightly.

If you prefer a smooth dal, liquidise it in a blender at this point; it's very much up to you how you'd like the texture and consistency to be. I like to give half the lentils a quick blend, then mix it with the more rough-textured dal in the pan. Add a splash more water if you feel the lentils need it and season with salt and pepper.

Now the tempering. Heat the oil in a small frying pan and toss in the cumin seeds followed by the chilli flakes. Swirl them around for about 20 seconds until they darken. Add the onion and fry until golden. Stir in the ginger and garlic and cook for another minute. Now add the tomato and garam masala and continue frying for two minutes, or until the tomato has softened.

Tip this masala into the hot dal and add the coriander (if using). Stir well and serve with brown rice or wholemeal flatbread. Fresh chutney and some plain yogurt are good alongside.

also try… **a south indian version** Leave out the cumin from the tempering spices and cook 2 tsp mustard seeds in the oil for 30 seconds (until they pop), then add about 8 curry leaves and ¼ tsp fenugreek seeds. Add the onion and continue to cook as in the main recipe. This usually has 250g–300g (9–10½oz) shredded spinach leaves (coarse stems removed) added at the end; they will wilt in the heat.

divine dal

'My daughter is coming home,' sighs my friend Roopa, 'We ought to be having something celebratory to eat but she says, "Mama, all I want is *dal chawal*".' I understand Roopa's daughter. 'Dal chawal' is just dal and rice. My comfort dish from childhood is mince and potatoes. To a child of Indian heritage it is *dal chawal*. And I yearn for it, too. Seat me in an Indian restaurant and *tarka dal* – the most basic, mellow, earthy lentil dish – will be the first thing I order.

There are lots of pulse and lentil dishes in this book, but not because they're healthy or because they're a good alternative to meat (offer me a sirloin steak or a bowl of dal and I'd have real trouble choosing). They're here because I love them. They are primarily earthy and comforting, but not always. Black lentils tossed with watercress, mango and a creamy Indian dressing is more of a Bollywood number than a gentle lullaby. And chickpea mash, the beans crushed with sautéed onions, loads of garlic, cumin, lemon and a big dollop of harissa, isn't mellow either. Beans and pulses are, in fact, good for you (that's their bonus). They make you feel full, they're 'good' carbs and they're a great source of protein. They're cheap, too. My particular love, in this world of dried things, is Indian dals.

The word 'dal' simply denotes a split pulse, but in India it has come to mean all dried beans and lentils, as well as dishes in which they are the principal ingredient. Apart from the not very specific 'tarka dal' (always on the menu in Indian restaurants), dals were rather a mystery to me. So I took some instruction from Roopa and can now dal-dance all over India. There is a world of dals and, despite their humble constituents, some of the dishes are, to me anyway, utterly luxurious. They are also simplicity itself. The key thing is creaminess – that's what makes dal such a soothing dish – and long, slow cooking delivers that. In fact the best dals in India are found at roadside shacks. Big pots – called *patilas* – of lentils are cooked on top of the tandoor ovens overnight (so the heat of the oven isn't wasted), ready to eat the next morning.

Dals can be as thin as a brothy soup, or as thick as porridge. They don't require stock, just water. As their distinctiveness lies in the spicing, there is no need for extra flavouring from stock. Vegetables – spinach or marrow – can be added, too (leafy veg go in at the end). Once you have the consistency you like (simply add more water, or keep cooking, to get there), the tempering or *tarka* is what both finishes and 'makes' the dal. Spices, red onions (and sometimes tomatoes) are fried, then scattered on top and stirred in. In Southern India the flavourings are curry leaves, fenugreek seeds and mustard seeds; in the Punjab, cumin, ginger, garlic, chilli and onion.

Now you just have to track down the various pulses and lentils (the only difficult thing), so find an Indian grocery store (or look at the sources on pages 328–329). Then there's the huge pleasure of unloading packages whose names evoke hot Delhi days and cool Bombay nights. Urad dal, chana dal, toor dal, moong dal… a world of comforting exoticism awaits.

indian-spiced spinach and mushrooms with black lentils and paneer

This is not at all authentic. I wanted something that had Indian spicing and ingredients but that kept its shape and had separate, though integral, parts and this is the result. You don't have to use paneer, it's good without it, but it adds another texture. And I love its creaminess against the lentils.

SERVES 6

3½ tbsp groundnut oil, plus more for the paneer

2 onions, chopped

2 small red chillies, deseeded and finely chopped

5cm (2in) cinnamon stick

175g (6oz) black lentils

salt and pepper

juice of 1 lime

2 tbsp finely chopped coriander leaves

3 garlic cloves, finely chopped

3cm (generous 1in) root ginger, peeled and finely chopped

600g (1lb 5oz) chestnut mushrooms, sliced

15g (½oz) unsalted butter (optional)

¾ tsp ground cumin

¾ tsp ground coriander

2 large tomatoes, chopped

300g (10oz) baby spinach

125g (4½oz) paneer, cut into squares

1 tsp garam masala

3½ tbsp plain yogurt

Heat 1 tbsp of the oil in a saucepan and add one of the chopped onions. Sauté until soft and golden, then add one of the chillies and the cinnamon and cook for a minute. Add the lentils, cover with plenty of water and bring to the boil. Reduce the heat and simmer until the lentils are tender, anything from 15–30 minutes, depending on the age of the lentils. Quickly drain the lentils and return them to the warm pan. Season well with salt and pepper and stir in the lime juice and coriander. Cover to keep warm.

Meanwhile, sauté the remaining onion in a sauté pan in another 1 tbsp of the oil. When the onion is pale gold, add the garlic, remaining chilli and the ginger and cook for another minute.

In a separate frying pan, using the remaining oil, sauté the mushrooms briskly over a fairly high heat, in batches, until they are a good colour. Add them to the onion mixture. Add the butter (if using, it is really for flavour) and cook for another few minutes, then stir in the ground cumin and coriander and the tomatoes. Sauté these until the tomatoes are soft. Reduce the heat and cook until the tomatoes are almost collapsing and have reduced, about 10 minutes. Add the spinach, in batches, and turn it over in the mixture; the leaves will wilt and give off moisture. Whack up the heat to boil off some of the liquid if it's very watery.

Brush the cubes of paneer with a little oil and either griddle them or quickly brown them in a frying pan.

Stir the garam masala and the yogurt into the mushrooms and heat through, though don't boil. Check for seasoning. Serve the mushrooms with the paneer scattered on top and the lentils spooned round the side.

pilaf of mixed grains, sweet potato and fennel with avocado 'cream'

This is lovely but pretty starchy when served as a main course, even with the purée. It needs a spicy vegetable dish alongside and plenty of fresh salad leaves. It works as a good side dish with meat, too. The quinoa doesn't have to be red, but it does look good if you can find it.

SERVES 4 AS A MAIN DISH, 6–8 AS A SIDE

2 sweet potatoes (about 500g/ 1lb 2oz), peeled

3 tbsp olive oil

1½ tbsp balsamic vinegar

salt and pepper

2 small fennel bulbs

80g (2¾oz) wild rice

100g (3½oz) red quinoa

1 onion, finely chopped

2 garlic cloves, finely chopped

2 red chillies, deseeded and finely chopped

100g (3½oz) bulgar wheat

400ml (14fl oz) chicken or vegetable stock

FOR THE AVOCADO CREAM

2 ripe avocados

juice of 2 limes

1 red chilli, deseeded and finely chopped

1 garlic clove, crushed

1 tbsp olive oil

¼ tbsp sherry vinegar, or more to taste

Preheat the oven to 190°C/375°F/gas mark 5. Cut the sweet potatoes into 3.5cm (1½in) chunks. Put these in a roasting tin and toss with 2 tbsp of the oil, the balsamic vinegar and seasoning. Put into the hot oven and cook for one hour.

About halfway through, trim the tips from the fennel (reserve any fronds), quarter the bulbs and remove any tough or discoloured outer leaves. Carefully cut out the core at the base of each (don't cut off so much that the fennel falls apart). Add to the sweet potatoes for the last 20 minutes of their cooking time, tossing in the juices. When ready, both should be tender and slightly charred.

Meanwhile, put the wild rice into a saucepan and cover with water. Bring to the boil and cook for 45 minutes.

Toast the quinoa in a dry frying pan for two minutes. Put the remaining 1 tbsp of oil into a saucepan and sauté the onion until soft and golden. Add the garlic and chillies and cook for a couple of minutes, then add the toasted quinoa, bulgar and stock. Season. Bring to the boil, then reduce to a simmer, cover and cook for 15 minutes. You should get a panful of dry-ish, fluffy grains.

Drain the wild rice, rinse in boiling water and gently fork it into the quinoa and bulgar with the vegetables. Check for seasoning.

Prepare the avocado just before you want to serve, as it discolours if it sits for long. Halve, pit and scoop out the flesh, then mash it with all the other ingredients until smooth. Taste for seasoning (you may want a little more vinegar). Serve with the pilaf.

try this... with minted yogurt
Mix together 225g (8oz) Greek yogurt, 1 crushed garlic clove, about 20 mint leaves, roughly chopped and 2 tbsp extra virgin olive oil. Serve instead of, or as well as, the avocado cream.

autumn menu go east my friend

persimmon and avocado salad | burmese chilli fish | citrus compote with ginger snow

Eating more healthily has drawn me deeper and deeper into the cuisines of the east,
particularly the food of Vietnam and Japan. The ingredients are healthy, the flavours are
clean, hot or mouth-puckeringly citrussy and attack the front of your mouth. You quite
often leave the table feeling that you've had a jog round a forest. The food is usually very
pretty too, your pleasure starts as you look at your plate. This menu is a perfect illustration
of why the east is a good hunting ground for dishes that are irresistible and good for you.

japanese persimmon and avocado salad with ginger

I serve the dressing on the side here for guests to add their own, as the platter topped with snowy
white mooli furls just looks so lovely as you take it to the table. It's hard to find perfectly ripe
persimmons, so you need to think ahead: buy them in advance and let them ripen at home.

SERVES 4

FOR THE DRESSING

1 tbsp rice vinegar, or to taste

juice of ½ lime

2½ tbsp ginger syrup from a
preserved ginger jar, or to taste

2 tbsp groundnut oil

2 tsp dark soy sauce, or to taste

3cm (generous 1in) root ginger,
peeled and grated, or to taste

FOR THE SALAD

2 large, just-ripe avocados

juice of 1 lime

salt and pepper

3 just-ripe persimmons

175g (6oz) mooli (daikon), peeled

50g (1¾oz) mizuna and baby leaves
(ideally including microleaves)

about 4 tsp black sesame seeds

To make the dressing, just whisk everything together. Taste for a
balance of hot, sour, salty and sweet, adjusting the ginger, vinegar,
soy or syrup as you like.

Halve the avocados and remove the stones (hit the blade of a
broad knife into the stone, twist and pull the stone out; it should
attach to the blade). Cut into slim slices and carefully peel each
slice (I find this approach produces the most intact, neat slices).
Immediately squeeze on some lime juice and season; you always
seem to get a better salad if you season the avocado separately.

Halve the persimmons and cut out the calyxes. Cut into slices and
carefully peel each slice. Squeeze lime juice on these, too.

With the mooli you can do one of two things: either shave into
slices (use a mandoline or a very sharp knife); or cut into furls by
shaving off slices, using your knife in a circular movement (the
results look a bit like pencil shavings rather than slices).

Spread the leaves in a broad shallow bowl, then arrange slices of
persimmon, avocado and mooli on top. Scatter on the sesame
seeds and serve immediately with the dressing on the side.

burmese chilli fish with hot and sour salad

This is adapted from a recipe in Naomi Duguid's *Burma: Rivers of Flavor*, one of my favourite cookbooks. It's a great quick dish.

SERVES 4

750g (1lb 10oz) fish fillets (I like bream), skinned

2 tsp turmeric

½ tsp salt

8 shallots, very finely chopped

½ tsp sea salt flakes

3cm (generous 1in) root ginger, peeled and chopped

4 garlic cloves, peeled and chopped

1½ tbsp groundnut oil

1 dried red chilli, crumbled

1 tbsp fish sauce

lime juice, to taste

FOR THE HOT AND SOUR SALAD

¼ Savoy cabbage

8 shallots

10 radishes, topped and tailed

1 red chilli, deseeded and finely sliced

3 tbsp fish sauce

3 tbsp lime juice

1 tsp caster sugar, or more to taste

Rinse the fish, pat dry and feel along the surface for any little bones that may be left. Pull out any you find. Cut the fish into 5cm (2in) pieces and toss it in a bowl with the turmeric and salt. Turn the fish to coat and set aside for 15 minutes.

Pound the shallots in a large mortar with half the sea salt flakes (the salt acts as an abrasive) until you have a paste, remove, then do the same with the ginger and garlic, using the rest of the salt.

Make the salad so that it's ready to go once the fish is cooked. Remove and discard any discoloured or tough outer leaves and the core of the cabbage and shred the leaves very finely. Put into a serving bowl. Slice the shallots as finely as you can (use a mandoline if you have one) and do the same with the radishes. Add to the bowl with the chilli. In a little cup or bowl, mix the fish sauce, lime juice and sugar, stirring to help the sugar dissolve. Taste; you may want a little more sugar. Toss the vegetables with the dressing. (There should be plenty of dressing on this; all the vegetables should be coated.)

Heat ½ tbsp of the oil and sauté the ground shallots over a medium heat until soft and starting to turn golden. Add a little more of the oil, the pounded garlic and ginger and the dried chilli and cook for another couple of minutes until the whole mixture is soft and golden. Add a little more oil (you may not need all of what remains), add the fish and cook for 1½ minutes, then turn the pieces over and cook for another minute or so on the other side. It should be lovely and golden. Add the fish sauce and taste; you may want to add more. Squeeze on some lime and serve with the hot and sour salad and some brown rice.

citrus compote with ginger snow

This is quite magical – the granita does look like snow – and very cleansing. It's so thirst quenching it makes me think of the little boy, Nene, in Leonardo Sciascia's novel *The Wine-dark Sea*. Nene tells his travelling companions that when he gets to Catania he is 'going to eat a bucketful' of granita. He must have had this one in mind.

It might seem like a lot of citrus fruits but, as you remove the segments, quite a lot of the fruit gets left behind. (If you prefer not to segment the fruits you can slice them instead and use only four of them.) You don't have to make a syrup for the fruits at all, of course. You can just remove the segments and serve them with the granita.

SERVES 4–6

FOR THE GINGER SNOW

155g (5½oz) granulated sugar

finely grated zest of 2 limes
(removed with a zester),
plus the juice of 3

40g (1½oz) root ginger, peeled
and grated

FOR THE COMPOTE

2 pink grapefruits

2 red grapefruits

2 oranges or white grapefruits

100g (3½oz) granulated sugar

juice of 2 limes

To make the granita, mix the sugar, zest and ginger in a saucepan, pour in 600ml (1 pint) of water and gently bring to the boil, stirring to help the sugar dissolve. Once it's come to the boil, reduce the heat and simmer for two minutes. Let the liquid cool.

Strain the liquid, add the lime juice and pour the mixture into a freezer-proof shallow container, preferably a metal one. Put this into the freezer. Once the liquid has started to set, stir it with a fork to break up the crystals. Do this three or four times during the freezing process; you should be left with a lovely mixture of glassy shards.

For the compote, cut the tops and bottoms from all the fruits so they have a flat base on which to sit. Using a very sharp knife, cut the peel and pith from each, working around the fruit and cutting it away in broad strips from top to bottom. Working over a bowl, remove the segments by inserting a knife between the membrane surrounding each. Let the segments drop into the bowl.

Carefully drain off the citrus juice from the bowl into a saucepan. Add 5 tbsp of water, the sugar and lime juice and heat, stirring from time to time to help the sugar dissolve. Bring to the boil, then reduce the heat and simmer very gently for five minutes. Leave to cool, strain and put into the fridge until well-chilled.

Put the fruit segments into a serving bowl and pour over the cold syrup. Serve with the granita spooned on top.

roast tomatoes, houmous and spinach on toast

Roast tomatoes and houmous are good things to make ahead and have to hand in the fridge for lunch for one, or for breakfast. (And as you're putting the oven on you might as well roast some peppers to keep in the fridge as well.) If you are into gilding the lily (and why not?) then a poached egg perched on top is just fab and makes the dish more substantial.

SERVES 4

FOR THE TOMATOES, SPINACH AND TOASTS

6 large plum tomatoes

1½ tbsp olive oil

½ tbsp balsamic vinegar

about ½ tsp harissa, if you fancy some heat (optional)

1 tsp caster sugar

salt and pepper

4 slices of wholemeal bread

15g (½oz) baby spinach leaves

FOR THE HOUMOUS

400g can of chickpeas

4 tbsp tahini

2 fat garlic cloves, crushed

juice of 1 lemon, or to taste

½ tsp ground cumin

3 tbsp extra virgin olive oil, plus more to serve

1 tbsp Greek or Turkish yogurt (optional)

Preheat the oven to 190°C/375°F/gas mark 5.

Halve the tomatoes and lay them in a single layer in a small roasting tin or ovenproof dish. Mix the regular olive oil, balsamic and harissa (if using) together and pour over the tomatoes. Turn the tomatoes over in the oil to make sure they are well coated, ending with them cut side up. Sprinkle with sugar and season. Roast in the hot oven for 45 minutes, or until the tomatoes are caramelized and slightly shrunken.

For the houmous, drain and rinse the chickpeas and put them into a food processor. Add the tahini, garlic, lemon juice, cumin, salt and extra virgin oil with 3 tbsp of warm water. Whizz to a purée. Taste and add the yogurt if you want (I like it). Taste again and see whether you want to add more lemon juice or not. You may want to add more water to thin the mixture a little more as well. Scrape into a bowl, cover and put in the fridge until you want it.

To assemble, just toast the bread and drizzle a little extra virgin oil on it. Put the spinach on top, add a good spoonful of houmous, then arrange three tomato halves on top of that. Serve.

scallops with anchovy and caper dressing

A real treat for two. And a healthy one. Protein, omega-3 fatty acids and vitamin B12, they're all here. The richness of scallop flesh makes them filling, too. You can serve this with some lightly dressed leaves; bitter endive is good against the sweetness of the scallop flesh, or go with watercress.

SERVES 2

6 king scallops

2 tbsp extra virgin olive oil

2 garlic cloves, sliced

3 anchovies, drained of oil, finely chopped

1 tbsp capers, rinsed of salt or brine

2 tbsp lemon juice

olive oil

salt and pepper

½ tbsp roughly chopped flat-leaf parsley leaves

Prepare the scallops. Look at the side and you may see a little firm piece that is whiter and a different texture to the rest of the flesh. (It's a little bit of muscle and some fishmongers leave it on.) Pull or cut it off. Dry the scallops by blotting them with kitchen paper (wet scallops don't colour so well).

Prepare the dressing. Heat the extra virgin oil and gently sauté the garlic, but don't let it colour (about 30 seconds). Add the anchovies and cook gently for another 45 seconds or so, pressing them with the back of a wooden spoon to help them disintegrate a little. Add the capers and lemon juice and leave the dressing sitting in its pan while you quickly cook the scallops.

Brush the scallops all over with a light coating of the regular olive oil and season. Heat a frying pan or griddle until really hot and cook the scallops for a minute on each side – you want a good golden colour – then reduce the heat and cook for 30 seconds. The scallops should be cooked on the inside, but be careful not to overcook as it makes them rubbery. Take a look inside one of them with the tip of a small sharp knife to check how they are.

Reheat the dressing – it doesn't have to be hot, just warm – and add the parsley. Put the scallops on two plates, drizzle with the pan juices and spoon the dressing on top. Serve immediately. This is even better with some bread on the side to mop up the juices.

squid with smoky almond tarator, peppers, freekeh and spinach

A big unarguable-with plateful. Of all the grains, freekeh is the one that can cope best with big flavours, so it's perfect with squid, peppers and smoked paprika. If you can't find freekeh, use wheat berries or kamut (see page 224 for how to cook those).

SERVES 6

FOR THE PEPPERS AND SQUID

3 red peppers

olive oil

salt and pepper

900g (2lb) squid, cleaned weight

juice of ½ lemon, plus lemon wedges to serve

2 red chillies, deseeded and shredded

2 tbsp chopped coriander leaves

FOR THE FREEKEH

200g (7oz) freekeh (whole grains, not broken freekeh)

2 tbsp olive oil

3 tbsp coarsely chopped flat-leaf parsley leaves

juice of 1 lemon

3½ tbsp extra virgin olive oil

50g (1¾oz) baby spinach

FOR THE TARATOR

25g (1oz) coarse country bread, crusts removed

4 tbsp milk

50g (1¾oz) blanched almonds

¾ tsp smoked paprika

¼ tsp cayenne pepper

2 garlic cloves

125ml (4fl oz) extra virgin olive oil (Greek is good for this)

juice of ¾ lemon, or more to taste

Preheat the oven to 180°C/350°F/gas mark 4. Brush the peppers with regular olive oil, season and put into a roasting tin. Cook for 35–40 minutes. They should be completely tender and slightly blistered. I don't skin them as I love the charred skin, but do so if you prefer. Slice into strips once they are cool enough to handle.

Make the tarator. Soak the bread in the milk for 15 minutes. Purée in a food processor with the almonds, smoked paprika, cayenne, garlic and seasoning, adding the extra virgin oil and lemon juice as you go. Add 75ml (2½fl oz) of water and whizz again. It should be thick but not stiff, so add more water if you need to. Taste and adjust the seasoning. You could very well need more lemon.

Put the freekeh into a saucepan with plenty of water, ½ tsp salt and the regular olive oil. Bring to the boil. Cover with a tight-fitting lid, reduce the temperature and simmer for 20–25 minutes. It should be tender but will retain a firmness in the middle. Drain and toss with the parsley, lemon juice and extra virgin oil and season. This is nice warm, so cover while you cook the squid.

Wash the squid, removing any whitish gunge from inside, and pat dry. (If it's damp it won't fry well.) If they're small, leave them whole. Otherwise, cut the little wings off and put them aside with the tentacles. Cut the bodies down one side to open out. If they are very big, halve the bodies lengthways and score them on the inside with a cross-hatch. Put in a bowl with olive oil to moisten.

Heat a griddle pan until really hot. Season the squid and cook it on both sides in batches, pressing it down to pick up the griddle marks. It needs only about 20 seconds on each side to turn opaque and a lovely golden colour. As soon as each batch of squid is ready, remove it to a plate and squeeze lemon juice over it. Add the chillies and coriander once it's all cooked and toss together.

Toss the spinach with the freekeh and divide between plates or spread out on a platter or a broad shallow bowl, top with the squid and peppers and put a dollop of tarator on the side of each plate, serving the rest in a bowl. Serve with wedges of lemon.

smoked mackerel, beetroot and poppy seed relish and treacly brown bread

I love this kind of food. It's partly Scandinavian, partly Irish. The bread is sweet and quite cake-like (it's a form of soda bread). I like the slight sweetness contrasting with the saltiness of the mackerel but, if you want something lower in carbs, use plain rye bread instead.

The bread recipe here is enough to make two small loaves. Just halve it if you only want one… but it always seems a bit pointless to put the oven on for just one loaf.

SERVES 4

FOR THE BREAD

500g (1lb 2oz) malted brown flour (see page 328 for stockists)

175g (6oz) plain flour

75g (2½oz) medium oatmeal

1 tsp salt

2½ tsp bicarbonate of soda

50g (1¾oz) butter, cut into small cubes, plus more for the tins

4 tbsp molasses sugar

175ml (6fl oz) stout

80ml (2½fl oz) treacle

400ml (14fl oz) buttermilk

jumbo oats, for the top

FOR THE REST

1 apple

1 tbsp cider vinegar

¼ red onion, very finely sliced

1½ tbsp olive oil

3 large Savoy cabbage leaves

1 tsp soft light brown sugar

2 tsp poppy seeds

salt and pepper

3 small-ish cooked beetroots, total weight about 300g (10½oz)

a few microleaves, ideally red-veined (optional)

4 smoked mackerel fillets

To make the bread, preheat the oven to 180°C/350°F/gas mark 4. Mix the flours and oatmeal with the salt and bicarbonate of soda. Add the butter and rub it in with your fingertips. Stir in the sugar. Make a well in the centre of the mixture and gradually pour in the stout, followed by the treacle and then the buttermilk. Mix these liquids in with a butter knife as they are added. You will end up with a pretty wet mixture and won't believe it will ever turn into bread. Divide it between two small buttered loaf tins (each should measure 19 x 9 x 5cm/7½ x 3½ x 2in and they should be 5cm/2in deep), and sprinkle each with the jumbo oats.

Put into the oven and bake for 40–50 minutes. To test whether the loaves are ready, remove one of them from the tin and tap the bottom. If it sounds hollow, it is ready. If not, return to the oven for a little while longer. Be sure not to overcook, though, or it will be dry. Turn out of the tins and leave to cool on a wire rack.

Peel the apple, core and cut the flesh into matchsticks. Put immediately into a bowl with the vinegar and mix to coat. Sauté the onion gently in ½ tbsp of the olive oil for about 1½ minutes. You don't want to colour or even soften it much, just take the raw edge off it. Add to the bowl with the apples. Remove the thick central rib from each of the cabbage leaves then roll the leaves up and cut them into shreds. Add this to the bowl with the remaining olive oil, sugar, poppy seeds and seasoning.

Peel the beetroots and cut into matchsticks. Add to the bowl at the last minute (if you add them earlier, they bleed over the other ingredients; a little of this is fine but it looks better when it hasn't gone too far), then scatter the salad with microleaves (if using).

Serve the smoked mackerel with the bread and salad.

bream with ginger, soy and spring onions

One of the cleanest, simplest recipes in the book. If you're trying to cut down your fat intake for whatever reason you don't have to fry the chilli and ginger, though the contrast in texture with the steamed flesh of the fish is wonderful. You can just steam them on top of the fish fillets along with the rest of the ginger instead.

SERVES 4

3½ tbsp soy sauce

3½ tbsp rice wine

4 tsp caster sugar

4 x 175g (6oz) bream fillets (or similar; sea bass is lovely, but more expensive)

2.5cm (1in) root ginger, peeled and shredded

6 tbsp groundnut oil

2 red chillies, deseeded and shredded

8 spring onions, trimmed, cut in half horizontally, then julienned

Mix the soy sauce, rice wine and sugar. Put the bream fillets on a plate and sprinkle 4 tbsp of the soy sauce mixture and half the ginger over them. Leave for 15 minutes.

Pour water into a large saucepan on top of which a steaming basket will fit. Bring the water to the boil. Set the steamer basket on top and put the fish in, on its plate (you can shake the soy mixture off, but leave the ginger). Cover tightly. Steam for seven minutes, remove from the heat and allow to cook in the residual heat for one minute. Check to see that the fish is cooked through.

Heat the oil and quickly fry the chillies and the rest of the ginger until pale gold. Serve the fish with the spring onions strewn over them, then pour on the hot oil with the chillies and ginger. Spoon on some of the remaining soy sauce mixture and put any that remains in a bowl for guests to help themselves at the table.

another way… scallops with ginger, soy and spring onions

Chop 4cm (1½cm) peeled root ginger into matchsticks. Divide about one-third of this between 4 clean scallop shells, then top each with 3 scallops and their roes. Chop 6 trimmed spring onions on the diagonal and scatter over the scallops with 6 tbsp of soy sauce. Get a two-tiered steamer ready and put two shells in each of the levels. Steam for six to eight minutes, depending on their size (you should ideally swap the tiers halfway through to ensure they all cook at the same rate). Heat 1 tbsp groundnut oil in a frying pan and sauté the rest of the ginger and 2 finely sliced garlic cloves. The garlic should be pale gold and the ginger like little golden shreds. Scoop out and drain on kitchen paper. Plate the scallops and sprinkle the top with the fried ginger and garlic, adding a drop of toasted sesame oil. Serve immediately. This makes a substantial starter or, with rice and stir-fried greens on the side, a main course for 4.

sashimi

Raw fish isn't to everyone's taste, and you do have to get spankingly fresh stuff (you need an excellent fishmonger), but it quickly grows on you. In fact I find it quite addictive (except for the squid option). It isn't a cheap dish – unless you make it with mackerel only – but it is incredibly filling (a massive hit of protein) and brilliant if you're watching your weight.

Wasabi varies hugely in quality. It comes in tubes, in powder form to mix yourself and as the fresh root (see a photo of the root on page 59). Fresh is the best option, but it's difficult to find (see page 329 for an online stockist); it can be grated on a special Japanese grater. Japanese soy sauce is lighter and more refined than others and doesn't overwhelm the taste of the fish.

SERVES AS MANY AS YOU LIKE

about 90g (3oz) sushi-quality skinned fish fillets per person (tuna, salmon, sea bass, mackerel, sardine)

TO SERVE

shredded mooli (daikon)

julienned carrots

sprigs of cress or other microleaves

finely chopped spring onions

finely sliced radishes

pickled ginger

wasabi

Japanese soy sauce

Using a very sharp knife – preferably a fish filleting knife – cut the fish at an angle into slices about 3mm (⅛in) thick and 2.5cm (1in) wide. You shouldn't need to 'saw' the fish, just slice through it.

Arrange each type of fish – slightly overlapping – in a line. You can serve the various vegetable possibilities (mooli, carrots, leaves, spring onions, radishes) in little piles on the plate, though when it comes to arranging everything you can do your own thing. One of the thrills of serving and eating sashimi is just how simple and beautiful a plateful can look.

Serve other accompaniments – ginger, wasabi and soy sauce – in little bowls.

mackerel with hazelnut picada

Picada is generally used as a thickener in Catalan cookery, added to braises at the last minute, but some Spanish cooks now use it as a final flourish in much the same way that Italians use gremolata. A watercress salad and some lentils are perfect with this.

SERVES 4

FOR THE PICADA

4 tbsp extra virgin olive oil

50g (1¾oz) chewy peasant-style bread, crusts removed, sliced about 1cm (½in) thick

40g (1½oz) unblanched hazelnuts

zest from ½ orange, removed with a zester, then finely chopped

1 garlic clove, finely chopped

2 tbsp finely chopped flat-leaf parsley leaves

1 tbsp sherry vinegar, or to taste

salt and pepper

FOR THE FISH

4 large mackerel fillets, each about 150g (5½oz), or 8 small fillets

2 tbsp olive oil

good squeeze of orange juice

To make the picada, preheat the oven to 190°C/375°F/gas mark 5. Pour 3 tbsp of the oil into a small frying pan and set it over a medium-low heat. To test for the correct temperature, dip a piece of bread in the oil. If it sizzles a bit, reduce the heat slightly and add the bread in a single layer. Fry for two to three minutes, until the bread is a pale caramel colour. Remove the bread and spread it out on kitchen paper to cool.

Toast the hazelnuts in a roasting tin in the oven for 10 minutes, or until the skins have darkened but not burned. Put them in a tea towel and rub while they are still warm to remove most of the skins. Finely chop the nuts. Break the bread into chunks, put these in a paper bag and crush them into coarse crumbs using a rolling pin. Add the rest of the ingredients, including the remaining 1 tbsp of virgin olive oil, season to taste and mix together.

For the fish, season the mackerel fillets. Heat the regular olive oil in a non-stick frying pan, then quickly fry the fillets over a medium heat for three minutes on each side, skin side down first if you have larger fillets. Put on warm plates, skin side up, and squeeze over orange juice. Spoon some picada on top and serve.

more mackerel… **japanese mackerel with mushrooms** I fancy the Japanese might call this 'dying leaves in rain'. (You have to put yourself in a Zen place not to snigger at that, I know… get yourself to that place!) It's a beautiful mix of golden mushrooms and shimmering mackerel skin. Heat 2 tbsp rapeseed oil in a pan and cook 4 fillets of mackerel (each 115g/4oz) skin side down, until golden, about 3 minutes. Turn and cook for 3 minutes on the other side. Remove. Add 2 finely sliced garlic cloves and cook for 1 minute, then 100g (3½oz) shiitake – halved or sliced, depending on size – and 100g (3½oz) enoki mushrooms. Fry briskly for 3 minutes, then return the mackerel with 4 tbsp sake or dry sherry and 1 tbsp soy sauce, and heat through. Scatter on some black or white sesame seeds. Serves 4.

hot chilli-ginger stir-fried squid

Hot, quick, good for you and relatively cheap as well. Seriously, what more could you want?

SERVES 4

1 lemon grass stalk, trimmed, coarse outer leaves removed

1 tbsp groundnut oil

2 garlic cloves, finely sliced

2cm (¾in) root ginger, peeled and very finely chopped

1–2 red chillies, deseeded and shredded

900g (2lb) cleaned and prepared squid, cut into rings

4 spring onions, chopped

1 tsp caster sugar, or to taste

splash of fish sauce

salt and pepper

juice of ½ lime, or to taste

2 tbsp chopped coriander or mint leaves

Chop the lemon grass and bash it in a mortar with a pestle. Heat the oil in a wok or frying pan and add the lemon grass, garlic, ginger and chillies. Cook over a medium heat for one minute.

It's very important that the squid is dry, otherwise it won't fry properly, so pat it dry with kitchen paper. Add it to the pan and cook over a very high heat for one minute. Reduce the heat, add the spring onions, sugar, fish sauce, salt and pepper and lime juice.

Cook for another 30 seconds or so, quickly taste to check the seasoning (and sweet-tart balance, adjusting the levels of sugar and lime if you want), toss in the herbs and turn on to warm plates. Serve with brown rice and a salad or stir-fried greens.

more superquick seafood… prawns with lime and bok choi Heat 1 tbsp groundnut oil in a wok and throw in a 2cm (¾in) piece of root ginger, peeled and finely chopped, 1 lemon grass stalk, coarse leaves removed and tender heart finely chopped, 1 red and 1 green chilli, deseeded and shredded, and 4 spring onions, trimmed and chopped on the diagonal. Cook over a medium heat until the ginger is soft and beginning to colour. Increase the heat and add 500g (1lb 2oz) raw, shelled and deveined tiger or king prawns (ideally organic). Cook until they start to colour, then add the juice and finely grated zest of 1 lime, 1 tbsp fish sauce and 1 tbsp caster sugar. Cook until the prawns are pink. Scoop them out with a slotted spoon and add 250g (9oz) bok choi, sliced lengthways, to the wok. Allow it to wilt and the 'sauce' to reduce. Chuck the prawns back in with 15g (½oz) very roughly chopped coriander and 10g (¼oz) torn basil leaves. Taste for sweet-tart (sugar-lime) balance and serve immediately. You can eat this on its own or with brown rice. Offer wedges of lime. Serves 4.

warm duck salad with plum-ginger dressing and sesame

Many large supermarkets now seem to stock Japanese pickled plum paste (if you can't find it, see pages 328–329 for online stockists). Its fresh, sour quality is great in dressings and marinades. I remove the skin and fat from the duck breasts: it still makes a lovely salad, but you can leave it on if you prefer.

SERVES 4

FOR THE DRESSING

3½ tbsp mirin

2 tbsp rice vinegar, or to taste

2½ tbsp groundnut oil

2½ tbsp olive oil

2 tsp pickled plum paste, or to taste

2 tsp soft light brown sugar, or to taste

½ globe preserved (stem) ginger in syrup, finely chopped

FOR THE SALAD

2 avocados

salt and pepper

10 radishes (preferably nice firm French Breakfast radishes)

2 large Gressingham duck breasts, skin and fat removed

1 tbsp groundnut oil

150g (5½oz) French beans, topped but not tailed (or sugar snap peas, or a mixture)

125g (4½oz) baby spinach

2 tbsp sesame seeds (preferably black sesame)

Preheat the oven to 220°C/425°F/gas mark 7.

Make the dressing by simply whisking everything together. The pickled plum paste won't completely blend in; there will still be little pale pink pieces in the dressing. Taste for a balance of sweet and tart, adjusting the sugar, vinegar and plum paste accordingly.

Get the vegetables ready. Halve, pit and slice the avocados, peel each slice, and immediately season and toss with some of the dressing. Wash the radishes, snip off the tail and slice, lengthways, very thinly.

Season the duck breasts. Heat the oil in a frying pan and brown the duck breasts on both sides, then put them in a roasting tin and cook in the hot oven for five minutes. (You can check whether the meat is done by slicing through the centre of a breast. It should be pink, like rare steak.) Remove the duck breasts, cover with foil to insulate and leave to rest for three or four minutes.

Meanwhile, steam or boil the green beans until tender, then immediately rinse in cold water. Slice the duck breasts and season, then combine with all the other ingredients (except the sesame seeds) and toss with the dressing. Arrange on a large platter or divide between four plates. Sprinkle the sesame seeds on top and serve immediately.

thai-style chicken and mango salad

To be strictly Thai you can leave out the watercress and increase the quantity of herbs. If you can't find green mangoes, or prefer to eat ripe ones, you can use 1 ripe mango and 1 tart green apple (core removed). As well as sourness the green mangoes provide crunch, so apple is a fine substitute.

SERVES 4 AS A MAIN COURSE

salt and pepper

4 skinless boneless chicken breasts or thighs

5 tbsp groundnut oil

6 spring onions, trimmed and sliced on the diagonal

8 garlic cloves, peeled and finely sliced

2 green mangoes, peeled

3 red chillies, deseeded and shredded

2 tbsp fish sauce

1½ tbsp caster sugar

juice of 1½ limes

50g (1¾oz) coriander leaves

40g (1½oz) mint leaves

50g (1¾oz) watercress leaves, coarse stalks removed

1½ tbsp roughly chopped roasted peanuts

Lightly season the chicken and sauté in 2 tbsp of the oil until cooked through. Leave to cool. (Or you can use the same amount of leftover chicken, shredded.)

Sauté the spring onions, using ½ tbsp more oil, in the same pan, then put them in a broad flat bowl. Quickly fry the garlic until golden; be careful not to burn it. Add to the bowl as well.

Slice the flesh from the mangoes and cut it into lengths about the thickness of two matchsticks. Put these in the bowl with the chillies, fish sauce, sugar and lime juice.

Finally, cut the chicken into strips and add to the bowl with the herbs, watercress and the remaining 2½ tbsp of oil. Mix everything together. Scatter the peanuts over the top and serve.

and also… burmese-style chicken salad Soak 2 sliced shallots in cold water for 10 minutes, then drain. Put these in a dish with 200–250g (7–9oz) shredded cooked chicken (but use whatever you have, I generally make this with leftovers). Add the juice of 3 limes, ½ green chilli, deseeded and shredded and a really generous handful of coriander and mint leaves. Slice another 4 shallots and fry these in 2 tbsp groundnut oil until golden brown. Pour this over the salad, season and toss. Sprinkle on about 1 tbsp of chopped roasted peanuts, if you want. I also sometimes add matchsticks of carrot or shredded cabbage, especially if I am short of chicken. Serves 2 as a light main course.

shawarma chicken with warm chickpea purée and sumac onions

This is a great mixture of flavours and temperatures and people always love it. You can prepare the purée in advance, then all you have to do is griddle the chicken. The purée is also excellent with lamb or with roast Mediterranean vegetables.

SERVES 4

FOR THE CHICKEN AND MARINADE

4 garlic cloves, crushed

1 tsp ground ginger

1 tsp mixed spice

½ tsp turmeric

2 tsp ground cumin

3 tbsp olive oil

juice of 1 lemon

salt and plenty of pepper

8 skinless boneless chicken thighs

FOR THE PURÉE

1 onion, finely chopped

1 tbsp olive oil

4 garlic cloves, finely chopped

3 tsp ground cumin

½ tsp ground mixed spice

400g can of chickpeas, drained and rinsed

150ml (5fl oz) extra virgin olive oil

2 tbsp tahini

juice of 1 lemon, or to taste

FOR THE ONIONS

½ small red onion, peeled and very finely sliced

seeds from ½ pomegranate

½ tsp sumac

TO SERVE

really fresh sprigs of coriander

Greek or Turkish yogurt

lemon wedges

Prepare the marinade by mixing everything together (except the chicken) in a shallow, non-reactive dish that will hold the chicken pieces in a single layer. Put them in this, turning them over to make sure they are well coated. Cover. Ideally you should leave the chicken for a couple of hours in the fridge (or put it in the fridge in the morning and leave to marinate all day), but I leave it for 30 minutes when pushed. Turn the chicken every so often.

To make the purée, sauté the onion in the regular olive oil until soft and golden. Add the garlic and cook for another two minutes, then add the spices for another minute. Toss in the chickpeas and heat them through, tossing them with the onions and spices. Tip all this into a food processor with the extra virgin oil, tahini, lemon juice, salt and pepper, adding 6–8 tbsp of water. Purée and taste; you may want to add more lemon juice or seasoning (it needs good, assertive seasoning). You might also need to add more water so you get the right texture (if you do, adjust the seasoning again). Scrape out into a clean pan so you can reheat the purée (though you can serve it at room temperature if you want).

Put the red onion into a bowl of very cold water and leave to crisp up for 15 minutes or so.

Lift the chicken out of the marinade and season with salt. Heat a frying pan or griddle pan until really hot, then cook the chicken for 1½ minutes on each side (you don't need to add any oil). Reduce the heat and cook for a further 2½ minutes on each side. The chicken will be golden and gorgeously singed in places.

Drain the red onion, pat dry, mix with the pomegranate seeds and sprinkle with sumac.

Reheat the purée if you prefer it hot. Serve the chicken thighs with some of the purée, add the sprigs of coriander and top with the pomegranate and red onion mixture. Provide a bowl of yogurt and some lemon wedges too. You can offer flatbread or bulgar wheat on the side but you really don't need it; a salad of bitter leaves (chicory or radicchio) is better.

chicken and pumpkin with soy and star anise

This is slightly adapted from an excellent American book (*All About Braising*, by Molly Stevens). It quickly became one of the most cooked dishes in my house, as it's easy and children love it. You might feel that there isn't enough soy but, as the chicken exudes its juices, you end up with enough liquid.

Don't be tempted to add more star anise; one really is enough. It's a powerful spice.

SERVES 4

1 tbsp groundnut oil

8 bone-in chicken thighs

2 tbsp soy sauce

2 tbsp rice vinegar

2 tbsp fish sauce

2 tbsp soft dark brown sugar

1 red chilli, deseeded and shredded

2.5cm (1in) root ginger, peeled and very finely chopped

3 garlic cloves, very finely chopped

8 spring onions, trimmed and chopped on the diagonal

900g (2lb) pumpkin or squash, peeled, deseeded and cut into chunks

3 strips of orange zest

1 star anise

2 tbsp orange juice

pepper

Preheat the oven to 180°C/350°F/gas mark 4.

Heat the oil in a casserole or sauté pan (something in which all the chicken thighs can lie in a single layer). Remove the chicken skin if you prefer, then brown the chicken on both sides. Don't try to turn the thighs until they are easy to move, as pulling will tear them. Take the chicken out of the pan and set aside. Pour the fat out of the pan into a cup.

Mix the soy sauce, vinegar and fish sauce with the sugar and stir. Put 1 tbsp of the reserved fat back in the pan, heat it and add the chilli, ginger and garlic. Keep some of the greener bits of spring onion back to sprinkle on at the end and add the rest to the pan. Cook over a medium heat for a couple of minutes, until the garlic is golden, then add the soy sauce mixture. Return the chicken, along with any juices that have seeped out, plus the pumpkin, orange zest, star anise, orange juice and 3–4 tbsp of water. Grind on some pepper. Cover and put in the hot oven for 40 minutes in total. After 15 minutes' cooking time, turn the chicken pieces over, then cover once more. After 30 minutes' cooking time, uncover and return to the oven to cook for the remaining 10 minutes.

Scatter with the reserved spring onion greens and serve. Any grain is good on the side: brown rice, kamut, quinoa or wheat berries (see pages 223–224 for how to cook them). Just season the grain well and toss it with lots of chopped coriander leaves and some lime juice.

spiced pork chops with ginger and mango relish

Don't keep this relish just for chops, as it's brilliant with any spicy meat (and grilled salmon and mackerel, too). I've called it a relish but it's chunky, almost like a salad, and people usually end up filling a third of their plate with it (and asking for more). You can treat chicken in the same way as the chops. If you prefer to cut down on fat, then remove it from the chops, or let guests do it for themselves, but not until after cooking (you need it for the flavour).

SERVES 6

FOR THE CHOPS

2 tbsp groundnut oil

juice of 3 limes

2 red chillies, deseeded
and chopped

2 garlic cloves, crushed

2cm (¾in) root ginger, peeled
and grated

6 pork loin chops

FOR THE RELISH

2 mangoes

finely grated zest and juice of
1 lime

1 tbsp groundnut oil

10 garlic cloves, grated

120g (4¼oz) root ginger, peeled
and grated

2 tsp wholegrain mustard

caster sugar, to taste (about 1 tsp)

salt and pepper

1 green chilli, deseeded
and shredded

1 red chilli, deseeded
and shredded

leaves from a small bunch of
coriander, roughly chopped

Mix everything for the chops (except the meat itself) together to make a marinade and place in a shallow, non-reactive bowl. Put the chops into this, turn to coat, cover and marinate in the fridge for a couple of hours. Turn the chops over every so often.

Peel the mangoes and cut the cheeks from each side of the stones. Remove whatever flesh you can slice off into neat strips from the mango stones. Cut the mango cheeks into wedges about the thickness of a pound coin and toss with the lime zest and juice.

Heat the oil in a frying pan and add the grated garlic and ginger pastes. Cook over a medium-low heat until it smells cooked and no longer raw. Pull off the heat and stir in the mustard, then stir this mixture into the mangoes. Gently stir in the sugar, salt, pepper, chillies and coriander.

Heat a frying pan until it is really hot and take the chops out of the marinade. Scrape the marinade off the chops and back into the bowl in which they were lying. Season the chops. Cook them over a high heat for about three minutes, or until you get a good colour, then turn and do the same on the other side. Now reduce the heat to low and continue to cook until completely cooked through; this takes at least 10 minutes. There should be no pink juices when you pierce them. When you get towards the end of the cooking time, add the marinade and let it glaze the pork chops and bubble away in the pan. Serve the chops with the ginger and mango relish.

crazy grains

It's great when a previously unglamorous and relatively cheap ingredient becomes the *dernier cri*. I love an underdog making it to the top, so I have to smile when I think that whole grains – once the domain of the sandal-wearing muesli brigade – are now eaten by minxes shod in Christian Louboutin. Whole grains are hip. And don't assume they're all chewy and taste of straw. Quinoa has small grains and a delicate flavour, bulgar is gently nutty. I especially like the stronger grains – deeply earthy rye berries and smoky, sexy freekeh – and they've all made me more inventive as a cook.

The consensus is that they're good for us, certainly preferable to processed grains that have had most of their nutrients stripped away. Refined carbohydrates are quickly converted by our bodies into sugar, and the surges and dips in blood sugar this causes provoke a rise in insulin. High levels of insulin are increasingly blamed for weight gain and obesity (and their attendant problems). Whole grains, on the other hand, don't produce such spikes. A meal of slowly digested whole-grain carbohydrates and proteins smooths out the blood sugar-insulin roller coaster. Whole grains make you feel fuller for longer and also send the 'satiety' signal to your brain relatively quickly, so you feel full sooner. Fans also see them as a good alternative to meat and point out how important fibre is in our diet.

I am pretty convinced by the findings of The Nurses' Health Study, one of the longest-running, most intensive investigations into health and nutrition ever conducted. (Started in 1976 with funding from the National Institutes of Health in the USA, it is still going, with the nurses' children now taking part as well.) It has looked at the whole question of fibre, and found that participants who ate most fibre from whole grains (about 7.5g a day) were thirty per cent less likely to develop type-2 diabetes than those who ate less (2.5g), while those who ate two servings of whole grains a day were thirty per cent less likely to develop heart disease than those who ate only one serving a week. There's no arguing with that.

There are negative murmurings. The investigative food journalist Joanna Blythman, in her book *What to Eat*, argues that all the vitamins and minerals in whole grains are found in greater quantities in meat, fish and eggs (though for various reasons animal proteins are not always an option and some grains – such as buckwheat, kamut, oats, quinoa, rye and spelt – provide good levels of protein). The anti-carbists aren't keen on them either, because although they're 'good carbs' they're still carbs.

Whole grains are so filling you're not going to gorge yourself on them, though, so unless you have real problems with carbohydrates, I'd put them on the menu. And I'm not saying never have a bowl of white rice with your curry again, just not too often. Besides, you'll get to love the brown stuff... honest.

barley

Banish all thoughts of sensible Scotch broth, barley has been liberated and is now found in trendy salads everywhere. Pearl barley is the type most commonly available. This has been processed – the germ and some of the bran removed – but, unlike most grains, barley's fibre is found right through the kernel. Pearl barley cooks in 25–30 minutes. Drain, dress in vinaigrette and use as a salad base, or make a pilaf with it by the absorption method (cooking it in stock and other flavourings, allowing the liquid to become absorbed as the grain cooks), or cook it like risotto rice, stirring so it becomes creamy. The unprocessed type, pot or 'Scotch' barley, takes an hour to cook (and needs overnight soaking).

brown long-grain rice

This retains a certain firmness after cooking. Cook it in boiling water for about 25 minutes, or make it by the absorption method (see above). It doesn't need pre-soaking. Because the grains stay separate (like many whole grains), it makes a great salad base.

buckwheat

A staple in Russia and Eastern Europe, both buckwheat groats and roasted buckwheat (also known as kasha) have a robust, 'beefy' flavour (particularly the roasted variety). Start with the unroasted type and fry it in oil before adding water and cooking for 15 minutes.

bulgar

This, much used in Middle Eastern food, is a boon, it's so quick to prepare. It is produced when wheat (usually durum) is boiled, dried and cracked. Cook in boiling water or stock: the time depends on the size of the grain (medium, the type I mostly use, takes 15 minutes). For salads, where it requires a less fluffy texture, just soak it in water for 15 minutes.

camargue red rice

This, cultivated in the Camargue wetlands, has a gorgeous colour and is great mixed into salads or pilafs of brown rice, wild rice or quinoa. It cooks – boiled or by the absorption method (see above) – in 25 minutes, and shares the chewy nuttiness of brown rice.

farro

An ancient grain, believed to have sustained the Roman legions. It's pale brown, has a real hazelnutty flavour and makes a superb salad base. Most commonly available is semi-pearled; this doesn't need soaking and cooks in 20–25 minutes. Use the unpearled type if you prefer; it needs overnight soaking and cooks in one hour. I used to cook farro only in autumn and winter, but a summery farro salad in Rome – containing tomatoes, olives, basil and grassy Tuscan oil – won me over to using it all year round.

freekeh

Freekeh is assertive. Smoky. Chewy. It's roasted young green wheat, cooked mostly in the Middle East, and is the coolest grain around. It stands up well to big flavours such as preserved lemons, pomegranate molasses and oily fish. Just boil it in water for 20–25 minutes, drain and use in salads, or cook in stock by the absorption method (see page 223).

kamut

The brand name for khorasan, an ancient variety of wheat that's still rather under the radar. Flavour isn't its chief attraction – it's fairly bland – but the large, honey-coloured kernels make a great salad base. Soak overnight, then cook for 50–60 minutes.

oats

See page 240 for everything you need to know about oats.

quinoa

This pseudo grain – really a seed – is a health wonder. It's a complete protein (rare in the plant world). In texture and size it's somewhere between couscous and bulgar and is lovely hot or cold. Toast it for a few minutes in a dry pan – it helps the flavour – then add 675ml (1 pint 2½fl oz) liquid for every 300g (10½oz) quinoa and cook for 15 minutes for plump, dry grains. It can be cream, black or red, so you also get to be a painter when you use it.

rye

The cold grain, easily grown in the wet and chilly north. I love it for its deep, dark, fruity flavour. It's fantastic teamed with other 'northern' ingredients, try it with beetroots, smoked fish, dill, caraway and buttermilk. Soak the grain overnight and cook it for 50–60 minutes.

spelt

Because the name sounds rather austere (just say it out loud), I usually team spelt with northern ingredients such as smoked foods and buttermilk. Spelt is often used interchangeably with farro, but pearled spelt, the type most commonly available, is more refined (and makes a better risotto, nice and creamy) than semi-pearled farro. Pearled spelt cooks in 20–25 minutes. Substitute non-pearled spelt, the whole grain version, if you want – find it online – except for in risottos (soak it overnight and cook for about one hour).

wheat berries

These are wheat grains, but Americans generally call them 'berries' and we are adopting the term. Both soft and hard varieties are available (the latter is more chewy) and both need to be soaked overnight. Soft wheat cooks in 40 minutes; hard wheat can take about 90.

wild rice

This is the grain from a native American water grass. It stays very firm and is great mixed with quinoa, red rice or brown rice, mainly because of its colour but also texture (on its own I find it too chewy and robust, it's better as a 'mixer'). It's ready in about 45 minutes.

griddled chicken, kale and farro with creamy garlic and anchovy dressing

You won't get this at all until you taste it, but I think of it as healthy chicken Caesar. It's got all the same elements, but with the addition of grains. And it uses great greens. The farro can be substituted with spelt and the kale with cavolo nero. You don't have to use griddled chicken. Just roast a whole chicken, carve the meat and serve it on the grains and greens.

SERVES 4

200g (7oz) farro

2½ tbsp olive oil

1 small onion, finely chopped

250g (9oz) kale

½ tbsp extra virgin olive oil

good squeeze of lemon, plus lemon wedges to serve

4 boneless chicken thighs

FOR THE DRESSING

6 anchovies, drained of oil

30g (1oz) pine nuts or blanched almonds

1 fat garlic clove

salt and pepper

2 tbsp extra virgin olive oil

juice of ½ lemon

½ tbsp finely chopped flat-leaf parsley leaves

Put the farro in a saucepan and cover with plenty of water. Bring to the boil, then reduce the heat to a lively simmer and cook for 20–25 minutes, or until the farro is just tender. (It doesn't completely soften like rice, but retains a slight 'bite'.)

Meanwhile, for the dressing, put the anchovies, nuts, garlic and some pepper into a small food processor. With the motor running, add the extra virgin oil, lemon juice and 2 tbsp of water. Process until smooth. You can add a little more water if you would like the dressing to be thinner, it should be about as thick as double cream (though not as smooth). Scrape into a bowl and stir in the parsley.

Heat 1½ tbsp of the regular olive oil in a frying pan and cook the onion over a medium-low heat until pale gold and soft. Set aside.

Remove the ribs from the kale and discard, then tear the leaves into pieces. Put it into plenty of boiling water and cook for four minutes. Drain really well and add to the onion in the pan. Set over a medium heat once more, stirring the kale to ensure it gets coated in the oil. It should be deep green and glossy.

Rinse the farro in boiling water then immediately toss with the kale, extra virgin oil and lemon juice. Season to taste (but remember you are going to add a really punchy dressing).

Brush the chicken thighs on both sides with the remaining regular oil and season. Heat a griddle pan until really hot, then cook the chicken for two minutes on each side. Reduce the heat and cook for another two minutes on each side, or until the chicken is cooked through (there should be no trace of pink in the centre).

Divide the farro and kale between four plates and drizzle with the dressing (serve the rest on the side). Put the chicken on top; you can slice it or leave the thighs whole. Serve with lemon wedges.

autumn menu **indian warmth**

lentil, roast tomato and saffron soup | indian-spiced beetroot, pumpkin and spinach | mangoes

The kind of menu that surprises people. There's no meat, but diners don't realize it until they've finished. You certainly don't feel anything is missing. I crave Indian spices as soon as the weather starts to get cold. They render food warming in a sweet, fragrant, 'alive' kind of way. For pudding, simply serve perfectly ripe mangoes and good juicy limes. Allow people to cut their own mangoes into slices and squeeze on the lime. A bowl of fresh lychees (available from November to January) would be good, too. If you want to serve a 'proper' pudding, Citrus compote with ginger snow (see page 200) would be lovely.

lentil and roast tomato soup with saffron

The tomatoes give real depth. It makes a hearty opener, but the main course is deceptively light.

SERVES 6

10 plum tomatoes, halved

4 tbsp olive oil

2 tsp harissa

salt and pepper

2 tsp brown sugar (optional)

2 tsp cumin seeds

1 tsp coriander seeds

1 tbsp groundnut oil

1 large onion, chopped

4 garlic cloves, chopped

½ tsp turmeric

good pinch of saffron stamens

2cm (¾in) root ginger, chopped

1 green chilli, finely chopped

150g (5½oz) split red lentils

900ml (1½ pints) vegetable stock

4 tbsp chopped coriander leaves

plain yogurt (optional)

toasted flaked almonds

Preheat the oven to 190°C/375°F/gas mark 5. Put the tomatoes in a roasting tin in which they can lie in a single layer. Mix the olive oil, harissa and salt and pepper together in a cup and pour this over them. Turn them over to coat, ending with them cut side up. (If your tomatoes aren't the best, sprinkle the brown sugar over them, though their natural sweetness comes out as they roast.) Cook for 45 minutes until slightly shrunken and charred in places. Pick out the six nicest looking tomato halves and set aside.

Toast the cumin and coriander seeds for two minutes in a dry pan. Grind them in a mortar and set aside. Heat the groundnut oil in a saucepan and sauté the onion until soft and golden. Add the garlic, all the spices, ginger and chilli and cook for two minutes. Tip in the lentils, stirring to coat in the cooking juices, tomatoes with their juices and the stock. Season well. Bring to the boil, reduce the heat to a simmer and cook for 15–20 minutes, or until the lentils have collapsed into a purée. The tomatoes should have disintegrated too. Now either purée the soup or leave it chunky. Check the seasoning and stir in most of the coriander. Serve each bowlful with a swirl of yogurt (if you want), a reserved tomato half, a few toasted almonds and some of the remaining coriander.

indian-spiced beetroot, pumpkin and spinach

This started out as a thoran, a stir-fry from Kerala with the key flavourings of mustard seeds, curry leaves and coconut. But then I decided I wanted something more substantial, so it's not an authentic dish, but it is delicious. One of the boons is that it doesn't use many spices. You can buy curry leaves in Indian groceries, large supermarkets and online. They freeze very well. If you can't find them, just leave them out (don't substitute dried). It won't be the same, but it will still be good.

SERVES 6

1½ tbsp groundnut oil

4 tsp mustard seeds

handful of curry leaves (about 30)

3 tsp chilli flakes (or more, depending on how hot you want it)

2 small red onions, sliced

4cm (1½in) root ginger, peeled and shredded

1 tsp turmeric

200g (7oz) beetroot, peeled and cut into chunks

400g (14oz) pumpkin, peeled, deseeded and cut into chunks

salt and pepper

175g (6oz) waxy potatoes, peeled and cut into chunks

200g (7oz) baby spinach leaves, washed well

juice of 1 juicy lime

6 tbsp freshly grated coconut

Heat the oil in a large wok or saucepan set over a medium heat. Toss in the mustard seeds followed by the curry leaves and chilli flakes. Swirl everything around until the leaves and mustard seeds stop spluttering. Reduce the heat to low.

Tip in the onions and ginger and cook for five minutes, until they have softened. Add the turmeric and cook for another minute.

Add the beetroot and pumpkin. Stir well to coat them with the spices. If you have bought a fresh coconut to make this recipe, add the coconut water to the pan, plus another 75ml (2½fl oz) of water. If you don't have any coconut water, just add about 120ml (4fl oz) of water to the pan. Season well. Bring to the boil, then reduce the heat, cover and cook over a gentle heat for about 15 minutes. Stir in the potatoes and continue to cook until all the vegetables are tender. Keep an eye on the pan to make sure the vegetables aren't catching on the bottom and add a little more water if you need to, though this dish should end up quite 'dry'.

When the vegetables are soft add the spinach, mix together, and cook, stirring a little to help incorporate the spinach, until wilted (this only takes a few minutes). Add the lime juice and check the seasoning. Scatter with the coconut before serving. Offer brown rice alongside, and some plain yogurt.

crazy salad

This is one of my favourite dishes in the book. I wanted to come up with a salad, especially one that would be good in the colder months, that was robust, really healthy and irresistible ('accidentally healthy'). When I served this, the kids said 'Crazy, mum,' because they said it was hippy salad reborn. I wasn't sure whether that was a criticism or a compliment, and then sat back and watched them eat platefuls of it.

This recipe is a starting point. Cook other grains – kamut or wheat berries (see page 224 for how to cook those) – and add peas, cucumber, crumbled feta and mint, other beans, black or red lentils instead of Puy, blueberries or chopped apples instead of pomegranates. There are all sorts of things you can do if you just start off with a cooked grain as a salad base. As long as you stick to the basic quantities for the dressing (1 tbsp of vinegar, 4 tbsp of oil), you can flavour it that bit differently, too.

SERVES 6 AS A SIDE DISH

FOR THE SALAD

90g (3oz) semi-pearled farro or pearled spelt

55g (2oz) Puy lentils

125g (4½oz) carrots, cut into matchsticks

100g (3½oz) cooked chickpeas, drained and rinsed

2 tbsp mixed seeds (sunflower, pumpkin, sesame, whatever you have)

seeds from ½ pomegranate

30g (1oz) watercress, coarse stalks removed

FOR THE DRESSING

1 tbsp white balsamic vinegar, or to taste

½–1 tsp harissa, or to taste

4 tbsp extra virgin olive oil

½–1 tsp runny honey

¾ tbsp pomegranate molasses

salt and pepper

Put the farro or spelt into a saucepan and cover with water. Bring to the boil, reduce the heat to a simmer and cook for 20–25 minutes, or until the grain is cooked but still has a nutty bite. Cook the lentils at the same time, again in water, until they are tender. (Cooking time varies depending on their age, so it could take as little as 15 or as much as 35 minutes.)

Meanwhile, make the dressing by mixing all the ingredients together, seasoning well. Drain the grains and lentils, run cold water through them to cool them down, shake the sieve vigorously to get rid of as much water as possible and tumble them into a serving bowl. Season and add half the dressing.

Toss in all the other ingredients (if you want to assemble this ahead of time, don't add the watercress until just before serving) and add the rest of the dressing. Taste for seasoning: you might want a little more salt, pepper or harissa, or you may even want more white balsamic.

pears poached in earl grey

These pears end up a lovely rich toffee colour and, if you are able to leave them sitting in the reduced syrup overnight before serving, they will absorb more of the subtly smoky tea flavour. Serve them with Greek yogurt.

SERVES 4

4 Earl Grey tea bags

150g (5½oz) granulated sugar

juice of 2 lemons, plus 2 broad strips of lemon zest

2 broad strips of orange zest

4 pears, peeled, halved and cored

Put three of the tea bags into a jug with 1 litre (1¾ pints) of boiling water and leave it to brew. Discard the tea bags and pour the tea into a saucepan broad enough to take all the pear halves in a single layer. Add the sugar.

Stir over a medium heat to dissolve the sugar, then add the lemon juice, lemon and orange zests and the pears. Bring the liquid to a simmer, then reduce the heat and gently cook the pears until they are tender. How long this takes depends on how ripe your fruit is. Keep checking, sticking the tip of a sharp knife into the flesh. Once the pears are ready, scoop them out with a slotted spoon and set them in a dish where they are not touching each other, so they can cool down and stop cooking (if you pile them on top of each other, the heat means they will continue to soften).

Remove the zest from the poaching liquid and bring it to the boil. Add the final tea bag and simmer until the liquid is reduced to about 275ml (9½fl oz). The syrup will thicken more as it cools. Leave to cool completely, strain, then put the pears into a serving dish and pour over the syrup.

turkish quince sorbet

Quince flesh is so honeyed that I think it needs a little help from acidity, hence the tart apples and lemon juice here. You need to leave this a decent amount of time for the sorbet to soften before serving as it sets pretty solid, due to the high proportion of pectin in it. You can replace some of the water with pomegranate juice (pure stuff, not sweetened or 'pomegranate juice drink') for a beautifully coloured sorbet with a slightly different flavour.

SERVES 8

100g (3½oz) tart eating apples (I use Granny Smith)

400g (14oz) quinces

315g (11oz) granulated sugar

juice of 1 lemon

1–2 tsp flower water (rose or orange), optional

seeds from 1 pomegranate, to serve (optional)

Peel and core the apples and quinces and chop the flesh into chunks. Put in a saucepan and add water to just cover. Cover and cook the fruit gently until soft – it could take as much as 30 minutes as quince flesh is so hard – by which time there should be very little liquid left. (Do keep a careful eye on it to make sure it doesn't boil dry, but don't add too much water as it will affect the sorbet. If you really need it, add just 1–2 tbsp at a time.)

Make a sugar syrup by gently dissolving the sugar over a medium heat in 315ml (11fl oz) of water. Set aside to cool.

Purée the apple and quince flesh in a food processor or blender, then push it through a nylon sieve (quince is so fibrous you really have to do this to get a decently smooth sorbet). Add the lemon juice, then a small amount of flower water and taste; brands vary in strength so you might want a little more. Add the sugar syrup too, then chill in the fridge. Freeze in an ice-cream machine according to the manufacturer's instructions. If you don't have an ice-cream machine, put the mixture in a shallow, freezer-proof container in the freezer. When it has frozen round the edges but is still slushy in the middle, churn the mixture in a food processor (or use a fork and beat vigorously). Repeat three or four times during the freezing process.

Serve sprinkled with the pomegranate seeds.

blackberry and red wine jellies

This may seem like a lot of gelatine, but alcohol inhibits its setting qualities so you do need this much. This is not a pudding for every day (that alcohol!), but a weekend treat. It's best to make these the day before serving, so they have time to set.

SERVES 6

5 large or 10 small sheets gelatine (about 18g/generous ½oz in total)

475ml (17fl oz) red wine

150g (5½oz) granulated sugar

400g (14oz) blackberries, stalks removed

Put the gelatine into a shallow bowl and cover with water. Soak for five minutes, until completely soft. Scoop up the gelatine and gently squeeze out the excess water. Meanwhile, heat the wine and sugar with 175ml (6fl oz) of water, stirring gently to help the sugar dissolve. The wine shouldn't get any hotter than hand warm. Add the soaked gelatine and stir to dissolve. (Gelatine can't go into boiling liquid or it will lose its setting properties.)

Divide the berries between six glasses and pour over the liquid. Put in the refrigerator to set. There is a lot of fruit here, so it shouldn't bob too much to the top as it is tightly packed. Leave overnight to set before serving.

more fruit jelly please… cardamom-scented plum jellies

Make these in early autumn before the plums have disappeared. Halve and pit 700g (1lb 9oz) red-fleshed plums and put them in a saucepan with 400ml (14fl oz) apple juice, 100ml (3½fl oz) of water, 125g (4½oz) granulated sugar and the ground seeds of 4 cardamom pods. Heat gently, stirring to help the sugar dissolve and, when nearly boiling, reduce the heat to a simmer and cook until the fruit is completely soft and falling apart. Leave to cool a little, then purée in a blender or food processor. Measure how much you have and make up the quantity to 1 litre (1¾ pints) with either more apple juice or water. Put 4 large or 8 small sheets of gelatine in a bowl and cover with cold water. Leave for 10 minutes until it goes completely soft. Meanwhile, heat some of the plum purée to hand heat (it must be hot enough to melt the gelatine but not so hot that it destroys its setting properties). Squeeze the excess water out of the gelatine and put it into the warm purée. Stir to dissolve, then add this back to the rest of the purée. Pour into six glasses and leave in the fridge to set overnight. Serve with some Greek yogurt sweetened slightly with sugar. Serves 6.

date, apricot and walnut loaf cake

This is not so healthy that you can eat it with abandon (it is full of dried fruits which are high in sugar, not to mention the stuff that comes in a bag), but it uses good whole grain flours and has plenty of good-for-you nuts and seeds in it, too. It's a great Saturday or Sunday afternoon treat as it's so easy and quick to make (mix, scrape into the tin, put it in the oven). My kids like it just as much as chocolate cake. They eat it warm spread with butter, though… what's not to like?

SERVES ABOUT 10

175g (6oz) unsalted butter, plus more for the tin

150g (5½oz) pitted dates, chopped

75g (2¾oz) ready-to-eat dried apricots, chopped

75ml (2½fl oz) apple juice

140g (5oz) soft dark brown sugar

finely grated zest of 1 orange

1 egg, lightly beaten

100g (3½oz) plain flour

125g (4½oz) malted brown flour (see page 328 for stockists)

1 tsp baking powder

good pinch of mixed spice

really generous grating of nutmeg

50g (1¾oz) walnuts, chopped

2 tbsp pumpkin seeds, plus more for the top (optional)

2 tbsp sunflower seeds

1 tbsp sesame seeds (optional)

Butter a loaf tin measuring 22 x 11 x 6cm (9 x 4½ x 2½in) and line the base with baking parchment. Put the dates and apricots in a saucepan with the apple juice and 3–4 tbsp of water. Bring to the boil, then reduce the heat right down and simmer for 15 minutes. You will have something that looks like a purée. Leave to cool. Melt the butter and allow it, too, to cool. Meanwhile, preheat the oven to 180°C/350°F/gas mark 4.

Add the butter to the dates and apricots with the sugar, zest and egg. Sift the flours into a bowl, then tip the bran caught in the sieve back into the bowl. Add the baking powder, mixed spice, nutmeg, nuts, pumpkin and sunflower seeds. Add the date and egg mixture, stirring it into the dry ingredients. Make sure everything is combined, but don't overwork. Scrape into the tin and sprinkle with the sesame seeds and extra pumpkin seeds (if using).

Bake in the hot oven for 1¼ hours, until a skewer inserted into the middle comes out clean. Leave to cool for 10 minutes, then turn out on to a wire rack, remove the paper and set the right way up. Leave to cool. Eat in slices, either plain or – if you are that way inclined – with butter.

ballymaloe brown bread

My go-to loaf from the celebrated Ballymaloe House. It's fantastic – very easy – and I've been making it for years. It doesn't even require kneading. Darina Allen from Ballymaloe writes that, 'white or brown sugar, honey, golden syrup, treacle or molasses may be used. Each will give a slightly different flavour to the bread. Different flours produce breads of different textures and flavours... the quantity of water should be altered accordingly. The dough should be just too wet to knead.' At Ballymaloe, their favourite variation uses wholemeal with a little added rye flour.

MAKES 2 SMALL LOAVES

butter or light oil, for the tins

60g (2¼oz) fresh yeast or 30g (1oz) dried yeast

700–850ml (1¼–1½ pints) water, at blood temperature

2 tbsp black treacle

1kg (2lb 4oz) wholemeal flour

2 tsp salt

2 tbsp sesame seeds

Lightly butter or oil two loaf tins, each measuring 22 x 11 x 6cm (9 x 4½ x 2½in). Mix the yeast with 250ml (9fl oz) of the water and the treacle and leave in a warm place until frothy. This will take 10–15 minutes.

Sift the flour and salt into a bowl. Make a well in the centre and pour in the yeast mixture. Bring the flour into the well and mix, adding enough of the remaining water to make a wettish dough (it shouldn't be so wet that it won't come together, though).

Divide the mixture in two and put in the tins. Leave to rise in a warm place, loosely covered with a couple of cloths, for about 30 minutes. Preheat the oven to 230°C/450°F/gas mark 8.

Sprinkle on the sesame seeds and cook in the hot oven for 45–50 minutes, but take them out of their tins after 30 minutes and put them on the bars of the oven to finish cooking. When they are cooked they should sound hollow when you tap the bottom.

clare's wheaten bread

Everyone in Northern Ireland has a recipe for wheaten bread – a no-knead bread made with buttermilk and baking soda – and it is the quickest and easiest bread in the world. Versions vary in sweetness and oatiness and you can embellish them by mixing in other ingredients (as in the version at the bottom of this page). This recipe is from my sister-in-law, Clare Henry.

MAKES 1 LOAF

70g (2½oz) cold butter, cut into little chunks, plus more for the tin

250g (9oz) wholemeal flour

115g (4oz) plain flour, plus more if needed

1 tsp bicarbonate of soda

40g (1½oz) soft light brown sugar

300ml (½ pint) buttermilk, plus more if needed

a little whole milk, if needed

sesame seeds and oats, for the top

Preheat the oven to 180°C/350°F/gas mark 4 and butter a 19 x 9 x 5cm (7½ x 3½ x 2in) loaf tin.

Sift the flours and bicarbonate of soda together into a large bowl, mix in the sugar and rub in the butter with your fingers.

Add the buttermilk. You may find you need a little more liquid than suggested here. If you don't have any more buttermilk, then normal milk will do. On the other hand you may need a little more flour, so have more available.

Bring everything together with your hands – this is a sticky dough, not one you could ever hope to knead even if you had to – and put it into the prepared tin. Smooth the top. Sprinkle with sesame seeds and oats and bake in the oven for 50 minutes.

a fruity version Make as above but add 175g (6oz) chopped, ready-to-eat dried figs (snip the stems off) or the same amount of chopped apricots or dried cranberries, plus 100g (3½oz) blanched hazelnuts (leave them whole). Add these to the mixture before you start mixing in the buttermilk. Bake the fruit version – which will turn out a bit bigger – in a 1kg (2lb 4oz) loaf tin.

breakfast in the cold months

Some of our best breakfast dishes were made for cold weather. It's good, as in the warm months, to get some protein under your belt to keep you going, but cold weather requires you to heat your body too. Porridge settles in your insides like a soft, warm blanket. Fruit – dried or fresh – can be baked or stewed and served warm instead of cold. A dish of smoky kedgeree or bosky mushrooms topped with a poached egg reflect the season outside. Those dark frosty mornings can be grim and a 'good' breakfast isn't merely nutritionally sound, but gives you pleasure and makes you feel cared for as well. A bowl of cold cereal just doesn't cut it. The next few pages offer a few better ways to start those cold days.

roast tomatoes and avocado on toast

Cooked tomatoes are one of the healthiest things you can eat. I roast tomatoes even in the winter. The heat condenses their flavour and sweetness. I nearly always have them in the fridge to form the basis of breakfast or lunch dishes. Double the amount of tomatoes and you have enough for two breakfasts (if you're putting the oven on for 40 minutes, it's best to make good use of it).

SERVES 2

6 large plum tomatoes

1½ tbsp olive oil

½ tbsp balsamic vinegar

a little harissa (about ½ tsp), if you fancy some heat

½ tsp caster sugar (only if your tomatoes aren't very sweet)

salt and pepper

1 ripe avocado

2 slices of whole grain bread

about 2 tbsp avocado oil, or extra virgin olive oil

lemon or lime juice

Preheat the oven to 190°C/375°F/gas mark 5.

Halve the tomatoes and put them in a single layer in a small roasting tin or ovenproof dish. Mix the olive oil, balsamic and harissa (if using) together and pour it over the tomatoes. Turn the tomatoes over with your hands to make sure they get well coated, and leave them cut side up. Sprinkle with the sugar (if using) and season. Roast in the hot oven for 45 minutes, or until the tomatoes are caramelized in patches and slightly shrunken.

Halve and pit the avocado and scoop out the flesh. Toast the bread, then drizzle it with some of the avocado oil, spread the avocado flesh roughly on each piece, sprinkle with the lemon or lime juice, season, then put the tomatoes on top. Drizzle with some more of the avocado oil and serve.

multi-grain porridge with blueberries and honey

You don't have to use the grains suggested, you can use any mixture you want as long as they add up to the same weight. (Make mixtures up in advance and keep them in the cupboard.) You can get loads of different flakes these days (see pages 328–329 for stockists). And of course the topping can be whatever and wherever your taste, budget, cupboard and fridge take you…

SERVES 4

FOR THE PORRIDGE

40g (1½oz) rye flakes

40g (1½oz) spelt flakes

40g (1½oz) quinoa flakes

40g (1½oz) barley flakes

1.2 litres (2 pints) milk, or water, or a mixture, plus more to serve (optional)

soft light brown sugar, to taste

TO SERVE

4 big tbsp Greek yogurt

3 tbsp runny honey

125g (4½oz) blueberries

1 tbsp sunflower seeds

Toast the flakes in a dry frying pan for a minute. Tip into a saucepan and add the milk for a creamier porridge, or water, or a mixture. Bring to the boil, then reduce the heat and simmer, stirring from time to time, until the mixture is thick and soft, about 20 minutes. Add sugar to taste.

Divide between four bowls and add a drizzle of milk if you want. Top with the yogurt, honey, blueberries and sunflower seeds.

spelt and oat porridge with pomegranates and pistachios

Porridge and then some, this is breakfast for a lumberjack. Replace the spelt with farro, if you prefer. Cook the grains the night before, stick them in the fridge, then finish off in 10 minutes the next morning. Use any topping (this is quite fancypants). Spelt feels northern, so I also like this with Shaken currants (see page 158), or stewed apples with honey.

SERVES 4

75g (2¾oz) pearled spelt

75g (2¾oz) jumbo porridge oats

300ml (½ pint) milk, or mixed milk and water

soft light brown sugar, to taste (I use 2 tsp)

seeds from 1 pomegranate

1½ tbsp chopped pistachios

Put the spelt into a saucepan and cover with plenty of water. Bring to the boil, reduce the heat and simmer for 20–30 minutes. Drain.

Return the spelt to the pan with the oats, milk (or milk and water) and sugar, bring to just under the boil, reduce the heat and simmer for 10 minutes, stirring all the time. It will be thick and creamy.

Top with the pomegranate seeds and pistachios, or whatever other topping you like.

proper slow-cooked porridge with maple apples

Having only tasted joyless porridge that was surely meant to punish (made with salt, I know many Scots like it but I can't take such a dour start to the day), I eventually tasted the kind that lulled Goldilocks to sleep. Now I like porridge so much I limit it to a couple of times a week (I know it's made of healthy oats and has a low GI, but if you like it as much as I do you'll eat too much of it).

Here's the knowledge. Freshly harvested oats contain about 14 per cent moisture, so they have to be dried and lightly toasted. Their outer casing is then removed by grinding to leave the groat or kernel. Pinhead and steel-cut oats (they're the same thing) are produced by passing these through steel cutters, which chop them. These are the ones I like, they make a good chunky, rough porridge.

Rolled oats are whole or split groats that have been steamed and flattened to make oat flakes that we call 'porridge oats'. Whole flakes are called 'jumbo' oat flakes and are popular in the US. These make quick porridge, derided by porridge aficionados: they do have a slightly pappy texture and less flavour, but cook in a fraction of the time… and we do live in the real world.

At the weekend do whatever you like (as far as I'm concerned weekends are for treats), adding a splash of cream and topping with soaked dried fruit in winter or fresh raspberries in the summer and early autumn. And you can add a dash of whiskey. (Pretend that, in the middle of a healthy cookbook, I didn't really say that last bit… but boy, it's good.)

SERVES 2–3

FOR THE PORRIDGE

100g (3½oz) steel-cut oats

400ml (14fl oz) mixed milk and water, or just water

soft light brown sugar, to taste (optional)

FOR THE APPLES

1 cooking apple, peeled

maple syrup, to taste

TO SERVE

milk, plain yogurt, maple syrup, flax seeds (all optional)

Put the oats into a bowl and cover with half the milk and water, or water. Leave overnight to soak. (You can omit the soaking, but then you'll need to add about 10 minutes to the cooking time.)

Slice the apple into a small pan until you have worked your way through to the core, then throw away the core. Add about 2 tbsp of water and set over a medium heat. Keep an eye on the apple and, once you can see that it is hot and starting to cook, reduce the heat and cover. Allow to cook, stirring and pressing the mass with a wooden spoon every so often, until completely soft. Leave to cool, then sweeten with maple syrup to taste.

Put the oats into a pan and add the remaining liquid. Slowly bring to the boil, then reduce the heat to low and cook, stirring (you can stir just occasionally, but I prefer to stir nearly all the time as it produces a creamier porridge) for 20 minutes. Add more water if needed (I tend to add only water once it is cooking, otherwise it is quite a rich porridge). Add some sugar if you want to.

Divide between two or three bowls. You can pour on a little more milk to cool it if you want, then add yogurt and a big dollop of the apples. Drizzle on a little more maple syrup if you want to, or sprinkle with some flax seeds, and eat immediately.

toasty rye muesli with hazelnuts and dried cranberries

This makes a change from regular muesli, but you can use the same basic quantities and substitute oats or quinoa flakes instead and use whatever nuts you like. I have to admit I do add a little brown sugar (½ tsp per bowl) or a drizzle of maple syrup, but you do what you like. Or you could increase the quantity of dried fruit. Another nice touch – though it won't be to everyone's taste – is to add some toasted and crushed caraway seeds. Very Scandi.

The muesli can be eaten plain with cold milk, or heated with milk as in this recipe. (See pages 328–329 for where you can find the ingredients online.)

MAKES ABOUT 500G (1LB 2OZ)

100g (3½oz) rye flakes

50g (1¾oz) spelt or barley flakes

100g (3½oz) toasted malted wheat flakes

25g (1oz) wheat bran

20g (¾oz) sesame seeds

50g (1¾oz) sunflower seeds

10g (¼oz) hemp seeds

10g (¼oz) linseeds

60g (2oz) unblanched hazelnuts

60g (2oz) dried cranberries or dried sour cherries

2 tbsp raisins

2 tbsp poppy seeds

TO SERVE

milk

Greek yogurt and chopped fresh fruit (both optional)

Preheat the oven to 180°C/350°F/gas mark 4. Put all the flakes, the bran, the sesame, sunflower, hemp and linseeds into a roasting tin and spread them out. Bake for about 15 minutes, turning the contents over a couple of times. (You can also do this in a dry frying pan if you prefer, it just takes minutes. You'll smell the toasty aroma.)

Roughly chop the hazelnuts and put them into a roasting tin too. Bake for about four minutes (you can also do these in a dry frying pan and in fact it's easier to make sure they don't burn that way).

Mix all the ingredients for the muesli together. You can store this in an airtight container for up to two weeks.

To cook, put 50g (1¾oz) of the muesli mix and 75ml (2½fl oz) milk per person into a saucepan. Heat until almost boiling, stir gently, then cover and leave to sit for five minutes so that the ingredients can soften.

Serve the muesli and milk, and add yogurt and fresh fruit as well, if you want. I especially like blueberries with the rye flavour.

soy mushrooms with egg ribbons and black sesame

These are shamelessly stolen from Caravan, a London restaurant that has made a bit of name for itself in the breakfast department. I have no idea how they make them, but this is my take. The omelette strips are a little Japanese touch. The strange thing is that the mushrooms don't taste at all Eastern, just deeply savoury. A lip-smacking serving of umami.

SERVES 1

1 tbsp groundnut or sunflower oil

150g (5½oz) field or button mushrooms, sliced

1½ tsp soy sauce

1½ tbsp crème fraîche

pepper

tiny knob of butter

1 egg, lightly beaten

white or black sesame seeds, to serve

Heat the oil in a frying pan and cook the mushrooms over a high heat, stirring with a wooden spoon to make sure they get a good colour all over. As soon as they are a lovely golden brown (about two minutes), add the soy sauce and let it bubble away for a few seconds, then immediately add the crème fraîche and pepper. Stir it in and as soon as it is warmed through – a matter of seconds – pull it off the heat.

Melt the butter in a small non-stick frying pan. Season the egg with pepper, add it to the pan and swish it round and cook as you would an omelette, but don't fold one half on top of the other, instead slide it on to a board and cut into ribbons. Serve the mushrooms with the egg ribbons and scatter with sesame seeds.

winter

eating in winter

This is the season we profess to dread. We think grey skies mean brown food. But it's not true; flick through these pages for proof. Just when we need it most, splashes of colour appear at the greengrocer: crimson blood oranges, jewelled pomegranates, purple-sprouting broccoli and candy pink rhubarb. And let's not forget those bitter leaves: this is the time for magenta chicory and radicchio, too.

Cold weather makes us crave internal central heating and we want psychological succour too, so our appetites become conservative. Although it's a fantasy, we feel we need to eat for survival. We bolster ourselves with mashed potato and buttery white rice, but we don't have to. Pulses and grains – spiced or well-seasoned – are deeply satisfying, better for you and keep you feeling full for longer. You can get sleepy after a dish of pommes dauphinoise, but a bowl of spicy dal, or borlotti beans tossed with a garlicky anchovy purée, will both sooth and invigorate. So don't just think about the fruit and vegetables that are available, remember all those pulses that can be cooked to softness and comfort.

early winter

beetroots
brussels sprouts
cauliflowers
celeriac
celery
chard
chestnuts
chicory
hazelnuts
horseradish
jerusalem artichokes
kale
kohlrabi
leeks
parsnips
potatoes
swedes
turnips
walnuts
wild mushrooms
winter cabbages

apples
clementines
cranberries
passion fruits
pears
pineapples
pomegranates
quinces
satsumas
tangerines

duck
goose
grouse
guinea fowl
partridge
pheasant
rabbit
venison

bream
clams
cod
coley
dover sole
gurnard
haddock
halibut
lemon sole
mackerel
monkfish
mussels
plaice
red mullet
scallops
sea bass
skate
turbot

mid winter

blood oranges
forced rhubarb
lemons
oranges

late winter

purple-sprouting broccoli
chard

salmon

crimson and white

Delicate and very pretty. You can increase the amount of feta used, but it's better not to muck about with this dish too much. It's one of those salads where you taste every ingredient because it isn't complicated. It does look lovely if you can get microleaves, or see page 329 for where you can find the seeds to grow them yourself. (It's easy. Really.)

SERVES 6 AS A STARTER

2 pink grapefruits

150g (5½oz) radishes (preferably French Breakfast radishes)

1 chicon of red chicory

1 small fennel bulb

juice of 1 lemon

½ tsp caster sugar

4 tbsp extra virgin olive oil

salt and pepper

125g (4½oz) feta cheese, ideally barrel-aged, crumbled

handful of crimson microleaves (if available)

leaves from 5 sprigs of mint, torn

Cut the grapefruits into segments: cut a slice from the bottom and top of each fruit so they have a flat base on which to sit. Using a very sharp knife, cut the peel and pith off each grapefruit, working around the fruit and cutting the peel away in broad strips from top to bottom. Working over a bowl, slip a sharp fine-bladed knife in between the membrane on either side of each segment and ease the segment out.

Cut the leaves from the radishes (if they are really fresh and perky, set them aside to add to the salad). Trim off and discard the unsightly bit from the tail of each radish, then wash really well. Using a knife or a mandoline, cut into wafer-thin slices.

Discard any blemished outer leaves from the chicory and cut the remaining leaves, lengthways, into slices. Trim the tips from the fennel (keep any little fronds for the salad) and quarter. Remove the tough outer layer of leaves and cut a little slice off the core. Again using a knife or mandoline, cut the fennel into very thin slices. As soon as you cut each piece, toss it with half the lemon juice (otherwise the fennel will discolour).

Whisk together the rest of the lemon juice with the caster sugar, extra virgin oil and salt and pepper to make the dressing and taste.

Arrange all the fruits and vegetables you've prepared on individual plates – or one large platter – and add the feta, the microleaves (if you're able to get any) and the mint. Spoon the dressing on top and serve immediately.

eat your greens (and your reds and your pinks…)

When I was little I was given the *Ladybird Book of Trees*. It had pictures of all the major species, so I could recognize them and remember their characteristics. I loved the book but refused to take it 'tree spotting', arguing that too much information would ruin my enjoyment of trees. I have always felt much the same about food. I don't want to sit down to blocks of nutrients, but to a meal. I take a particular joy in soft-boiled eggs with antipasti (the recipe's on page 30). Salty, melting anchovies and sweet purple-sprouting broccoli mollified by a rich, runny egg yolk, it gives mouthful after mouthful of pleasure. Taking the dish apart, though – labelling its properties – or cooking it only because it's 'healthy', would kill it stone dead. So I've always been vague about what fruits and vegetables do for you. But when I started looking at my eating I found there was an additional pleasure in knowing about the health-giving properties of this or that, even if it's just being able vaguely to remember what's good about tomatoes. And just as with the *Ladybird Book of Trees*, I can have the knowledge, then put it away.

I'm not going to list the properties of everything from apples to yams. If you want those details, consult Joanna Blythman's book *What to Eat*, a great reference on the health-giving properties of foods. Fruits and vegetables are the things most nutritionists and doctors agree on and governments encourage us to eat. Why? The report on food and cancer by the World Cancer Research Fund (2007) is clear: eat more fruits and vegetables. 'Eat mostly foods of plant origin' is the specific advice. There's one slight downer in the report. Studies since the mid-1990s have indicated that fruit and veg *may* help us fight cancer rather than that they definitely do. There's a lot of work still to be done. The good news, though, is that fruits and vegetables may help reduce the risk of developing heart disease, hypertension and diabetes as well as cancer because they're full of phytochemicals and antioxidants. Phytochemicals are naturally occurring chemicals, found in plants, which have properties that protect us from disease. Plants produce these to protect themselves, but research shows they can protect us, too. The action of phytochemicals varies by the colour and type of food, so it's best to eat as broad a range (and as many colours) of fruits and vegetables as possible.

Phytochemicals can act in the same way as antioxidants, and may even stop carcinogens (cancer-causing agents) from forming. Well-known phytochemicals are lycopene – found in cooked tomatoes – which appears to reduce the risk of heart attacks and cancer, and lutein – found in leafy greens – which seems to protect us against heart disease and breast cancer.

Antioxidants are a good thing, because they protect us from the damaging impact of free radicals. (Free radicals – by-products of the body's normal chemical processes – can attack healthy cells, damaging DNA and allowing tumours to grow). Antioxidants aren't yet fully understood, but as they appear to heal and protect (rather than harm) it makes sense to eat plenty of them. Foods strong in antioxidants are blueberries, cranberries, blackberries, raspberries, strawberries, apples, cherries, plums, avocados, oranges, red grapes and grapefruit (and there's nothing on that list I wouldn't eat with pleasure).

Cancer researchers Professor Richard Béliveau and Dr Denis Gingras from the University of Montreal have written the clearest, most authoritative work I have found on the link between nutrition and cancer. They list key 'good' foods in their book *Foods to Fight Cancer*, giving top marks to the following fruits and vegetables: cabbage and other cruciferous vegetables such as broccoli; garlic and other alliums; berries; tomatoes; citrus fruit; dark greens such as spinach; and other dark-coloured vegetables such as beetroot. (The other foods are soy bean products such as tofu; turmeric; green tea; oily fish; chocolate; and wine. Yes, you read that right, chocolate and wine!)

Looking at food this way can seem rather removed from the joy of eating. And it's easy to throw your hands up when every day new claims are made for particular foods. I'm sceptical about expensive 'superfoods'. Acai berries, chia seeds… let's see how they pan out in the long term. Anyway, good health comes from eating well across the board, not from sticking a handful of expensive berries on your muesli.

It's much easier to appreciate what a particular food can do if you enjoy it, or see how it's grown. I wasn't sure about watercress (was it just another hyped food?) until I went to see its cultivation in Hampshire. As I stood with Dr Steve Rothwell, the scientific brains behind much of what is grown there, he picked and ate watercress constantly. Nothing could have looked healthier than those dark green beds with spring water flowing through them, and indeed research carried out at the University of Ulster found that a daily portion of watercress (about 85g/3oz) reduced DNA damage to cells and increased the ability of those cells to resist further DNA damage caused by free radicals. I also discovered that watercress is at the top of something called the Aggregate Nutrient Density Index, a list collated by an American doctor that scores fruits and vegetables from one to one thousand for their nutrient qualities. Watercress has more vitamin C than oranges, more calcium than milk, more vitamin E than broccoli and more folate than bananas. I liked watercress anyway, but since my visit to Hampshire I eat it every day and it's been easy to incorporate. Experts I've talked to say you don't need to eat vegetables raw (light cooking is best for cruciferous vegetables, for example), but if you apply a mixture of approaches – raw, roast and steamed – just as you eat a range of colours, you will get the most out of them.

We don't yet fully understand the relationship between fruits and vegetables and health, but it seems a good idea to eat stuff that is very likely to help protect us from cancer and heart disease. And some major experts don't think five a day is enough; their advice is to eat them 'in abundance'. I wouldn't eat vegetables for health reasons alone, just as I don't down spoonfuls of cod liver oil. I eat them because I love them. Often, when I've eaten a vegetable dish from this book, I think, 'Meat; who needs it?' A piece of meat is, well, a piece of meat. There's a limit to what you can do with it. But vegetables? Colour, texture, flavour, the different cooking methods they can take… they're a marvel. Eat the rainbow.

roast pumpkin, labneh, walnut gremolata and pomegranates

One of my favourite dishes. Instead of pumpkin you can use carrots or beetroots (or a mixture of the two) and you can also replace the spinach leaves with watercress if you prefer.

SERVES 4

FOR THE LABNEH

300g (10½oz) Greek yogurt

1 garlic clove, crushed

good pinch of salt

FOR THE PUMPKIN AND SALAD

1.2kg (2lb 11oz) squash or pumpkin

4 tbsp olive oil

½ tsp ground cinnamon

½ tsp cayenne pepper

5cm (2in) root ginger, peeled and finely chopped

pepper

juice of ½ small lemon

125g (4½oz) baby spinach leaves

small bunch of coriander leaves

seeds from ¼ pomegranate

FOR THE GREMOLATA

35g (1¼oz) walnut pieces

zest of 1 lemon (removed with a zester)

2 garlic cloves, very finely chopped

2 tbsp chopped flat-leaf parsley

FOR THE DRESSING

2 tsp pomegranate molasses

smidgen of Dijon mustard

4 tbsp extra virgin olive oil

pinch of caster sugar (optional)

squeeze of lemon

Make the labneh the day before you want to serve the dish, as on page 104, using the yogurt, garlic and salt.

Preheat the oven to 190°C/375°F/gas mark 5. Halve the squash and scoop out and discard the seeds and fibres. Cut into slices about 2cm (scant 1in) thick at the thickest part. (If you are using a long butternut squash you can halve it horizontally as well as lengthways before cutting the wedges, otherwise you could have very long slices.) Peel each slice if you want, or you can leave the skin on if you don't mind discarding it when you are eating the dish. (Sometimes it is actually thin enough to eat.)

In a small saucepan, heat the regular olive oil, cinnamon, cayenne and ginger. Put the wedges of squash into a roasting tin and pour the spicy mixture over them, using your hands to make sure the squash gets well coated. Season with salt and pepper.

Put into the hot oven and roast for 35 minutes, or until tender and slightly caramelized, basting every so often. Put on to a serving dish and squeeze the lemon over.

Make the gremolata by toasting the walnuts in the oven for five minutes (keep an eye on them as they burn easily). Now simply chop everything for the gremolata together.

Take the drained labneh out of its muslin or J-cloth and gently break it up into nuggets.

Put the pomegranate molasses, mustard and salt and pepper into a small jug and whisk in the extra virgin oil. Taste and add the sugar (if using) and lemon; you really have to work on this dressing to get a good sweet-sour balance, so use your taste buds.

Using about three-quarters of the dressing, gently toss the spinach, coriander and pumpkin together in a wide shallow bowl.

Dot nuggets of labneh over this. Scatter on the gremolata and pomegranate seeds, drizzle on the rest of the dressing and serve.

beetroot and carrot fritters with dill and yogurt sauce

The beetroots make these an amazing colour but, if you prefer something mellower in tone, use parsnips or butternut squash instead. You can make different versions too: add 200g (7oz) crumbled feta to make Greek-style fritters; or add a chopped, deseeded chilli, 2 tsp ground cumin, 2 tsp ground ginger and 1 tsp ground coriander to the onions and fry for a couple of minutes to make Indian-spiced fritters. (Use coriander leaves in the yogurt if you make the latter.)

SERVES 4 (MAKES 8 FRITTERS)

FOR THE FRITTERS

2½ tbsp groundnut oil

1 small onion, finely chopped

2 garlic cloves, crushed

150g (5½oz) potatoes

200g (7oz) carrots

200g (7oz) beetroots

2 eggs, lightly beaten

salt and pepper

FOR THE SAUCE

200g (7oz) Greek yogurt

2 garlic cloves, crushed

1 tbsp extra virgin olive oil

1 tbsp chopped dill fronds, plus more to serve

Heat ½ tbsp of the groundnut oil in a large non-stick frying pan and gently sauté the onion until it is soft but not coloured. Add the garlic and cook for another two minutes. Put into a bowl.

Coarsely grate all the other vegetables, keeping them separate. After you finish grating each variety, put them into a tea towel and squeeze out excess moisture. (Better use a clean J-cloth for the beetroots as they will really stain your tea towel.) Add the vegetables to the onion with the eggs, season well and mix together. Make the sauce by mixing all the ingredients together.

Heat another 1 tbsp of groundnut oil in the frying pan. Spoon enough mixture into the pan to make a batch of fritters each about 8.5cm (3½in) in diameter. Cook over a medium heat until a crust is formed on one side, then carefully turn each over and cook on the other side again until a crust is formed. Don't over-brown them or they will burn on the outside before they are cooked. After the crust is formed, reduce the heat right down and cook for four to five minutes on each side, or until the vegetables are cooked through. (You'll know from the taste whether they are cooked right through. The potato becomes sweet.) You can keep the cooked fritters in a low oven while you finish the others, adding more oil to the pan to fry them if necessary.

Serve the fritters with the yogurt sauce, sprinkled with more dill.

japanese family chicken, egg and rice bowl (oyaka domburi)

This is a classic Japanese dish. It has a lovely name: 'oyaka' means 'parent and child'. It's not quite clear whether my interpretation of that – calling it 'family soup' – is right, or whether the name is a play on the fact that this dish contains both chicken and egg (which is the parent, which the child?)

This recipe does require dashi (Japanese stock), but making dashi is very easy and quick, so don't be daunted. Dried bonito flakes are expensive, but you don't need much. Follow the instructions for making it carefully: the temperature and the stage at which you do things is important, or it can turn out slightly bitter, or too fishy. Dashi can be kept for three or four days in the fridge, but doesn't freeze well (it tends to impair the flavour).

Traditionally this dish is made with white rice, but brown gives a good deep flavour. All the Japanese ingredients you need can be bought online (see pages 328–329).

SERVES 4

FOR THE DASHI

12.5cm (5in) square of kombu

25g (1oz) bonito flakes

FOR THE REST

150g (5½oz) brown rice

4 eggs

400ml (14fl oz) dashi

2 tbsp soy sauce

1 tsp caster sugar

1 tbsp sake or dry sherry

175g (6oz) skinless chicken breast, cut on the diagonal into slices about ½cm (¼in) thick

90g (3oz) onion, cut into very fine slices (almost shaved)

15g (½oz) watercress sprigs, coarse stalks removed

1 sheet of toasted nori, crumbled (optional)

To make the dashi, put the kombu into a saucepan with 1 litre (1¾ pints) of water. To get the maximum flavour, leave it soaking for 15 minutes, then place over a medium heat. As soon as little bubbles appear on the surface and at the sides, pull the pan off the heat. Scatter the bonito flakes on to the water and allow them to sink by themselves. After four minutes, pour the stock through a sieve lined with a coffee filter. (If you leave the bonito flakes too long, the stock becomes fishy.) Discard the solids.

Cook the rice in plenty of boiling water until it is tender (a matter of 25–30 minutes), then drain and return it to the pan. Cover to keep warm.

Beat the eggs very lightly; the Japanese like to see streaks of white in the finished dish.

Put the measured dashi into a deep frying pan or a sauté pan with the soy sauce, sugar and sake and gently heat. When bubbles start to appear, add the chicken and onion and poach for about two minutes. The chicken will turn white.

Pour the eggs over the poaching chicken and cook for about a minute, or until you can see that the egg is set but still moist. You are basically making an omelette but in a little liquid instead of fat. The omelette should come away from the sides of the pan. Break it up into four.

Divide the rice between four bowls and put the chicken and egg mixture on top, spooning it on to the warm rice. Garnish with the watercress and the nori (if using) and serve immediately.

winter greens with crispy onions, tahini and sumac

Savoy and cavolo nero (or kale) are really good together because the first is quite sweet and the second robust and bitter. You could also add cooked lentils to this at the last minute (just toss them in the pan and heat through when you are sautéing the cavolo nero). I know it seems like a pain to cook the two cabbages differently, but they do require different treatments before being tossed together. If you don't want to have the crispy fried onions, just leave them out.

SERVES 6 AS A SIDE DISH

FOR THE TAHINI DRESSING

4 tbsp tahini

2 tbsp extra virgin olive oil, plus more if needed

juice of ½ lemon

2 tbsp plain yogurt

2 small garlic cloves, grated

salt and pepper

FOR THE GREENS

½ Savoy cabbage (or any other soft-leaved winter cabbage)

300g (10½oz) cavolo nero or kale (or a mixture)

3½ tbsp olive oil

1 onion, very finely sliced

4 garlic cloves, finely sliced

1 tsp chilli flakes, or to taste (you might want a little more)

small knob of unsalted butter

good squeeze of lemon juice

½ tsp sumac

To make the tahini dressing, beat the tahini (just use a fork) and then gradually add 3½ tbsp of water, the extra virgin oil, lemon juice, yogurt and garlic. It might look, at some stages, as if it's going to split, but just keep going, it will come together. Taste and season with salt and pepper. You may also want to add a little more water or extra virgin oil to thin the mixture. Different brands of tahini have different consistencies, so you have to alter the amount of water and seasonings you add. Your finished mixture should be about the thickness of Jersey cream.

Remove the hard core from the Savoy cabbage. Keeping them separate, tear the leaves of the Savoy and the cavolo nero from their tough central ribs and cut the leaves into strips. Plunge the cavolo nero into boiling water for five minutes, then drain well.

Meanwhile, heat 1½ tbsp of the regular olive oil and fry the onion over a fairly high heat until golden and crispy. Set aside.

Heat the rest of the regular olive oil in a saucepan that has a lid and sauté the Savoy cabbage for one minute with the garlic and chilli. Now add 1 tbsp of water, salt and pepper and the butter. Put the lid on and cook over a medium heat for about two minutes, shaking the pan every so often. Remove the lid, add the drained cavolo nero, season to taste and fry for another couple of minutes until everything is hot. The garlic should be golden. Squeeze on the lemon juice. Put on a serving plate and drizzle with the tahini dressing (serve the rest on the side), top with the crispy onions and sprinkle on the sumac.

spinach, pomegranate and bulgar soup

This is based on an Azerbaijani soup, but I've taken liberties with the amount of pomegranate molasses (their version is very sweet-sour) and cooked the vegetables for much less time. The result manages to be very grounded and earthy – all those pulses, lots of greenery – yet with plenty of 'top' notes (the fruity acidity of pomegranates, the cleanness of dill and mint). You don't have to make the chunky walnut and garlic relish for the garnish, you can just scatter the soup with chopped toasted walnuts and pomegranate seeds if you prefer.

SERVES 6

FOR THE SOUP

2 tbsp olive oil

1 large onion, finely sliced

2 garlic cloves, finely chopped

2½ tsp ground cumin

¼ tsp ground cinnamon

100g (3½oz) yellow split peas

100g (3½oz) brown lentils

1 litre (1¾ pints) vegetable
or chicken stock or water,
plus more if needed

50g (1¾oz) bulgar wheat

6 tbsp pomegranate molasses

salt and pepper

200g (7oz) spinach leaves, coarse
stalks removed, torn

10g (¼oz) dill fronds, chopped

10g (¼oz) mint leaves, torn

15g (½oz) flat-leaf parsley leaves,
roughly chopped

TO FINISH

1 garlic clove, chopped

sea salt

25g (1oz) coarsely chopped
toasted walnuts

2 tbsp extra virgin olive oil

2 tbsp torn dill fronds, and/or mint
or flat-leaf parsley leaves

seeds from ½ pomegranate

Heat the regular olive oil in a heavy-based pan and sauté the onion until it is soft and pale gold, about 10 minutes. Add the garlic and cook for another couple of minutes, then add the cumin and cinnamon and cook for another minute. Add the split peas, lentils and stock or water and bring to the boil. Reduce the heat, cover and simmer for about 25 minutes.

Add the bulgar wheat, pomegranate molasses and 300ml (½ pint) of water and season. Return to the boil, then reduce the heat and simmer once more for 15 minutes.

Now add the spinach and all the herbs and heat through. Traditionally this is cooked for about 20 minutes, but the soup is much fresher tasting – not to mention greener looking – if you give it only a couple of minutes now, just enough time for the spinach to wilt. (If you're making the soup in advance, add the spinach and herbs when you are reheating the soup.)

Adjust the thickness if you need to by adding more water or stock. It's a thick soup, but it's not supposed to be like a purée. Taste for seasoning as well.

To finish the dish, put the garlic and a little sea salt in a mortar and grind to a paste. Add the walnuts and pound to a coarse mixture, then stir in the extra virgin oil. Put spoonfuls of this on each bowl of soup and strew with herbs and pomegranate seeds.

kale, salmon and barley soup with buttermilk

I grew up with vegetable and barley broth – it's both filling and restorative – and this is just a Scandi version. The fish is supposed to season the dish, it's not the main attraction. If you prefer something richer, serve this with soured cream mixed with dill rather than buttermilk. You can leave out the potato if you like and increase the amount of barley by 75–100g (2¾–3½oz).

SERVES 6–8

1.7 litres (3 pints) fish or light chicken stock, plus more if needed

100g (3½oz) pearl barley

1 large carrot, finely chopped

1 large leek, trimmed, chopped and washed

150g (5½oz) waxy potatoes, peeled and cut into small cubes

salt and pepper

40g (1½oz) kale, tough ribs removed and discarded, leaves torn

200g (7oz) raw or hot-smoked salmon, skinned and cut into chunks

150ml (5fl oz) buttermilk

1 tbsp lemon juice

1 tbsp chopped dill fronds

Put the stock, barley and carrot into a saucepan and bring to the boil. Reduce the heat and simmer for 15 minutes. Add the leek, potatoes and seasoning and cook for another 30 minutes.

If your stock has really reduced, top up with water. In the last five minutes, add the kale and, in the last two minutes, add the salmon and cook gently (this will cook the raw salmon, or warm through the hot-smoked fish). You can add more stock or water if it seems too thick.

Mix the buttermilk with the lemon juice and dill and season. Serve each bowl of soup topped with a generous spoonful of the dilled buttermilk, and offer the rest in a bowl on the side.

winter menu jewels in cold weather

red lentil kofte | spiced quail with blood orange and date salad | yogurt and apricot compote

A grand meal – it's so beautiful it's almost regal – though the only big expense is the quail. The blood oranges used in the main course salad aren't in season for long, so grab them while you can.

red lentil and carrot kofte with pomegranates, coriander and tahini

Really easy to make, pretty and moreish. If you can't get Turkish pepper paste – which has a really vibrant flavour – use harissa. (Find a recipe for Turkish pepper paste in my book *Salt Sugar Smoke*.)

MAKES ABOUT 30 (SERVES 6)

35ml (1¼fl oz) tahini

juice of 1¾ lemons

4 garlic cloves, crushed

salt and pepper

6 tbsp extra virgin olive oil

90g (3¼oz) red lentils

50g (1¾oz) bulgar wheat

200g (7oz) carrots

pinch of caster sugar

150ml (5fl oz) carrot juice or water

1 tbsp olive oil

1 red onion, very finely chopped

1 tbsp ground cumin

1 tsp ground paprika

1 tbsp Turkish pepper paste

1 tbsp tomato purée

leaves from 2 bunches of coriander, finely chopped

seeds from 1 pomegranate

25g (1oz) baby salad leaves

To make the tahini sauce, mix the tahini with 75ml (2½fl oz) of water, then the juice of ½ lemon, 1 crushed garlic clove, salt and pepper and 2 tbsp of the extra virgin oil. Taste for seasoning. You need to get the consistency right so you may need more water. It should end up about as thick as double cream.

Put the lentils in a pan with 250ml (9fl oz) of water. Bring to the boil, reduce the heat to a simmer, cover and cook for 20 minutes, until completely soft. Remove from the heat and add the bulgar, stir, cover and leave for 20 minutes so the grains can plump up.

Cook the carrots with the sugar and salt and pepper in the carrot juice or water (the carrot juice intensifies their flavour). When completely soft, drain, mash and mix with the lentil mixture.

Heat the regular olive oil and sauté the onion until completely soft, about seven minutes. Add the cumin, paprika and remaining garlic and cook for another two minutes. Stir in the pepper paste and tomato purée and cook for 30 seconds. Stir this into the lentil and carrot mix. Mix in the juice of 1 lemon, half the coriander, seasoning and 2 tbsp of the extra virgin oil. Taste for seasoning.

Shape the kofte mix into balls the size of a walnut in its shell, with an indentation in one side. Put them on a serving platter. Fill each indentation with pomegranate seeds. Toss the remaining coriander and baby leaves with the remaining extra virgin oil and lemon, put on a platter and drizzle with tahini. Serve the kofte with the salad.

spiced quail with blood orange and date salad

Sweet, sour and juicy. If you find dates too sweet, you can cut the amount. Or temper the sweetness by tossing shaved raw fennel in with the blood oranges and dates.

SERVES 6

FOR THE MARINADE

5 tbsp olive oil

3 tbsp pomegranate molasses

1½ tsp ground cumin

½ tsp ground cinnamon

6 tsp harissa

4 garlic cloves, crushed

4 tsp soft light brown sugar

4 tbsp lemon juice

salt and pepper

FOR THE QUAIL AND SALAD

12 quails

6 blood oranges

12 medjool dates, pitted and quartered lengthways

2 red chillies, deseeded and shredded

leaves from 1 bunch of coriander (about 20g/¾oz)

leaves from 12 sprigs of mint

seeds from ½ pomegranate (or buy a pack and use 2 heaped tbsp)

FOR THE DRESSING

2 garlic cloves, crushed

6 tbsp extra virgin olive oil (fruity rather than grassy)

6 tbsp blood orange juice

4 tbsp pomegranate molasses

2 tsp runny honey

drop of orange flower water (really, just a tiny splash)

To make the marinade, just mix everything together. Put the birds into a non-reactive shallow dish and pour the marinade over them, turning them to make sure they are coated. Cover with cling film and put in the fridge for a few hours (overnight is even better if you have time).

When you're ready to cook, preheat the oven to 190°C/375°F/ gas mark 5. Put the birds into a small roasting tin and pour the marinade over. Season with salt and pepper. Roast for 25 minutes.

Meanwhile, make the salad (or make it immediately before you cook the starter). Slice the ends off the oranges so they have a flat base on which to sit. Using a very sharp knife, cut the peel and pith off each, working around the fruit and cutting the peel away in broad strips from top to bottom. Working over a bowl, slip a sharp fine-bladed knife in between the membrane on either side of each segment and ease the segment out. Put these into a bowl with the dates, chillies, herbs, salt and pepper.

Whisk all the dressing ingredients together. Pour two-thirds of this over the orange salad.

Spoon the salad on to six plates and scatter with the pomegranate seeds. Put the spicy quail on top and pour the rest of the dressing over. Serve with bulgar wheat or couscous on the side.

yogurt with honeyed saffron syrup, almonds and apricot compote

A really simple pud that looks beautiful. If you don't usually like saffron have a go anyway, it's quite subtle and provides much of the visual impact.

SERVES 6

FOR THE COMPOTE

225g (8oz) dried apricots

75ml (2½fl oz) apple juice

juice of 1 lemon

broad strip of lemon zest

broad strip of orange zest

4 tbsp agave syrup

crushed seeds of 8 cardamom pods

FOR THE HONEYED SYRUP

good pinch of saffron stamens

100ml (3½fl oz) runny honey (ideally orange blossom honey)

½–¾ tbsp orange flower water, or to taste

TO SERVE

200g (7oz) Greek yogurt

2 tbsp toasted flaked almonds

The night before you want to eat it, put all the ingredients for the compote in a saucepan with 275ml (9½fl oz) of water and bring slowly to the boil. Immediately reduce the heat to a simmer and cook for 10–15 minutes. It's important that you keep an eye on them, some dried apricots are much softer than others and you don't want them to all fall apart (though it's fine if some do). Sometimes it takes 10 minutes for them to soften and plump up, sometimes quite a bit longer. You should end up with fat apricots in a syrup. If the syrup is a bit thin (it depends how long the apricots have cooked), remove the apricots with a slotted spoon and boil the juices until they get a bit thicker before returning the apricots. Leave to cool in the syrup, then put into a bowl, cover and leave overnight (remove the strips of peel before serving). You can keep the apricots, covered, in the fridge for a week.

It's best to prepare the honeyed syrup the day before, too, as the saffron continues to flavour it. Put 2 tbsp of boiling water into a teacup and add the saffron. Stir well to release the saffron's colour and flavour, then add to the honey with the orange flower water. Mix together, then cover and leave overnight.

To serve, put the apricot compote into little glasses or bowls, top with some of the yogurt, then spoon on the saffron honey. Scatter on some almonds and serve.

mustardy farro and roast winter vegetable salad

This dish has lovely muted colours, and it's really adaptable. You can serve it as a side dish with a vegetable or meat main course, or as a main course in its own right, adding sautéed mushrooms (wild if you have them), toasted walnuts or hazelnuts, crumbled goat's cheese or shavings of Gouda. Spelt or wheat berries can be used instead of farro (see page 224 for how to cook them). Those of you on a carb watch can omit the parsnips and increase the quantity of the other vegetables.

SERVES 6 AS A SIDE DISH,
4 AS A MAIN COURSE

FOR THE SALAD

6 carrots, trimmed, peeled and halved lengthways (quartered if very fat)

3 parsnips, prepared as for the carrots

300g (10½oz) celeriac, peeled and cut into wedges

½ cauliflower, broken into small florets (use the central base to make soup)

3 tbsp olive oil

salt and pepper

150g (5½oz) semi-pearled farro

1 tbsp extra virgin olive oil

2 tsp white balsamic vinegar

¾ tbsp mixed seeds: hemp, sesame, sunflower and pumpkin seeds are all good

FOR THE DRESSING

1 tsp wholegrain mustard

1–2 tsp runny honey

5 tsp cider vinegar

8 tbsp extra virgin olive oil (fruity rather than grassy)

2 garlic cloves, crushed

pinch of chilli flakes (optional)

1 tbsp finely chopped flat-leaf parsley leaves

Preheat the oven to 190°C/375°F/gas mark 5. Put the carrots, parsnips, celeriac and cauliflower into a roasting tin in which they can lie in a single layer: you want them to roast, not sweat. Drizzle with the regular olive oil, season and turn over to make sure they all get well coated in the oil. Roast for about 40 minutes, or until tender and slightly burnished in patches.

Meanwhile, cook the farro. Put it into a saucepan and cover with plenty of cold water. Bring to the boil, then reduce the heat and cook until tender, 20–25 minutes (even when cooked it retains a bite in the centre). Drain and immediately dress with the extra virgin oil, white balsamic and seasoning (this keeps the grain moist and seasons it thoroughly).

To make the dressing, put the mustard, honey and vinegar into a cup or small jug, season well and, using a fork, whisk in the extra virgin oil in a steady stream. Now mix in all the other dressing ingredients and taste.

Gently toss all the vegetables together with the farro and the dressing, adding any seeds you fancy.

also try this raw... Make this with raw vegetables, omitting the parsnips. Raw cauliflower should be in small florets. Shave the carrots into ribbons, chop the celeriac into matchsticks (immediately squeeze lemon juice all over to stop it discolouring) and cut the same weight of beetroots as parsnips (a range of coloured beetroots is especially lovely) into thin discs or matchsticks. Cook the farro and toss with the veg and dressing. You can add watercress, too.

quinoa, black lentil, mango and smoked chicken salad with korma dressing

I love the look of this dish, it is such a fantastic array of strong colours. Use regular chicken if you don't like smoked, or flaked cooked salmon, or even sliced raw salmon that you've marinated in the juice of two limes for five minutes.

SERVES 4 AS A MAIN COURSE

250g (9oz) black lentils

250g (9oz) cream-coloured quinoa

1 just-ripe mango

35g (1¼oz) watercress leaves, coarse stalks removed

300g (10½oz) smoked chicken, skinned and neatly sliced

10g (¼oz) mint leaves, torn

2 tbsp olive oil

juice of ½ lime

FOR THE DRESSING

juice of 1 lime

½ tsp caster sugar, or to taste

1 tsp fairly hot curry paste

4 tbsp groundnut or rapeseed oil

salt and pepper

3 tbsp single cream

Put the lentils in a saucepan and cover with water. Bring to the boil and cook for 15–30 minutes, or until the lentils are tender but not falling apart (the length of time it takes depends on the age of the lentils). Meanwhile, toast the quinoa in a dry frying pan for about two minutes, then put it into a separate saucepan, add boiling water, cover and cook for 15 minutes.

Peel the mango and cut off the 'cheeks' (the fleshy bits on each side of the central stone). Carefully cut the cheeks into slices about the thickness of a pound coin. It is very difficult to remove the flesh nearer the stone neatly, so just use the cheeks for this dish and use the remaining flesh for something else (or eat it).

Make the dressing. Using a fork, whisk everything together except the cream, then whisk that in too. Taste for seasoning.

Drain the lentils, quickly rinse them in hot water, then toss in a serving bowl with the drained quinoa, the mango, watercress, chicken, mint, olive oil, lime juice and seasoning (taste and adjust it if you need to, grains and lentils need assertive seasoning). Drizzle on the creamy korma dressing just before serving.

a veggie version If you want a vegetarian dish, replace the chicken with 3 avocados and add 3 finely chopped spring onions.

carrot love

Yes, three carrot salads (and there are more in the pages that follow, too). Since I first tasted *salade de carottes râpées* (grated or julienned carrots tossed with vinaigrette) on an exchange trip to France, I have thought them a brilliant salad ingredient. Crunch. Texture. Sweetness. Colour. And more filling than leaves. Carrot salads span the globe, too, so they take you places. And what about health? Carrots are rich in vitamins C and E, which help neutralize the damage done to cells by free radicals, and are a great source of betacarotene (the deeper the orange the more betacarotene they contain), which converts to vitamin A. And it's thought they help protect vision against degenerative conditions (such as cataracts) too. So carrots do (among other things) help you see... Get crunching.

moroccan carrot salad

There are salads in Morocco (some very sweet), made with raw or cooked carrots. The cooked carrot versions, while good, have a slightly 'boiled carrot' flavour rather than a fresh taste. I prefer to half-cook the carrots. They are no longer raw, they retain bite, but are certainly not tender. Herbs are optional; sometimes coriander and mint make every Moroccan dish you cook taste the same, so add herbs – or not – depending on what else you are serving with this dish.

SERVES 4

450g (1lb) carrots

2 garlic cloves, bruised

2 tbsp lemon juice

salt and pepper

¼ tsp harissa

½ tsp soft light brown sugar

good pinch of ground cinnamon

¼ tsp ground cumin, or to taste

¼ tsp sweet paprika, or to taste

2 tbsp extra virgin olive oil

2 tbsp chopped coriander leaves (optional)

torn leaves from 4 sprigs of mint (optional)

Peel and trim the carrots and cut them into rounds or batons. Put them into a saucepan, cover with water and add the garlic. Bring to the boil and cook the carrots until they are no longer raw, but not cooked. They should still have bite (though not be crunchy). I can't give you an exact time for this as it will depend on how you have cut the carrots, so keep checking the texture.

Meanwhile, mix the lemon juice, salt and pepper, harissa, sugar and spices together with the extra virgin oil. Drain the carrots as soon as they are ready and immediately add the dressing. Taste for seasoning and spicing. Add the herbs (if using) and serve.

japanese carrot and mooli salad

Very simple. I like this with boiled brown rice and a watercress salad – it is very more-ish – but you can use it as an accompaniment to lots of the Eastern dishes in the book, such as the Japanese rice bowl, Japanese ginger and garlic chicken, Seared tuna with avocado and wasabi purée, or Avocado, raw salmon and brown rice salad (see pages 43, 63, 291 and 306).

SERVES 4–6

250ml (9fl oz) rice vinegar

3 tbsp caster sugar

700g (1lb 9oz) mooli (daikon)

700g (1lb 9oz) carrots

1½ tsp salt

Heat the vinegar and sugar together gently in a saucepan, stirring a little to help the sugar dissolve. Leave to cool completely.

Peel and trim the mooli and carrots, keeping them separate, and cut into matchstick-sized pieces. Put them into colanders (or sieves). Mix 1 tsp of the salt into the mooli and ½ tsp into the carrot, mixing it well with your hands. Leave for 10 minutes, then squeeze out the excess water from both. Put both vegetables into a clean bowl and mix in the sweet vinegar mixture. Keep in the fridge and serve nice and cold. It will be fine for about five days.

spiced carrot, date and sesame salad

I never tire of this. It's great on its own, or have it with brown rice or houmous. If you don't have dates, raisins or dried apricots are good. Add extra seeds such as pumpkin or sunflower, they provide great crunch. (They're good for you, too.)

SERVES 4

4 carrots, peeled

juice of 1 lime (some can be dry, so you may need 2)

4 pitted medjool dates, sliced

2 tbsp roughly chopped coriander or mint leaves

1 tbsp black or toasted white sesame seeds

2 tbsp rapeseed or olive oil

1 tsp cumin seeds

1 tsp mustard seeds

good pinch of chilli flakes

2 small garlic cloves, finely sliced

50g (1¾oz) baby spinach, chopped

Grate the carrot coarsely into a bowl (or cut it into matchsticks, which takes longer but does give a great texture). Add the lime juice, dates, herbs and sesame seeds.

Heat the oil in a small frying pan and add the cumin and mustard seeds. Cook over a medium heat until they just start to splutter, then add the chilli and garlic and reduce the heat. Cook gently until the garlic is pale gold (about two minutes). Toss this immediately into the rest of the salad and add the spinach. Taste before adding any salt.

carrot and mooli salad with peanut-chilli dressing

Whenever I serve meat with this I wonder why I bother: nobody ever cares about the meat bit, this is what they want. It's fresh, crunchy, hot and very moreish. Have it on its own with brown rice or soba noodles or with other vegetable dishes such as Japanese aubergines with miso (see page 188).

SERVES 6 AS A SIDE DISH

FOR THE SALAD

150g (5½oz) mooli (daikon)

1 large carrot

6–10 pink radishes, depending on size

125g (4½oz) beansprouts

10g (¼oz) coriander leaves

25g (1oz) mizuna or watercress

1 tbsp rice vinegar

juice of 1 lime

1 tsp caster sugar

FOR THE PEANUT-CHILLI DRESSING

1½ tbsp groundnut oil

3 shallots, sliced

2 garlic cloves, finely chopped

2cm (¾in) root ginger, peeled and very finely chopped

1 red chilli, deseeded and cut into slivers

4 tbsp peanuts, roughly crushed

2 tsp golden caster sugar

juice of 1 lime

½ tbsp soy sauce

2 tbsp sesame oil

Peel the mooli and carrot, trim the tops and bases and cut into very fine batons. Put into ice-cold water, as this helps them to crisp up, while you make the rest of the salad.

Trim the radishes, then either slice them very finely (on a mandoline if you have one) or cut into matchstick-sized pieces. Throw into the cold water as well.

For the dressing, heat the groundnut oil in a frying pan and add the shallots. Cook over a medium heat until they are golden, then add the garlic, ginger and chilli and cook for another minute. Add the peanuts and sugar and stir for a couple more minutes. You should see and smell that the sugar is caramelizing. When this happens, pull the pan off the heat and add the lime juice and soy sauce. Add 1–2 tbsp of water (judge how much by the strength and consistency of the dressing), then the sesame oil.

Drain and dry the mooli, carrot and radishes and put into a broad, shallow bowl with the beansprouts, coriander and mizuna or watercress. Mix the rice vinegar with the lime juice and sugar, stir to dissolve the sugar, then toss this with the salad. Spoon the peanut dressing over the top and serve immediately.

winter menu spices and smoke

mandalay carrot salad | spiced smoked haddock stew | blood orange and cardamom sorbet

Sometimes you want to give your friends something grand, sometimes you just want a menu that uses everyday ingredients but uses them well. So it is with this. Carrots, lentils and smoked fish are about as down-to-earth as you can get. A good supper for a wet November night.

mandalay carrot salad

A very usable salad – easy to make and cheap – but quite addictive. It's lovely on its own with brown rice (and some dal or lentil salad), or used in sandwiches along with spinach and chicken, or with some kind of earthy bean purée.

SERVES 4–6

2 tsp chickpea flour (gram)

400g (14oz) carrots, coarsely grated

juice of 2 limes

1 tbsp fish sauce, or more to taste

1 green chilli, deseeded and very finely chopped

1 tsp caster sugar

½ tsp salt

6 shallots

2 tbsp groundnut oil

1 tbsp chopped roasted peanuts

2 tbsp chopped coriander leaves

2 tbsp chopped mint leaves

Put the flour into a small dry frying pan over a medium heat. Stir until it smells toasty and has turned a shade darker (don't take it too far). Tip into a bowl. Put the carrots in another bowl and add the lime juice and fish sauce. Press the carrots with the back of a wooden spoon to crush them a little. Spoon them into a serving dish, add the toasted chickpea flour, chilli, sugar and salt and toss.

Cut the shallots, lengthways, into thin slices. Heat the oil in a frying pan over a medium-high heat. Add the shallots and cook until they are golden brown, about 10 minutes. If they start to brown before that time, reduce the heat. Lift out of the pan with a slotted spoon on to kitchen paper. Separate out any clumps so that excess oil can be absorbed properly and leave to dry for about 10 minutes, until crispy and cool.

Just before serving, add the peanuts, crispy shallots and herbs to the carrot mixture.

smoked haddock with indian scented lentils

This, with its English and Indian flavours, was inspired by kedgeree. There is a little cream in it. You can either reduce it if you're bothered about your fat intake, or increase it a little if you're not. And if you're not sure whether you're bothered, have a read of pages 284–285 to see if that helps.

SERVES 4–6

2 large onions

15g (½oz) butter

3 tsp curry powder

¼ tsp turmeric

½ tsp ground ginger

½ tsp cayenne pepper

ground seeds of 10 cardamom pods

125g (4½oz) waxy potatoes, peeled (if you can be bothered) and cut into chunks

100g (3½oz) bulgar wheat

1 litre (1¾ pints) well-flavoured chicken stock (preferably home-made)

salt and pepper

150g (5½oz) Puy lentils

1 bay leaf

50ml (2fl oz) double cream

500g (1lb 2oz) smoked haddock fillet, skinned, cut into big chunks

2 tbsp chopped coriander leaves

1 tbsp groundnut or sunflower oil

1 tsp soft dark brown sugar

juice of ½ lime, plus lime wedges to serve

Finely chop one of the onions and cut the other into fine slices.

Heat the butter in a saucepan and sauté the chopped onion until soft and slightly coloured. Add the spices and cook for another two minutes. Add the potatoes, bulgar and stock and bring to the boil. Season. Reduce the heat to medium and leave to simmer gently until the potatoes are tender.

Meanwhile, put the lentils into a pan on their own and cover with water. Bring to the boil, add the bay, then reduce the heat and simmer the lentils until just tender. This could take 15 minutes, it could take 30 (it depends on the age of the lentils). When they are ready, drain them and season well. Add the lentils and the cream to the potato and bulgar wheat 'broth' to heat through, then add the fish and allow it to poach gently until cooked, about two minutes. Stir in most of the coriander.

While the fish is cooking, quickly fry the sliced onion over a high heat in the oil until golden. Add the sugar and allow it to caramelize and the onions to get darker. Squeeze on the lime juice. Divide the stew between warmed dishes, spoon the caramelized onions on top of each serving and scatter with the remaining coriander. Offer wedges of lime alongside.

blood orange and cardamom sorbet

This can vary a lot in colour depending on what the flesh of your blood oranges is like; sometimes it's an orangey-red, others more pinky. If you don't like cardamom just leave it out. It does tie the pudding to the other two dishes in the menu, though.

SERVES 4–6

135g (4¾oz) granulated sugar

8 cardamom pods, crushed

finely grated zest of 1 blood orange or regular orange

250ml (9fl oz) blood orange juice

juice of ½ lemon

pistachios, to serve (optional)

Put 150ml (5fl oz) of water and the sugar in a saucepan and heat, stirring to help the sugar dissolve. Add the cardamom, zest and juices and bring to the boil. Take off the heat and leave to cool.

Strain and put the liquid into an ice-cream maker to churn, or pour into a broad, shallow, freezer-proof container and put in the freezer. If you choose the latter method, when the bits round the outside have become firm, mix everything up together again with a fork. Do this three or four times during the freezing process, to break up the crystals and ensure a smooth sorbet. If you don't want to do it by hand you can put it in the food processor and whizz briefly, but I can never be bothered with the washing up.

Serve the sorbet with some pistachios – crushed or chopped – on top of each portion (if using).

also try... orange and rosemary sorbet. Make this in exactly the same way (using regular or blood oranges) and put a sprig of rosemary into the syrup instead of the cardamom. Strain it out it before churning. Citrus works brilliantly with rosemary. Lavender – to which rosemary is related – is also good (though only available in season in the summer).

kale pesto with wholewheat linguine

Yes, I know. This sounds really holier than thou. But it isn't. In fact I prefer it to basil pesto (which I've always found a bit perfumed and slightly cloying). If you're not the biggest fan of kale, this is the way to eat it; it's seasoned and enriched. You can also make this with cavolo nero in exactly the same way. I find wholemeal pasta a tough one. I can barely eat the shapes, they just seem chewy and punishing. But linguine and spaghetti are a different matter.

Toss steamed broccoli into this (yes, I mean it!) for a double dose of greens.

SERVES 4

450g (1lb) wholemeal linguine

sea salt

300g (10½oz) kale (the leaves should weigh about 250g/9oz once you've remove the tough stalks)

25g (1oz) butter

4 tbsp extra virgin olive oil (grassy rather than fruity)

10g (¼oz) flat-leaf parsley

2 good-quality anchovies, drained of oil

2 garlic cloves, roughly chopped

50–75g (1¾–2¾oz) grated Parmesan or pecorino

really good pinch of chilli flakes (optional)

Put the linguine into a big pan of boiling slightly salted water and boil until it is cooked but still al dente.

At the same time, make the pesto. Wash the kale well and strip the fibrous leaves from their stalks. Bring a large pot of water to the boil, plunge the leaves in and cook for five minutes. Drain well. Put the cooked kale into a food processor with the butter, extra virgin oil, parsley, anchovies, garlic and 50g (1¾oz) of the cheese. Add the chilli (if using). Blitz, using the pulse-blend button. I like this pesto when it isn't completely puréed but still has quite large flecks in it, so don't overdo it.

Taste, adding the rest of the cheese if you want. To be honest, I don't need any more, it has a great rich strong taste without it. But you decide.

Drain the linguine, then return it to the pan with a little of its cooking water. Mix in the pesto and serve immediately.

more greens please... **watercress pesto** Excellent with wholemeal linguine and a poached egg. And very good for you. Put 60g (2oz) watercress, 10g (¼oz) flat-leaf parsley (or basil) leaves, 30g (1oz) grated pecorino, 1 garlic clove, 40g (1½oz) toasted pine nuts (or sweeter cashews), 6 tbsp extra virgin oil and seasoning into a food processor and pulse-blend. Serves 4 with pasta.

calabrian pesto Even my fussy kids like this. Heat 2 tbsp olive oil and cook 1 finely chopped red pepper and ½ onion, chopped, until lightly caramelized, about 10 minutes. Add 50g (1¾oz) finely chopped aubergine and cook for 10 minutes, then add 1 chopped plum tomato, 1 chopped garlic clove and a good pinch of chilli flakes for five minutes. Pulse-blend with 60g (2oz) ricotta, 40g (1½oz) almonds, 2 tbsp extra virgin oil, seasoning and 10g (¼oz) basil leaves. Serves 4 with pasta.

good fat bad fat

The battle of the fats – saturated, polyunsaturated, monounsaturated – has been waged for more than fifty years. I used to ignore it. I couldn't keep up. I didn't understand the terms. And I love butter. But looking into it has been an eye opener: you could be eating stuff the World Health Organization, no less, labels toxic (no mincing of words there). So read on.

Butter was banned in our house – except for making cakes and pastry – in the mid-1970s. Mum put us all on low-fat spread. It seemed like the healthy option. Scientists had first sounded alarm bells about heart and circulatory disease in the 1950s. By the 1960s these were big killers, and still are. Saturated fat – found in butter and red meat – and cholesterol in the diet became the fall guys. The thinking on cholesterol has since changed. (Raised blood cholesterol is a risk factor for heart disease, but there is no direct correlation between cholesterol in your diet and levels of blood cholesterol.) Further, it's now accepted that margarines and spreads made by the hydrogenation process – the means by which polyunsaturated fats were made solid – are very bad for us ('toxic', as the WHO says). The process creates artery-clogging transfats that are a likely cause of heart disease. Producers now use a different process (called interesterification) to make low-fat spreads, but transfats are still around. *And you can't see them.* Factory-made biscuits, cakes and pastries, takeaways and processed foods may contain transfats (they are cheap and extend shelf life). The British Heart Foundation would like transfats eliminated and, until they are, be on the alert. Check labels (look for 'hydrogenated vegetable oil', 'partially hydrogenated vegetable oil', 'vegetable shortening' and 'margarine') and don't buy takeaways. This is the fat I can be clear on.

So where does this leave saturated fat? Plenty of people don't believe that fat equals heart disease. The French, they point out, eat red meat and cheese and don't have the high rates of heart disease found in Britain or America. The jury is out. There may be a correlation between saturated fat and heart disease but it's not as strong as that between, for example, tobacco and lung cancer. When we were instructed to watch saturated fat, the link was described as cause and effect. Some doctors specializing in obesity claim the emphasis on cutting fat has actually made us more overweight, because when we cut fat we tend to eat more refined carbohydrates. Experts also point out that foods high in fat fill you up, helping you eat less (which diets rich in refined carbs, with their blood sugar spikes, do not).

We've significantly reduced our intake of fat, eating thirty three per cent of our calorie intake as fats compared with forty per cent in the 1960s. But heart disease is still a huge problem and obesity rates are soaring. There's clearly something wrong with the way we eat, but is fat the *main* villain?

Before you dive into that block of butter, consider the research on high-fat diets, such as Atkins. An American study, in 2002, found people on a diet where they consumed sixty per cent of their calories as fats lost more weight, and had better cholesterol overall, than others on The American Heart Association diet, which is low in fat and relatively high in carbs. Five years later, another American study found that Atkins dieters had 'increased levels of

LDL ("bad") cholesterol'. Researchers also declared that the diet appeared to be 'potentially detrimental' for cardiovascular health. Confused? Me too. But it looks as though keeping an eye on saturated fats – until we know more – is sensible. We shouldn't replace saturated fats with refined carbs, though, otherwise we're dealing with one problem and creating another.

What about polyunsaturated fats, most often seen in cooking oils? We thought they were healthy, but corn, sunflower, safflower and grapeseed oils are high in omega-6 fatty acids and, used excessively, are now thought to be harmful. The good news is that research suggests olive oil (mainly monounsaturated fat) lowers blood pressure and the level of bad fats in the blood, and protects against heart disease. Two other monounsaturated fats – rapeseed and avocado oils – are good, too (avocado oil is luscious, gorgeously green with a rich, buttery flavour). Cold-pressed walnut, hazelnut and flaxseed oil are also good (though they're for dressings, not cooking).

Don't confuse omega-6 fatty acids with omega-3 fatty acids. Research clearly shows that omega-3 fatty acids, found in oily fish, help prevent strokes and heart disease and improve brain function. Everything good you've heard about oily fish seems to be true. So fill your boots with them! (Though the modern caveat has to be, 'as long as they are sustainable'.)

Trying to come to a clear conclusion, I went to the British Heart Foundation website. It's unequivocal. 'Avoid saturated fats wherever possible.' They also advise you to watch your intake of all fats, though many experts vehemently disagree with this last bit, advising us instead to replace saturated fat with good fats (such as olive oil).

Me? I'm cutting out 'low-fat' products – low-fat yogurt, low-fat cheese – since these often have something less healthy, usually sugar (which is *definitely* bad, see pages 24–26) added to replace the fat. I'm watching how much butter and cheese I eat (you'll know if you eat 'balanced' quantities or not). Red meat isn't a problem as I don't eat much. I enjoy it, but love vegetables and grains too and the ecological considerations of eating too much meat (the planet can't support its production) are important to me. I don't eat much polyunsaturated fat – except for a bit of frying – and use lots of monounsaturated fat (mainly olive oil). It's as wonderful as butter, and more varied, so I'm glad it gets the nod.

What seems clear is that adulterated foods – such as hydrogenated oils – can be a disaster. Spreads may be made differently now but, given our experience, I'm not inclined to be trusting. It's also clear that cooking your own food, rather than buying foods where fats are hidden, is the way to go. Some mornings I may put butter on my toast, another day it might be a slug of extra virgin olive oil and mashed avocado. Both sound great to me. And in each case I know what I'm eating and exactly how much.

Here's a thought to end on. The biggest source of fats in the UK, and particularly of saturated fats, is processed products such as burgers, sausages and pies. Biscuits and cakes are the next biggest source, then milk and, finally, butter. Perhaps it's not the butter on our toast we should be angsting about…

leek, spelt and goat's cheese risotto

It's usual to make 'risottos' now with barley, farro and spelt, as well as with risotto rice. Pearled spelt is the most successful as it becomes very creamy. Semi-pearled farro is delicious (and better for you), but the grains remain firmer and are less creamy. Use the same quantities of spelt and stock and you can make all sorts of risottos. You could also add kale to this at the end; just remove the thick stalks, blanch in boiling water for five minutes and drain.

SERVES 4 AS A MAIN COURSE

1 litre (1¾ pints) vegetable or chicken stock

2 tbsp olive or rapeseed oil

½ onion, peeled and finely chopped

4 leeks, trimmed, washed and cut into 2cm- (¾in-) thick rounds

2 garlic cloves, finely chopped

300g (10½oz) pearled spelt

80g (2¾oz) goat's cheese, crumbled

pepper

Put the stock in a saucepan, bring to a simmer, then reduce the heat to very low.

Heat the oil in a large saucepan over a medium heat. Add the onion and leeks and sweat gently for about 10 minutes, until soft. Add the garlic and cook for another couple of minutes, then stir in the spelt. Cook gently for a minute or two, stirring the grains in the fat and juices, then start adding the stock half a ladleful at a time, stirring often and letting each lot of stock become absorbed before you add the next. It should take about 35 minutes for the spelt to become tender with a little bite still in the centre of each grain. If you run out of stock, add a splash of boiling water.

Gently stir in most of the goat's cheese. Add pepper. Taste for seasoning (you shouldn't need any salt if you've used chicken stock, you might if you've used vegetable stock). Serve immediately with the remaining goat's cheese sprinkled over the top of each plate.

a barley version... pumpkin and chestnut risotto

Heat 2 tbsp olive oil in a pan and sauté 800g (1lb 12oz) of squash or pumpkin (pre-prepared weight), chopped, in two batches if you need to, until caramelized in patches. Set aside. Add another tbsp of oil and sauté 1 small finely chopped onion, 2 chopped garlic cloves and 1 chopped celery stick until pale gold. Add 300g (10½oz) pearl barley and stir to coat in the juices. Add 1 litre (1¾ pints) hot chicken or vegetable stock a ladleful at a time. (You don't have to stir continually, only from time to time.) In 30 minutes, it will soften and become creamy. Return the pumpkin after 15 minutes and add 75g (2¾oz) cooked, halved chestnuts five minutes before the end. Season. Add 1 tbsp chopped parsley or sage leaves, check the seasoning and serve with grated Parmesan. Serves 4.

fruited rye grains with gorgonzola

There's a mixture of warm and cold here, but it works nonetheless and is very adaptable; you can sauté the pear slices if you prefer (in which case use two pears and cut them into slices about ¾cm / ⅓in thick).

If you want this as a side to go with other dishes, you can leave out the pears and serve it in a big bowl, or it can be more of a carefully constructed salad served on individual plates. You can use raw radicchio or red chicory instead of warm red cabbage, and wheat berries or brown rice instead of the rye grains, if you prefer.

The whole is gorgeously nutty. The key thing is to get your seasoning right.

SERVES 6–8 (DEPENDS IF IT IS A STARTER OR SIDE SALAD)

FOR THE SALAD

200g (7oz) rye grains

salt and pepper

juice of 1 lemon, plus more for the dressing

40g (1½oz) dried cranberries

1 fat, perfectly ripe pear

½ tbsp olive oil

125g (4½oz) red cabbage, cut into strips about 2cm- (¾in-) thick

50g (1¾oz) watercress, coarse stalks removed

125g (4½oz) Gorgonzola, crumbled

40g (1½oz) pecans, toasted and roughly chopped

½ tbsp sunflower seeds

½ tbsp poppy seeds

FOR THE DRESSING

1 tbsp balsamic vinegar

1¼ tsp Dijon mustard

1¼ tsp maple syrup

4 tbsp walnut or hazelnut oil

1¼ tbsp extra virgin olive oil (fruity rather than grassy)

Soak the rye grains overnight, then rinse well. Put in a pan with plenty of water to cover, then bring to the boil. Reduce the heat a little and cook until tender, 50–60 minutes. Check during this time to make sure there's plenty of water in the pan and add boiling water if you need to. Drain it, season the rye and add the juice of ½ lemon. Put the dried cranberries in a small bowl, cover with boiling water and leave to soak for 15 minutes, then drain.

Meanwhile, halve and core the pear and cut it into thin slices. Squeeze the juice of ½ lemon over it to stop it discolouring.

To make the dressing, mix the vinegar, mustard, maple syrup and some seasoning together, then whisk in the oils with a fork. Add lemon juice to taste.

Heat the regular olive oil and sauté the red cabbage over a medium heat for about three minutes; it will wilt. Season. Put the rye into a broad shallow dish (or divide it between plates) and add the rest of the ingredients (except the poppy seeds). Gently toss the various components together (try not to crush the cheese) with the dressing. Check the seasoning again – grains do need a lot – and sprinkle the poppy seeds on top. Serve while still warm.

radicchio and red onions on white bean purée

It is truly amazing what you can do with a couple of cans of beans. Here they are transformed into a pretty classy dish (if you choose the right plate to serve it on, it even looks rather painterly). Bitter leaves, sweet onions, earthy beans, the different components work very well together.

Eat as a main course or with a range of vegetables. Italian dishes are best alongside: try Beluga lentil, roast grape and red chicory salad, though use watercress instead of red chicory as the leafy component, or Roast Jerusalem artichokes and pumpkin with agresto (see pages 172 and 178). It's also good with meaty fish.

SERVES 6

FOR THE BEAN PURÉE

2 tbsp olive oil

½ onion, roughly chopped

1 garlic clove, crushed

2 x 400g cans cannellini beans, drained and rinsed

150ml (5fl oz) chicken stock or water

salt and pepper

4 tbsp extra virgin olive oil, plus more to serve

good squeeze of lemon

FOR THE REST

2 large heads of radicchio

2 red onions, peeled

3 tbsp olive oil

4 tbsp balsamic vinegar

For the bean purée, heat the regular olive oil in a saucepan and gently cook the onion until it is soft but not coloured. Add the garlic, the beans, stock or water and seasoning. Cook over a medium heat for about four minutes.

Process the beans and their cooking liquid in a blender or food processor with the extra virgin oil and lemon juice. Taste and adjust the seasoning. You can set the purée aside to reheat later, or serve it at room temperature.

Now for the rest. Halve each head of radicchio, then cut each half into four sections. Trim the base and a little of the white heart from each piece, without letting the sections fall apart. Halve the onions and trim the base of each. Cut each half lengthways into crescent moon-shaped wedges, about 2cm (¾in) wide at their thickest part. (Or just slice them horizontally, if you prefer.)

Mix the regular olive oil, balsamic and seasoning together in a dish and put the onions and radicchio in it. Gently turn over to coat then leave for about 10 minutes.

Heat a griddle pan until really hot and cook the onions quickly until well coloured on both sides. Reduce the heat to low and let the onions cook until they are soft, turning frequently.

Meanwhile, spoon the bean purée into a serving dish, reheating it gently first if you want to.

Increase the heat under the griddle pan and add the radicchio. Let it colour on each side – this will happen very quickly – and wilt. Put the radicchio and onions on top of the bean purée. Season and serve with a little extra virgin oil drizzled over the top.

uzbeki carrots

It's just carrots, but not as you've ever had them before. You can, honestly, eat this just with rice or couscous and be happy. Add a dollop of yogurt, too. If you want another vegetable dish to serve alongside, make sure it contrasts, so definitely not something sweet.

SERVES 6

1 tbsp rapeseed or groundnut oil

1 onion, very finely sliced

2 tomatoes, peeled and cut into slim wedges

4 garlic cloves, finely chopped

2 green chillies, deseeded and shredded

¼ tsp ground cinnamon

½ tsp ground cumin

600g (1lb 5oz) carrots, cut into batons

75g (2¾oz) currants

1 tbsp dried barberries

¼ tsp saffron stamens

350ml (12fl oz) vegetable or chicken stock, or water, plus more if needed

1 tbsp tomato purée

2 tsp runny honey, or to taste

salt and pepper

1 tbsp shelled unsalted pistachios, roughly chopped

2 tbsp chopped coriander or mint leaves

Heat the oil in a large saucepan and fry the onion over a medium heat until golden, then add the tomatoes and cook until they are beginning to soften (about three minutes). Add the garlic and chillies and cook for another minute, then the cinnamon and cumin and cook for a further minute. Add everything else, except the pistachios and herbs, and bring to the boil.

Reduce the heat and simmer the carrots until totally tender, about 25 minutes. The mixture should remain moist but not be swimming in juice. If it gets too dry, add a little more stock or water. If it is too sloppy, whack the heat up and boil off some of the liquid.

Taste for seasoning and balance; the mixture should be sweet and savoury. Stir in the pistachios and herbs and serve.

seared tuna with avocado and wasabi purée

Ready in minutes, filling, zingy… everything you could possibly want.

SERVES 4

FOR THE TUNA

2 tbsp olive oil

3 garlic cloves, crushed

4 tbsp soy sauce

pepper

4 tuna steaks, 175g (6oz) each

pickled ginger, to serve

FOR THE PURÉE

2 completely ripe avocados

1 tsp wasabi paste, or to taste

juice of 1 lime, or to taste

salt

Mix the olive oil, garlic, soy sauce and pepper. Put the tuna steaks in a dish and pour the marinade over them, turning to coat. Leave for 30 minutes.

To make the purée, halve and pit the avocados and scoop out the flesh with a spoon. Mash with the wasabi and lime juice, add salt and taste. Add more wasabi, salt or lime, as you think is needed.

Heat a griddle pan until it's really hot. Lift the tuna out of the marinade and gently shake off the excess. Griddle the tuna for about one minute each side (this gives you a moist interior that is quite raw in the centre).

Serve the tuna with the avocado purée, with pickled ginger on the side. Offer brown rice as well, if you like.

try this with… leeks with miso mustard

Remove the tough outer leaves from 6 leeks and discard. Slice the base from each leek and trim the dark green leaves from the top end. Cut the leeks into 4cm (1½in) lengths. Wash really well, making sure you get rid of any grit or soil inside the layers. Steam over boiling water for four to six minutes. They should be completely tender to the middle; test with the tip of a knife. Tip on to a clean tea towel and gently pat to soak up excess moisture. Whisk ½ tbsp Dijon mustard, 1½ tbsp brown miso, 2 tbsp white miso, 1 tbsp runny honey and 1½ tbsp rice vinegar together with a fork. Gently toss this with the leeks and sprinkle with sesame seeds. Serves 4.

borlotti beans and kale with anchovy and rosemary sauce

If you are in a hurry you can make this with a couple of cans of drained and rinsed borlotti beans and it will still be good. But home-cooked beans just have that unctuousness and depth of flavour that canned beans don't. In summer, fresh borlotti beans would also be wonderful (use double the weight of fresh to dried beans, so 400g/14oz). Just shell the fresh beans and cook in simmering water for 30–40 minutes, or until tender, and replace the kale with 500g (1lb 2oz) of spinach, adding the leaves to the dish at the end of cooking just long enough to wilt them.

This is a very 'meaty' dish, despite there being no meat in it. It's lovely with farro (see page 223 for how to cook that). If you are in a meat-eating mood it's also great with roast lamb (and not bad with roast chicken). The anchovy sauce is definitely a recipe to keep. It's excellent with meaty fish such as monkfish.

**SERVES 4 AS A MAIN COURSE,
6 AS A SIDE DISH**

FOR THE BEANS AND KALE

200g (7oz) dried borlotti beans, soaked overnight and drained

½ head of garlic (halved horizontally), plus 2 garlic cloves, finely sliced

a few parsley stalks

1 dried chilli, crumbled

1 carrot, roughly chopped

1 bay leaf

3 celery sticks

8 tbsp extra virgin olive oil

juice of 1 lemon

salt and pepper

500g (1lb 2oz) kale

¼ tsp chilli flakes

FOR THE SAUCE

1 tsp rosemary leaves

6 cured anchovies, drained of oil

juice of ¼ lemon, or to taste

2½ tbsp extra virgin olive oil

Put the borlotti beans into a heavy-based pan with water to cover, the ½ head of garlic, parsley stalks, chilli, carrot, bay, two of the celery sticks, each broken in half, and 4 tbsp of the the extra virgin oil. Bring to the boil, then reduce the heat to its lowest, cover and cook for an hour, or until the beans are tender but not falling apart. Drain the beans and remove the garlic, parsley stalks, carrot, bay and celery. Return the beans to the pan with 2 tbsp more of the extra virgin oil and the juice of ½ lemon, salt and pepper.

To make the sauce, pound the rosemary in a mortar then add the anchovies and crush to a paste. Gradually add the lemon juice and then the extra virgin oil, a little at a time, grinding as you go. You aren't making a mayonnaise, so don't expect this to emulsify. You'll be left with a lumpy sauce, but the pounding just melds all the elements together. Add pepper and set aside.

Rip the kale leaves from their coarse ribs (discard the ribs) then plunge the leaves into a pan of boiling water. Cook for five minutes, then drain.

Dice the remaining celery stick and heat the remaining 2 tbsp of extra virgin oil in a large pan (preferably a sauté pan). Cook the celery for one minute, or just until it is beginning to soften but hasn't yet lost its bite. Add the sliced garlic and chilli flakes and cook for another minute, then add the beans and kale. Carefully heat these through without squashing them or overcooking. Check for seasoning, add some more lemon and serve with the sauce.

soba noodles with chilli, purple-sprouting broccoli and a fried egg

Made from buckwheat flour, Japanese soba noodles are healthier than regular pasta and have a gently meaty flavour. They can be eaten cold with dipping sauces, or hot (and are especially popular in broths in Japan). I also serve them in Japanese dishes where I would otherwise serve brown rice, such as in a Japanese rice bowl (see page 43). The following recipe makes a perfect lunch for one. Surprisingly filling.

SERVES 1

70g (2½oz) soba noodles

60g (2¼oz) purple-sprouting broccoli

1 tbsp groundnut oil

1cm (½in) root ginger, peeled and really finely chopped

1 red chilli, deseeded and finely sliced

2 garlic cloves, finely sliced

2 tbsp soy sauce

3 spring onions, chopped

1 large egg

black sesame seeds

Put the soba noodles in a saucepan of boiling water. It will take about seven minutes to cook them (though follow the packet instructions), and you need to have everything else ready.

Trim the base of the broccoli stems. Steam the broccoli until tender (two to four minutes, depending on thickness).

Meanwhile, heat half the oil in a frying pan and gently sauté the ginger, chilli and garlic until the garlic is pale gold. Add the soy sauce, then drain the noodles and add them to the pan. Toss in the purple-sprouting broccoli and the spring onions. In another small frying pan, quickly fry the egg in the remaining oil. Put the noodles and broccoli into a bowl and slide the egg on top. Sprinkle with black sesame seeds and serve immediately.

sea bass ceviche with avocado and grapefruit

This can be made with spanking-fresh mackerel if you would like a cheaper option than sea bass. It's gorgeous – bright-flavoured, slightly sweet because of the grapefruit, and hot – so much so that I can eat the ceviche completely on it's own.

SERVES 4 AS A STARTER OR LIGHT MAIN COURSE

FOR THE CEVICHE

400g (14oz) sushi-quality sea bass fillet

½ small red onion, peeled and sliced wafer-thin

1 red chilli, very finely sliced

1 garlic clove, peeled and very finely sliced

juice of 2 limes

salt and pepper

2 pink or white grapefruits

2 just-ripe avocados

10g (¼oz) coriander leaves, roughly chopped

FOR THE DRESSING

2½ tbsp olive oil

3 tbsp verjuice

Place the sea bass fillet skin side down on a board and, with a very sharp knife, cut slices on the bias as you would for smoked salmon, leaving the skin behind. Put the fish, onion, chilli and garlic into a non-reactive shallow dish. Mix the lime juice with ¼ tsp of salt, pour it in and gently turn the fish. Cover with cling film and refrigerate for one hour, turning the fish again halfway through.

Cut the grapefruits into segments: cut a slice off the bottom and top of each fruit so they have a flat base on which to sit. Using a very sharp knife, cut the peel and pith off each grapefruit, working around the fruit and cutting the peel away in broad strips from top to bottom. Working over a bowl, slip a sharp fine-bladed knife in between the membrane on either side of each segment and ease the segment out.

To prepare the avocados, halve and remove the stones. Cut each half into slices then peel each slice, working carefully to avoid squashing the flesh. Sprinkle with salt and pepper.

Once the fish is 'cooked', strain off the liquid. Whisk the olive oil, verjuice and a little salt together for the dressing. Arrange the marinated fish (with the onions, chilli and garlic) on plates with the avocados and grapefruit. Spoon the dressing over and sprinkle with the coriander.

goan baked fish with green chilli and coconut chutney

Every so often I buy a fresh coconut and smash it on the front door step (watching it bounce off into the lavender bushes), but now you can actually buy little packs of fresh stuff, which is a boon for recipes like this. This is a big impact dish. Everyone smiles as you take it to the table. It kind of smells of exotic holidays.

SERVES 6

FOR THE CHUTNEY

½ tbsp groundnut oil, plus more for the fish

½ onion, roughly chopped

¾ tsp cumin seeds

¾ tsp mustard seeds

3 garlic cloves, roughly chopped

leaves from a 100g (3½oz) bunch of coriander, plus more small sprigs to serve (optional)

4 green chillies, deseeded and roughly chopped

juice of 3 limes

1 tsp caster sugar

2.5cm (1in) root ginger, peeled and grated

125g (4½oz) fresh coconut, trimmed of dark skin and chopped, plus more coconut, shaved wafer-thin, to serve (optional)

salt

FOR THE FISH

6 bream, scaled, trimmed and cleaned (about 300g/10½oz each)

wedges of lime, to serve

Preheat the oven to 180°C/350°F/gas mark 4.

For the chutney, heat the oil in a frying pan and gently sauté the onion until softening but not golden; you just need to take off the raw edge. Scrape into a food processor. Put the cumin and mustard seeds into the frying pan and toast until they become fragrant. Scrape these into the food processor too with all the other chutney ingredients. Blitz, using the pulse-blend button, until you have a rough paste. Taste for seasoning.

Make two slashes on both sides of each fish. Season the fish inside and out with salt. Push some of the chutney into the slits and inside each fish too. Put the fish on a lightly oiled piece of foil or baking parchment on a baking sheet and brush the top of each with a little more oil. Put into the oven and cook for 20 minutes, or until the flesh near the bone is white and has lost its glassy look.

Serve each diner with a whole fish, more of the chutney and lime wedges, scattering the fish with coconut shavings and coriander sprigs (if using). Brown rice is a good side option, as is Kachumber (see page 89).

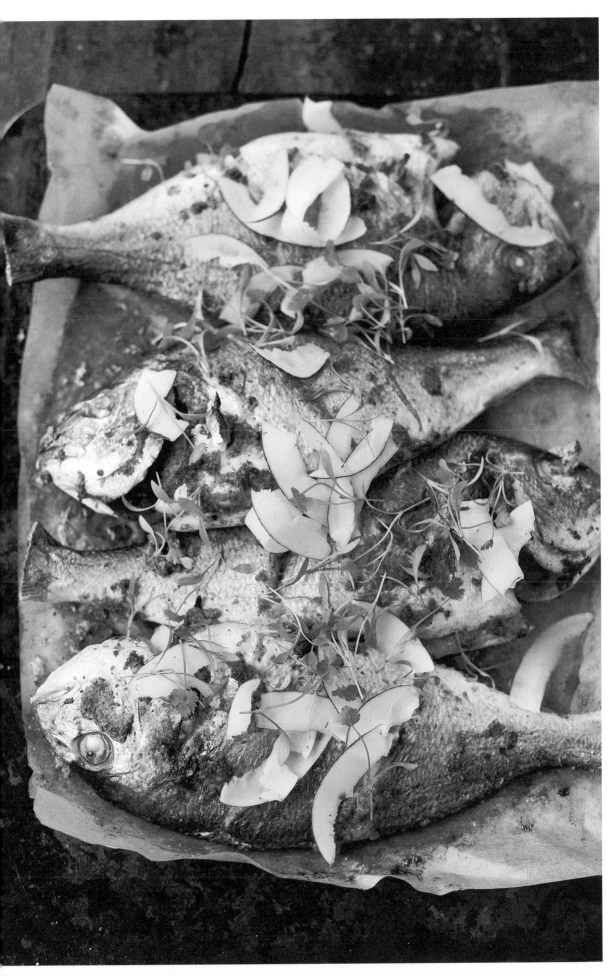

winter menu a painterly supper

bagna cauda | georgian chicken with walnut sauce | orange and pomegranate cake

A meal of fantastic colours – the bagna cauda on its own looks like an old master – that completely demolishes the notion that wintry food has to be brown.

cold weather bagna cauda

This recipe is from chef Brett Barnes who cooks at one of my favourite restaurants, Ducksoup in Soho in London. Bagna cauda is a Piedmontese sauce and I've eaten it there plenty of times, but Brett's is by far the best version I've ever tasted: pungent, earthy and rich. You don't have to stick to the vegetables I suggest here, you can serve cooked carrots, Jerusalem artichokes or cardoons.

Yes, the sauce is high in fat – and saturated fat at that because it's butter – but saturated fat may not be the bogeyman we once thought it was (see pages 284–285). And you don't eat this every day. You can make it with just half the butter given here, or replace the butter with extra virgin olive oil (plenty of bagna cauda recipes are made completely with olive oil). But this is true to Brett's recipe.

SERVES 6

FOR THE BAGNA CAUDA

75g (2½oz) best-quality canned anchovies (such as Ortiz), drained weight

1 head of garlic, cloves separated and peeled

250ml (9fl oz) milk, more if needed

30g (1oz) sourdough bread, crusts cut off

100g (3½oz) unsalted butter, diced

FOR THE VEGETABLES

bunch of French Breakfast radishes, leaves removed, trimmed

two chicons of red chicory, leaves separated

1 head of chard, leaves separated

18 stalks of purple-sprouting broccoli, bases trimmed

Chop the anchovies. Put the radishes and chicory on a platter.

Cook the garlic in the milk over a very gentle heat until completely soft, it will take about 10 minutes. Be careful not to let it go too far. At this point the milk should still just cover the garlic.

Take the pan of garlic and milk off the heat and add the bread, torn into really small chunks, then the anchovies. Return to a low heat and simmer for two minutes, whisking constantly (one of those small sauce whisks is ideal here). If you find that the mixture is so thick it won't move, add a little milk (only about 2 tbsp). Once you've cooked and whisked for a couple of minutes you should have a thick, homogenous mass. Whisk in the butter a little at a time until you have a creamy yet rough emulsion.

Meanwhile, lightly cook the chard and purple-sprouting broccoli (steam or boil them for two to four minutes, depending on size).

Put the chard and purple-sprouting broccoli on the platter with the other vegetables. Serve with the warm anchovy sauce.

georgian chicken with walnut sauce and hot grated beetroot

The walnut sauce here is based on a Georgian recipe called *satsivi*. The authentic sauce is thinner (diluted with chicken stock), but I prefer the chunkiness of this version. Bulgar wheat, farro or brown rice are good on the side (see page 223 for how to cook those). You could stir some greens through the grain – kale or spinach – but don't do anything too fancy, there's enough going on. You can buy the dried marigold flowers used in Georgian cookery online (see page 329 for stockists).

SERVES 6

FOR THE BEETROOT

400g (14oz) beetroots

1½ tbsp olive oil

salt and pepper

3 garlic cloves, crushed

½ tsp ground coriander

15g (½oz) flat-leaf parsley, stalks removed, leaves roughly chopped

2 tsp red wine vinegar

½ tbsp extra virgin olive oil

FOR THE CHICKEN

1.8kg (4lb) chicken

1 tsp cayenne pepper

2 tbsp olive oil

1 lemon, halved

FOR THE SAUCE

2 tbsp olive oil

1 onion, very finely chopped

75g (2¾oz) walnut pieces

2 garlic cloves, crushed

¼ tsp ground cinnamon

½ tsp ground coriander

¼ tsp cayenne pepper

¼ tsp paprika

good pinch of ground fenugreek

½ tsp dried marigold flowers, plus more to serve

½ tbsp red wine vinegar

235ml (8½fl oz) chicken stock

2 tbsp chopped coriander leaves

Preheat the oven to 190°C/375°F/gas mark 5. Trim the beetroots and put them on a double-thickness square of foil. Drizzle with the regular olive oil, season and pull the foil up round them, sealing to make a 'tent'. Place in a small roasting tin and bake for one hour, or until tender to the tip of a sharp knife.

Season the chicken inside and out and sprinkle the cayenne over it. Put into a roasting tin. Drizzle on the regular olive oil then squeeze the lemon halves over the bird. Put the lemon halves in the cavity and roast the chicken in the oven with the beetroot for 1¼ hours.

Meanwhile, grind the garlic, ground coriander and parsley for the beetroot together until you have a paste.

Make the walnut sauce while the chicken is in the oven. Heat the regular olive oil in a frying pan and sauté the onion until soft and pale gold, about 10 minutes. Add the walnut pieces, garlic, spices and marigolds and sauté for another four minutes or so, stirring frequently. Put this into a large mortar and pound to a coarse paste (traditionally this is pounded until smooth, but I prefer it to keep a bit of texture). Return this to the pan and add the vinegar. Leave it over a medium-low heat and gradually add the chicken stock, a little at a time, stirring and allowing the mixture to thicken. Taste for seasoning and stir in the chopped coriander.

Check to see whether the chicken is cooked by piercing the flesh between one of the legs and the breast of the bird: the juices should run clear, with no trace of pinkness.

When the beetroots are cool enough to handle, peel, grate into a bowl, add the ground garlic and herb paste, the vinegar and extra virgin oil. You can serve this at room temperature.

Serve the chicken, sprinkled with a few dried marigold flowers, with the warm walnut sauce and beetroot.

orange and pomegranate cake

Incredibly easy. Not sugar-free I know but, as cakes go, not bad. And it is for dessert. Serve thin slices with Greek yogurt. It's very, very moist (almost pudding-like) so be careful when you're moving it off the base of the cake tin and on to a plate.

SERVES 8

FOR THE CAKE

50g (1¾oz) wholemeal breadcrumbs

100g (3½oz) ground almonds

175g (6oz) soft light brown sugar

2 tsp baking powder

finely grated zest of 1½ oranges

215ml (7½fl oz) olive oil, plus more for the tin

4 eggs, lightly beaten

seeds from ½ pomegranate

FOR THE SYRUP

juice of 1 orange

100ml (3½fl oz) pomegranate juice (pure juice, not 'pomegranate juice drink')

1 tbsp pomegranate molasses

2 tbsp runny honey

In a bowl, mix together the breadcrumbs, almonds, sugar and baking powder. Add the orange zest, olive oil and eggs and stir well until everything is amalgamated.

Pour the batter into an oiled 20cm (8in) springform cake tin. Put it into a cold oven and set the heat to 190°C/375°F/gas mark 5. Bake for 45–50 minutes, or until the cake is browned and a skewer inserted into the middle comes out clean.

Meanwhile, make the syrup by gently heating all the ingredients together. Stir a little until the honey has dissolved, then increase the heat and simmer for five minutes. You should end up with about 100ml (3½fl oz) of syrup.

When the cake is cooked, pierce holes all over the surface and slowly pour the syrup all over it, allowing it to sink in. Leave the cake to cool completely in the tin. It will sink a little in the middle but don't worry, this makes a lovely dip for the pomegranate seeds to lie in. Scatter the pomegranate seeds on top just before serving.

avocado, raw salmon and brown rice salad

A very good midweek supper or lunch dish. If you aren't keen on raw fish you can cook it, but there is something very satisfying – and truly filling – about raw fish.

SERVES 4

salt and pepper

200g (7oz) brown rice

3 tbsp rice vinegar

2.5cm (1in) root ginger, peeled and grated

8 tbsp mild olive oil

1 tbsp sesame oil

2 tsp runny honey, or to taste

2 avocados

150g (5½oz) radishes (ideally French Breakfast), very finely sliced

2 spring onions, trimmed and finely chopped

75g (2½oz) watercress (only use sprigs with fine stalks, keep the rest for soup)

pickled ginger

wasabi paste (optional)

soy sauce, to serve

FOR THE SALMON

600g (1lb 5oz) sushi-quality salmon fillet, skinned, tiny bones removed, sliced about 2mm (⅛in) thick

juice of 2 limes

2 tsp caster sugar

Bring a saucepan of salted water to the boil, then cook the brown rice until tender (it can take as much as 25 minutes). While the rice is cooking, mix the rice vinegar with the ginger, olive oil, sesame oil, honey, salt and pepper.

You need to marinate the salmon while cooking the rice. The longer you marinate it the more the lime juice will 'cook' it, so you can just toss the salmon in a non-reactive dish with the lime juice, sugar and salt and pepper, or you can leave it for three to four minutes, to taste.

Halve the avocados and remove the stones. Cut each half into slices, then peel each slice.

When the rice is cooked, drain it and toss with most of the dressing (you need to keep some back for dressing the avocado), the radishes, spring onions and watercress. Taste for seasoning, rice does take a lot of seasoning. Spoon this on to plates and lay the salmon and the avocado slices alongside. Put some slices of pickled ginger over the salmon and drizzle the rest of the dressing over the avocados. Grind some black pepper on top. Add a little dollop of wasabi to each plate (if using) and offer soy sauce for people to help themselves.

north african spiced mackerel with kamut

Kamut has a nutty flavour and I love its texture – good big grains – but it's quite bland, so needs strong seasoning. It works really well with ingredients that have a good assertive flavour, such as mackerel, and is excellent with Moroccan dishes (read more about it on page 224).

SERVES 4

FOR THE KAMUT

250g (9oz) kamut

2 tbsp juice from the preserved lemon jar

2 tbsp extra virgin olive oil

50g (1¾oz) green olives, pitted and chopped

3 tbsp chopped coriander leaves

2 preserved lemons (1 if you are using larger home-made lemons)

FOR THE FISH

½ tbsp ground cumin

2 tsp cayenne pepper

½ tsp chilli flakes

½ tsp ground ginger

2 garlic cloves, crushed

4 tbsp olive oil

4 mackerel

salt and pepper

juice of ½ lemon

The day before you are going to eat it, put the kamut to soak in plenty of water in a large bowl. Next day, drain it well.

Put the soaked, drained kamut into a saucepan and cover with plenty of water. Bring to the boil, then reduce the heat to a brisk simmer. Cook for 50–60 minutes, or until tender. The grains will have plumped up and be soft but still 'nutty'. Keep an eye on the water level and make sure the grain is always covered.

Preheat the oven to 200°C/400°F/gas mark 6. For the fish, mix together the cumin, cayenne, chilli, ginger and garlic with the regular olive oil. Rub this all over the mackerel, inside and out, and season all over too. Put into a roasting tin and squeeze the lemon all over. Cook in the hot oven for 20 minutes.

Drain the kamut and immediately toss with the preserved lemon juice, extra virgin oil, olives, coriander and salt and pepper. Halve the preserved lemons and scrape out the flesh (discard it). Cut the zest into shreds and add that to the kamut as well.

Check the fish for doneness: look at the thickest part of the flesh near the bone, it should be white and not at all glassy. Serve the spiced mackerel with the kamut.

chicken with yogurt and pomegranates

Most of the dishes in this book have big flavours. They aren't subtle. This one is different. Apart from the tart juice of the pomegranates on top, all is creaminess and restraint.

SERVES 4

1½ tbsp olive oil

salt and pepper

8 skinless bone-in chicken thighs

1 large onion, finely sliced

1 tsp ground cumin

½ tsp cayenne pepper

¼ tsp chilli flakes

6 garlic cloves, crushed

400ml (14fl oz) chicken stock

250g (9oz) Greek yogurt

1 tbsp plain flour

seeds from ½ pomegranate

1 tbsp finely chopped coriander leaves

Heat the olive oil in a broad, heavy-based saucepan or sauté pan. Season the chicken pieces and brown them on both sides until pale gold. Remove from the pan and set aside. Add the onion to the fat and cooking juices and cook it until soft and a very pale gold. Sprinkle on the cumin, cayenne, chilli and garlic and cook for another couple of minutes.

Return the chicken pieces to the pan with any juices which have emerged and add the stock. Bring to the boil, then immediately reduce the heat to very low. Cover and cook for 20 minutes, then uncover and cook for a further 15 minutes. The liquid will reduce somewhat and the chicken should be cooked through (when you pierce the thickest piece there should be no pink juices). If you have more than about 200ml (7fl oz) of liquid, take the chicken pieces out and boil to reduce the liquid.

Mix the yogurt with the flour (this stabilizes it and stops it from splitting). Add a small ladleful of the cooking liquor to the yogurt and mix well. Now add the yogurt to the pan and mix carefully. If you have removed the chicken to reduce the cooking juices, return it now. Gently heat through, then scatter with the pomegranate seeds and coriander and serve.

lamb with kurdish rhubarb and split peas

The rhubarb and split pea braise here is actually served as a dish in its own right in Kurdistan, with grains on the side. I thought it made a good accompaniment to lamb, but you could try it as a main course too (we're not used to seeing rhubarb as a savoury ingredient, but it's good). My recipe is based on one in a brilliant book called *Silk Road Cooking* by Najmieh Batmanglij.

Cooking this with lamb fillets means you can make the braise in advance, then cook the lamb at the last minute. The sauce is also very good with venison (see below), though that's a bit unorthodox.

SERVES 6

5 tbsp olive oil

1 onion, finely sliced

4 garlic cloves, finely chopped

1 red chilli, deseeded and finely chopped

½ tsp turmeric

100g (3½oz) yellow split peas

800ml (1 pint 7fl oz) chicken, lamb or vegetable stock

½ tsp saffron stamens

1 large tomato, roughly chopped

juice of 1 lime

2 tbsp granulated sugar, or to taste

salt and pepper

450g (1lb) forced rhubarb, trimmed and cut into 3cm (1in) lengths

20g (¾oz) flat-leaf parsley leaves

leaves from 8 sprigs of mint

15g (½oz) dill fronds

20g (¾oz) coriander leaves

3 x 300g (10½oz) fillets of lamb, trimmed

Heat 2 tbsp of the olive oil in a saucepan and sauté the onion until soft, about five minutes. Add the garlic and chilli and cook for another two minutes, then add the turmeric and cook for another minute. Stir in the split peas and add the stock and saffron. Bring to the boil, then reduce the heat and simmer for about 30 minutes. Preheat the oven to 200°C/400°F/gas mark 6.

Add the tomato, lime, sugar and seasoning to the split pea mixture and stir them in. Return to the boil, reduce the heat to a simmer and put the rhubarb on top. Cover and cook for 15 minutes. The rhubarb should cook without completely falling apart. Gently stir it into the other ingredients with all the herbs, being careful not to make the rhubarb too mushy. Season and taste for salt, pepper and a sweet-sour balance.

Sprinkle the lamb with salt and pepper and heat the remaining 3 tbsp of olive oil in a sauté pan. Brown the fillets all over, then transfer to a roasting tin and cook in the oven for 10 minutes. Take the fillets out, cover and keep warm to rest for 10 minutes.

Cut the lamb fillet into thick slices. Serve with the rhubarb and split pea braise, some Greek yogurt and grains (bulgar is very good here). A watercress salad is good on the side as well.

try the braise with… venison. Brush 6 venison steaks (about 175g/6oz each, cut from the leg or the loin) with olive oil and season with salt and pepper. Heat a frying pan until really hot, then sear the steaks on each side so they get a really good colour. Reduce the heat and cook until rare, it should take about 2½ minutes on each side. Cut each steak into four slices, just to reveal the lovely pinkness inside, and serve on warm plates with spoonfuls of the braise alongside. Serves 6.

griddled vietnamese chicken with table salad

Vietnamese table salad isn't a salad as we know it, as the various elements aren't tossed together but are instead offered separately. The diner is supposed to take bits of chicken and various vegetables, then roll them all up in large lettuce leaves and dip the resulting package in a hot sauce. DIY eating of the most wonderful kind. Offer napkins, as you have to eat this with your hands.

SERVES 4

FOR THE CHICKEN

3 lemon grass stalks, white part only, finely chopped

4 garlic cloves, chopped

salt and pepper

1 tsp caster sugar

1 tbsp fish sauce

2½ tbsp vegetable or sunflower oil

4 skinless chicken breasts

FOR THE DIPPING SAUCE

8 garlic cloves

2 red chillies, deseeded and finely chopped

2cm (¾in) root ginger, peeled and grated

6 tsp caster sugar

juice of 2 limes

8 tbsp fish sauce

FOR THE SALAD

1 small, slightly under-ripe mango

3 carrots, peeled and cut into fine batons

½ cucumber, cut into fine batons

100g (3½oz) beansprouts

leaves from a small bunch of mint

leaves from a small bunch of basil

125g (4½oz) large lettuce leaves, such as Romaine, washed

First marinate the chicken. Using a mortar and pestle or a small food processor, grind the lemon grass and garlic together with some salt and pepper. Now work in the caster sugar, fish sauce and oil. Put the chicken in a bowl and pour over the marinade, turning to make sure everything gets well coated. Cover and leave in the fridge for a couple of hours, or overnight.

To make the dipping sauce, using a mortar and pestle or small food processor, pound or blitz the garlic, chillies, ginger and sugar together, then add the lime juice and fish sauce. Add 4–5 tbsp of water (according to how strong you want it) and mix well.

For the salad, peel the mango and cut the 'cheeks' off each side. (They are the halves which you can remove by cutting right next to the stone.) Cut the cheeks into slices or batons. Remove the rest of the flesh from the mango and do the same with it. The flesh must be intact and not soft or bruised, so keep any bits which are less than perfect for making a smoothie (or eat them).

Now, basically, you just provide the array of fruit, vegetables and herbs on a platter. You can either toss the ingredients together (except for the lettuce leaves), or keep them separate and let people pick what they want to add to their plates.

Heat a griddle pan until hot and take the chicken out of the marinade. Cook each bit on both sides over a medium-high heat at first, and then on a lower heat until the chicken is cooked through, turning it every so often.

Serve the chicken with the table salad, the dipping sauce and some brown rice on the side. Generally diners put their choice of fruit, vegetables, herbs and chicken together, roll them up in a lettuce leaf and dip in the dipping sauce. Let people help themselves.

beef carpaccio with beluga lentils, horseradish and buttermilk

Delicious, filling, luxurious, this is great for entertaining. Fillet steak is expensive, I know, but it is only a very small amount per head.

SERVES 6 AS A MAIN COURSE

FOR THE DISH

4 medium or 8 small beetroots

1 tbsp olive oil, plus more for the beetroots

salt and pepper

½ red onion, finely chopped

½ celery stick, finely chopped

1 garlic clove, finely chopped

250g (9oz) black lentils

5 tbsp extra virgin olive oil, plus more to serve

1 tbsp white balsamic vinegar

good squeeze of lemon juice

2 tbsp chopped dill fronds

450g (1lb) well-aged fillet steak, in one piece

4cm (1½cm) fresh horseradish, peeled and grated

FOR THE BUTTERMILK DRESSING

125ml (4fl oz) buttermilk

½ garlic clove, crushed

1 tbsp extra virgin olive oil

For the beetroots, preheat the oven to 220°C/425°F/gas mark 7. Remove any leaves from the beetroots. If they're nice and fresh, keep them (they can go on the plate, too). If they're at all withered then throw them out. Wash the beetroots and set them on a double sheet of foil in a roasting dish (use enough foil to make a kind of tent around them). Drizzle with olive oil and season. Pull the foil up around the vegetables, seal the edges and put into the hot oven. Cook for about 30 minutes, or one hour if using medium beetroots, then check for tenderness with the tip of a knife; if the beetroots aren't tender right through, return them to the oven and cook until they are.

Meanwhile, cook the lentils. Heat the 1 tbsp of regular olive oil in a saucepan and add the onion and celery. Sauté until the vegetables are soft but not coloured. Add the garlic and cook for another two minutes, then add the lentils and enough water to cover by about 5cm (2in). Bring to the boil, reduce the heat and simmer until the lentils are tender (check after 15 minutes, as cooking time depends on the age of the lentils). Drain and immediately add the extra virgin oil, white balsamic, lemon juice, salt and pepper and dill.

If you have reserved any beetroot leaves, wash them well, then blanch them in boiling, salted water for three minutes. Scoop them out with a slotted spoon on to a dry tea towel and carefully dry the leaves.

Wipe the meat with kitchen paper and remove any fat or sinew from the surface. Using a sharp, fine knife – I use a fish filleting knife – cut the beef into very thin slices across the grain. Put these between two sheets of dampened greaseproof paper and beat them with a mallet or rolling pin (do several pieces at once).

Mix all the ingredients for the dressing and season to taste.

Halve or quarter the roast beetroots depending on size and arrange on plates with the beef, lentils and blanched leaves (if using). Drizzle the beetroots and leaves with extra virgin oil. Season the leaves. Sprinkle on some of the horseradish and offer the rest in a small bowl, serving the buttermilk dressing in another bowl.

braised venison and beetroot with horseradish

There are a lot of light, bright, quickly cooked dishes in this book, but you crave dark, mellow stews in winter. They don't have to be rich in wine, though, and vegetables can play as big a role as meat. Venison is great – lean with a strong flavour – and brilliant with whole grains such as barley, bulgar wheat, farro or spelt on the side (see pages 223–224 for how to cook those). Just make sure to keep checking and stirring, venison can become dry so you need to keep an eye on it. A dish for a cold Scandinavian day.

SERVES 6

salt and pepper

25g (1oz) plain flour

1kg (2lb 4oz) braising venison, cut into cubes

1 tbsp groundnut or sunflower oil, plus more if needed

2 onions, roughly chopped

10 juniper berries, crushed

sprig of rosemary

500ml (18fl oz) beef or chicken stock, plus more if needed

1 tbsp plum or redcurrant jelly

300g (10½oz) beetroots, peeled

1½ tbsp chopped dill fronds

fresh grated horseradish, to serve

Preheat the oven to 150°C/300°F/gas mark 2. Season the flour, then toss the venison in it (you only need a light coating, so vigorously shake off the excess).

Heat the oil in a heavy-based ovenproof casserole. Brown the venison all over in batches, removing each once it has browned. Don't crowd the pan, or the meat will steam instead of brown. Sauté the onions in the same pan (you may need a little more oil) until soft and golden, then stir in the juniper and rosemary and return the meat. Add the stock and jelly, then season.

Cut the beetroots into wedges, about 1cm (½in) thick at the thickest part, and add to the pan. Bring to the boil, then reduce the heat to really low, cover and put into the oven. After 1½ hours, uncover and stir occasionally for up to another 30 minutes: the liquid will reduce and thicken and the venison should become completely tender. If it seems dry, add a little more stock or water. Taste for seasoning. Sprinkle on the dill and horseradish and serve.

for something different… You can replace the beetroot with pumpkin and use a little honey instead of redcurrant jelly. This is good with Walnut gremolata (see page 254) instead of dill and horseradish sprinkled on top. Or replace the beetroots with mixed fresh and dried wild mushrooms, or regular mushrooms.

lychees in jasmine tea

Very subtle and delicately perfumed. Be careful not to let the tea get too perfumed – don't brew it for long – and don't add too much lime juice, or the other flavours will be overwhelmed.

SERVES 4

2 jasmine-scented green tea bags

125g (4½oz) granulated sugar

squeeze of lime juice, to taste

24 lychees, peeled and pitted

Put the tea bags into a jug or teapot and add 300ml (½ pint) of boiling water. Leave for just 90 seconds, you don't want this to get too strong and perfumed. Remove and discard the tea bags and put the tea into a pan with the sugar. Heat the contents of the pan, stirring to help the sugar dissolve. Bring to the boil and cook until reduced by one-third. Add the lime but be careful, it's just supposed to heighten the flavours, not mask the delicate jasmine. Leave to cool completely.

Put the lychees into a dish and pour the syrup over the top. Serve on its own. Anything else would really mask the flavours.

an alternative for warmer months...

It's difficult to get hold of lychees in the summer, so you may have to use canned lychees for this (but they are a good product). Make the syrup as above, but use rose-scented green tea. Drain a 400g can of lychees, put the fruit into a bowl and add 200g (7oz) raspberries. Pour over the syrup. If you can't find rose-scented green tea, use green tea and add 1 tsp of rose water (taste as you add, as flower waters vary in strength). Raspberries, roses and lychees are just sublime together. You could also use geranium-scented water instead of rose water (see pages 328–329 for stockists). Serves 4–6.

pink rhubarb baked with star anise

Simple, not too sweet and good for breakfast as well as for pudding. Baking rhubarb is much easier than poaching (I invariably manage to let poached rhubarb fall apart, whereas, baked, the pieces stay intact and beautiful). If you want to extend it, add slices of ripe mango, or mango and lychees, or grapefruit (see below) to the cooked rhubarb; these all make a stunning looking dish.

SERVES 6

500g (1lb 2oz) young rhubarb

100g (3½oz) golden caster sugar

juice of 1 small orange

1 star anise

Preheat the oven to 170°C/340°F/gas mark 3½.

Trim the rhubarb stalks at each end and cut into lengths of about 3.5cm (1½in). Put into an ovenproof dish in which the pieces can sit in a single layer. Sprinkle with the sugar and add the orange juice. Break the star anise into 3–4 pieces and add to the liquid in the dish.

Cover with a piece of foil and bake in the oven for 20–30 minutes, until the rhubarb is tender but intact. It must not be at all mushy. Leave to cool.

try adding… **mango or grapefruit** This is lovely – and stunningly pretty – with the addition of mango or grapefruit. Add twice the amount of orange juice and another 25g (1oz) of sugar – so you end up with more syrup – cook the rhubarb and leave until it has completely cooled, then add 1 small mango. You need to peel it, cut the cheeks off (they're the bits on each side of the stone), then cut the cheeks into slices about the thickness of a 50 pence piece. Gently mix these into the rhubarb, being careful not to let the rhubarb fall apart. Pink or red grapefruit need to be segmented (see page 44). Add the segments from two fruits to the rhubarb once it's cool. Both versions serve 8 or more.

mulled quince and pear compote with cranberries

Quinces are luscious and honeyed so you don't need much to feel replete. They benefit from being mixed with pears – quinces can be almost *too* sweet on their own – and the cranberries cut this, too. Leftovers are fabulous on porridge.

SERVES 8

450ml (15fl oz) cranberry juice

135g (4¾oz) soft light brown sugar

½ cinnamon stick, broken

3 cloves

3 quinces, peeled, quartered and cored

juice of 1 lemon

2 strips of orange zest

3 fat pears (not too ripe), peeled, quartered and cored

150g (5½oz) cranberries

Put the cranberry juice, sugar, cinnamon and cloves into a broad, heavy-based pan with 150ml (5fl oz) of water and slowly bring to the boil, stirring a little to help the sugar dissolve. Reduce the heat to its lowest, add the quinces, lemon juice and orange zest and cook gently for 15 minutes. Add the pears and gently poach those for another 15 minutes (depending on how ripe your pears are). Turn the fruit every so often to make sure all sides get to sit in the poaching liquid.

Once the quinces and pears are almost tender, add the cranberries and gently stir them in. Cook for another five or 10 minutes. The cranberries should burst and colour the poaching liquid and the fruit should be completely tender. You shouldn't need to reduce the poaching liquid: quinces have loads of pectin in them so it should thicken as it cools.

Transfer the fruit and juices to a serving bowl (whip out the cinnamon and the cloves). Serve at room temperature with yogurt.

pomegranates, oranges and dates with flower water syrup

Fresh, light, scented, I get cravings for this dish. Don't assemble it too far in advance. It tastes good slightly chilled, but it's best not to put it in the fridge for too long as it loses its visual sparkle (and the oranges get a bit too soft).

SERVES 4–6

juice of 3 lemons

150g (5½oz) granulated sugar

1 broad strip of lemon zest

1 broad strip of orange zest

2 tbsp orange flower water

8 dates, pitted

5 oranges

120g (4oz) pomegranate seeds

Heat 325ml (11fl oz) of water, the lemon juice and sugar together with the strips of zest, stirring from time to time to help the sugar dissolve. Bring to the boil, then reduce the heat and simmer for 10–12 minutes until the mixture is syrupy. You will add oranges later and their juices will render it a bit thinner again. Leave to cool, then strain to remove the zests and add the flower water.

Halve the dates, then cut each half into three slices.

Cut the top and bottom off the oranges so they have a flat base on which to sit. Using a very sharp knife, cut the peel and pith off each, working around the fruit and cutting the peel away in broad strips from top to bottom. You can either cut the oranges into slices or into segments, whichever way you cut them catch the juice as you go along and add to the syrup.

Put the oranges in a shallow bowl, layering them up with the pomegranate seeds and dates. Pour over the syrup. Chill, this is lovely and refreshing served cold. Offer Greek yogurt – slightly sweetened if you like – on the side.

the good loaf

It's much easier to get proper, hand-made bread than it used to be, but beware the healthy pretender. The moniker 'wholemeal' is open to interpretation, likewise the term 'natural'. To think that all brown loaves are equal – and equally healthy – is like thinking a Trabant is as good as a Rolls Royce, because they're both cars.

Artisan bakeries are springing up everywhere and that's where you will find a good loaf. (And I mean *proper* artisan bakeries, not small-scale 'craft' bakeries that make better-looking breads with the same cocktail of artificial additives, 'improvers' and hidden processing aids as industrial bakers.) Proper artisan bakeries employ slower methods to make their bread, generally use less industrial (and so more wholesome) flours, smaller quantities of yeast and a wider range of grains. They have the skills to turn flour, water, salt and yeast into minor works of art, and to deal with natural variations in their product. They don't always have their own shops, but you can find their stuff at farmers' markets and delis. The Real Bread Campaign (www.realbreadcampaign.org), a charity promoting proper bread (as opposed to the industrial loaf made by the quick Chorleywood Bread Process), tells you where.

I realize this sounds rather precious, and that this kind of bread is not cheap. But why is it better not to care about what you eat, knowingly to eat inferior stuff and not to support small businesses who care about their produce? And just compare the experiences. Eat a piece of sliced wholemeal bread that you've bought in a supermarket alongside one from a proper artisan loaf. The one from the sliced loaf won't taste that good, in fact it has very little flavour. The loaf from the artisan bakery will taste much better – nutty and deep – but here's the crunch (especially if you're watching your weight): the artisan bread will also make you feel more satisfied, so you don't want another slice, and another. I can eat three slices of supermarket bread in a row (I'm sure I'm not the only one who, in times of stress, can live on toast). But the well-made loaf? One slice. Not only has the eating been pleasurable, but I'm much more satisfied. The bread is heavier and denser. And sourdoughs, which seem expensive when you buy them, last for days (you have to toast them on the third day, but that just enlivens that tangy flavour).

Is it okay to eat bread at all if you're watching your weight? All white breads and some wholemeal breads have high glycaemic indexes (GI): they cause surges in blood sugar and insulin (read more on pages 24–25). I haven't banned baguette, but eat it only occasionally. Long-fermented breads such as genuine sourdough, pumpernickel and some other ryes have a lower GI because of their long fermentation, so I go for those, though not *just* because it's better to eat complex carbohydrates; it's mostly because they have a great, full flavour that makes you experience bread as a proper food and not a 'filler'. I don't buy sliced white except for nostalgic tomato sandwiches (soggy tomato sarnies made with pappy white bread were in my childhood lunchbox). You can make your own bread, too (there are recipes in this book and, once you start, you get used to it). But if you're buying bread, shop well. You'll feel better, you'll eat better… and you'll eat less of it.

black bread

This – the classic Russian bread – is from Dan Lepard's fabulous baking book *Short and Sweet*. I have changed it only slightly. It is one of the most delicious breads I make, soft and yielding with a deep, dark flavour. One slice of it seems to be much more satisfying than two of any other type of bread. Eat it with raw or smoked fish, or as part of a Scandi-style breakfast.

Rye bread is easy to buy which is why I haven't given a recipe for it in the book, but black bread is much harder to find and, in any case, this is a joy to make. The dough is a gorgeous rusty colour and smells heady and sweet. The whole process is invigorating.

MAKES 1 LARGE LOAF

150g (5½oz) rye flour

2½ tsp dried yeast

3 tsp muscovado sugar

2 tbsp cocoa powder

2 tbsp instant coffee granules

75g (2¾oz) black treacle

4 tsp caraway seeds, plus
1 tsp for the top

50g (1¾oz) unsalted butter

425g (15oz) strong white
bread flour

2 tsp salt

150g (5½oz) finely grated
raw carrot

groundnut oil

1–2 tsp sesame seeds

Put 225ml (8fl oz) of cold water into a pan and bring to the boil. Whisk in 50g (1¾oz) of the rye flour with a fork – it will look like porridge – and leave to cool to lukewarm (about 15 minutes). Add the yeast and 1 tsp of the sugar, stir well, cover and leave at room temperature for 45 minutes. Heat 100ml (3½fl oz) more water and add the cocoa, coffee, treacle, 4 tsp of caraway seeds, the rest of the sugar and the butter. Stir until the butter has melted. Leave until lukewarm.

Put the white flour and the rest of the rye flour into a bowl with the salt. Make a well in the centre and pour the yeast mixture into it, followed by the treacle liquid and the carrot. Mix until you have a sticky dough. Lightly oil a small area of your work surface and your hands and put the dough on to it. Knead the dough on this, or in a food mixer fitted with a dough hook. If you are doing it yourself, knead for 10 minutes; if in the food mixer, knead for five minutes. The dough will be glossy, taut and a rusty mud colour, flecked with carrot. And it will smell delicious. Put into a lightly oiled bowl and cover with oiled cling film. Leave at room temperature for one hour (it should increase in size by about half).

Knock the dough back for 30 seconds, then shape into a round loaf with the seam underneath and put on an oiled baking sheet. Cover with the oiled cling film and leave at room temperature for about an hour. Preheat the oven to 220°C/425°F/gas mark 7.

Remove the cling film – the dough will be beautifully smooth and pillowy – and brush the surface with water. Sprinkle on the sesame and caraway seeds and cut a deep cross in the top with a serrated knife. Bake in the hot oven for 20 minutes, then reduce the heat to 180°C/350°F/gas mark 4 and bake for another 20 minutes. If you slide the loaf off and tap the underneath it should sound hollow. Slide on to a wire rack and leave to cool.

final thoughts

This book was finished when I started a list of guidelines (I forget things, so I love lists.) It wasn't a 'diet', but a way of eating that took my newly acquired knowledge into account. This is a personal aide mémoire, but I hope you find it useful.

Why should you care how a food writer eats? Because they love food and will not suggest a way of eating, however healthy, that isn't pleasurable. Also, as they are surrounded by temptation, they know well the pitfalls facing those who love food.

After reading this book, you might end up with your own guidelines. You know better than I what is possible in your life, as well as your personal weaknesses. You might put away half a pound of cheese while preparing dinner, or find it hard to stop at one glass of wine. The following sums up what I have taken to heart during my 'change of appetite'.

useful mantras

Mantras are good because you can call them to mind easily. One of my favourites is from the American journalist Michael Pollan. It is, 'Eat real food, mostly plants, not too much.' I would simply add, 'Savour it. Watch the carbs.'

We don't yet understand the relationship between fruits and vegetables and health. But this seems to be the area in which there is most agreement between experts. Fruit and veg are at most incredibly beneficial and, at least, benign. Majoring on them looks like a good idea and the bigger the variety the better (though cruciferous veg and 'greens' appear to offer the greatest benefits). So my second mantra is, 'Eat your greens, and your reds, and your pinks.'

One of the most shocking things I found was how sugar – even where it occurs naturally – is a major contributor to the growing problem of obesity. Obesity expert Robert Lustig believes fruit juice is every bit as bad as fizzy drinks. (As someone capable of downing half a carton of grapefruit juice in one fell swoop, I'm glad he told me.) Eating fruit is better, as it contains fibre. So one of Lustig's mantras has become mine: 'Eat the fruit, not the juice.'

fats

• Saturated fat, as found in butter, cheese and red meat, may not be as bad for us as we once thought (following low-fat diets hasn't cut rates of heart disease or cancer). But it still seems sensible to keep an eye on your intake. And eating small amounts of butter is preferable to switching to a low-fat alternative that has undergone an industrial process.
• Don't eat transfats (hidden in processed foods) *at all* and look for them on food labels.
• Use olive oil, avocado oil and rapeseed oil freely; cold-pressed hazelnut and walnut oils are good too (use those in dressings). Keep an eye on your intake of omega-6 oils (corn, sunflower, safflower and grapeseed).
• Don't buy 'low-fat' anything. If they've taken something *out* there's a good chance they've put something worse (such as sugar) *in*.

eggs
It appears that there is no link between dietary cholesterol and levels of cholesterol in your blood. Eggs are back on the menu.

oily fish
Full of omega-3 fatty acids. Fill your boots. As long as they are sustainable.

carbs
• Cut refined carbs and switch to whole grains. *Watch sugar like a hawk*, especially if you have trouble with your weight. You may have to limit all carbs, even whole grains, to lose weight.
• Be careful about snacking on fruit, it contains lots of natural sugar.
• Check the GI and GL of particular foods (especially those you like), so you know which cause insulin spikes. Check the great Australian website www.glycemicindex.com.

bread
• Eat proper whole grain breads, based on a variety of grains, from good artisan bakers.
• Remember that not all brown breads are 'healthy' (some are no better than white breads).

breakfast
Dump commercial breakfast cereal. Eat whole grains or protein to keep you full until lunch.

remember
• Nothing is forbidden. Healthy eating doesn't mean every meal has to be healthy. It means you should aim for *a balance overall*.
• It isn't a question of what you can't eat, more of what you can eat lots of.
• Don't eat in a hurry, and stop eating when you're full.
• Be aware of what you've learned, but don't think slavishly about health. Food is for enjoying. When you eat delicious food you know isn't doing you good – great croissants, home-made jam – don't angst over it. That's not what eating is about. Just *love* it.
• Plunder the healthy cuisines of the world – Middle Eastern, Mediterranean, Japanese, Thai, Burmese, Vietnamese – for dishes that are 'accidentally' healthy. (There's a list of good cookbooks in the bibliography.) There are masses of bright, strong 'front-of-the-mouth' flavours out there that can satisfy you (without the need for lots of sugar or stodge).

over to you...
This is my eighth book, and the one which has stretched me most (I prefer to think about flavours rather than food groups). It has also been the biggest surprise. In the past I groaned when people used the phrase 'healthy eating' (a mountain of Iceberg lettuce and cottage cheese as high as the sky would appear before my eyes). But of all my books, this is the one I keep right beside the cooker. I use it all the time. My cooking has changed and developed in a delicious way. I hope it does the same for you.

suppliers

grains and pulses

Supermarkets now stock a much wider range of whole grains and pulses than they used to and this is only likely to increase. But some things are still hard to find. Look in health food and whole food shops, or – even better – go online. There isn't a single ingredient I haven't been able to track down this way.

HEALTHY SUPPLIES
www.healthysupplies.co.uk
Fabulous. A one-stop online shop for a huge range of whole grains, whole flours (including Doves Farm), pulses, spices, nuts, seeds, dried fruits, mirin and oriental vinegars. They also have dried marigolds, used in Georgian food, and dried hibiscus.

MERCHANT GOURMET
www.merchant-gourmet.com
You can find these products in some supermarkets, but you can also buy directly from the website. They sell wholemeal giant couscous – which can be hard to find – and wheat berries. I don't use their ready-cooked grains and lentils – home-cooked, they keep their shape better – but I admit they can speed things up.

REAL FOODS
www.realfoods.co.uk
A great range of grains and pulses, including hard-to-find kamut, freekeh and Beluga black lentils. Excellent choice of flours, too, including a few favourites used in the recipes in this book: Doves Farm malthouse flour; and Marriages country fayre flour, a brown, malted flour with kibbled grains.

STEENBERGS
www.steenbergs.co.uk
Pulses, whole grains, nuts, seeds, baking ingredients, cereals, natural extracts and flavourings, plus a tremendous range of spices.

oils

I wish I had a pound for every time I recommend fruity rather than grassy extra virgin olive oil. Such is the marketing power of Tuscany that the biggest range of extra virgin olive oils come from there, or at least certainly from Italy. There's nothing wrong with them, but the more assertively grassy or bitter oils tend to dominate other flavours. This is fine if that's the result you want, but it's mostly not very user-friendly. For the fruitier oils, go to Liguria or to France. There's a good range of estate-bottled olive oils in supermarkets, so shop around, look in delis and go online. French oils are the hardest to find. Provençal extra virgin olive oil, from Les Baux, is my favourite all-rounder. Ligurian oils are also lovely and buttery and there are some fabulous – more assertive, but not 'grassy' – Sicilian oils, too.

A L'OLIVIER
www.alolivier.com
Wonderful oils in beautiful cans. And they have extra virgin olive oil from Les Baux. Also good vinegars, including raspberry vinegar made with raspberry pulp, and unusual oils such as argan oil.

THE OIL MERCHANT
www.oilmerchant.co.uk
Charles Carey, the owner, is the olive oil expert and he sells wholesale and mail order (though at the time of writing he doesn't have a fully functioning website). Contact him via the site to see what they have.

spices

GOUMANYAT
www.goumanyat.fr
It's worth going to Paris just to see this place, as you won't find spices like this anywhere else. Luckily their stock is now available online. They also have excellent flower waters.

SEASONED PIONEERS
www.seasonedpioneers.co.uk
Pretty much any spice you can think of.

THE COOL CHILE COMPANY
www.coolchile.co.uk
Every kind of dried chilli.

ethnic and hard-to-find ingredients

BELAZU
www.belazu.com
Barley couscous, preserved lemons, rose harissa, white balsamic and oils.

BRINDISA
www.brindisa.com
Canned smoked anchovies, Ortiz anchovies and canned tuna, as well as other wonderful Spanish things.

BUYWHOLEFOODSONLINE
www.buywholefoodsonline.co.uk
Grains, pulses, flours and some harder-to-find wholefood groceries such as nut butters.

HOMESTEAD FARM SUPPLIES
www.homesteadfarmsupplies.co.uk
To make your own goat's curd, this is where you can find animal rennet.

JAPAN CENTRE
www.japancentre.com
Everything Japanese…

MELBURY AND APPLETON
www.melburyandappleton.co.uk
Fabulous company supplying hard-to-find ingredients for Japanese, Vietnamese, Thai, Italian, Spanish and Middle Eastern cookery. Also a good source for whole grains, pulses, unusual things such as dried hibiscus, beluga lentils and verjus.

MULLACO
www.mullaco.com
If you don't live near a Middle Eastern shop, it's good to know about this Yorkshire-based company. They stock flower waters and pomegranate molasses, as well as lots of Indian ingredients.

NATCO
www.natco-online.com
Very big supplier of Indian ingredients.

ORIENTAL FOOD SHOP
www.orientalfoodshop.com
Rice vinegars, spices, soy sauce.

OTTOLENGHI
www.ottolenghi.co.uk
From food writer and restaurateur Yotam Ottolenghi, this sells grains, Middle Eastern storecupboard ingredients, olive oils and unusual items such as geranium flower water.

bibliography

SCANDINAVIAN KITCHEN
www.scandikitchen.co.uk
London-based café and online shop
for Scandinavian foods.

SOUSCHEF
www.souschef.co.uk
Excellent range of grains (including
freekeh) and just about everything
you've ever had trouble tracking
down. If you love finding unusual
ingredients, you'll be in heaven:
verjus, Aleppo pepper, dried
marigolds, yuzu juice, Japanese chilli
oil, it's all here…

THE ASIAN COOKSHOP
www.theasiancookshop.co.uk
There's an extraordinary range of
stuff here, from every single pulse
you might need for every kind of dal,
to specialist ingredients for Indian,
Burmese, Japanese, Thai, Chinese,
Mexican and Caribbean food. There
are things even I have never needed
(beetroot powder, Filipino cane
vinegar…?) A treasure trove.

THE WASABI COMPANY
www.thewasabicompany.co.uk
Fresh wasabi grown in England.
Expensive, but if you love your
wasabi, you might think it's worth it.

seeds for edible flowers and microleaves, and seeds for sprouting

Some farmers' markets now stock
fabulous edible flowers, while
microleaves are becoming more
available (even in supermarkets).
But if you don't have access to them
you can try growing your own, and
sprouting seeds as well. Growing your
own microleaves and sprouting seeds
is – honestly – very easy.

SKY SPROUTS
www.skysprouts.co.uk
Organic seeds for sprouting
(including China rose radish, which
look stunning).

WWW.OTTERFARM.CO.UK
WWW.REALSEEDS.CO.UK
WWW.SARAHRAVEN.COM
All suppliers of high-quality seeds,
with ranges of edible flowers.

essential reading

WHAT TO EAT? 10 CHEWY
QUESTIONS ABOUT FOOD
Hattie Ellis
Portobello Books, 2012
This is the best place to start: a
personal, accessible, wide-ranging
approach to the many conflicting
ideas that are out there. Ellis is not a
nutritionist or an 'expert', but a food
lover. This will get you thinking.

FOOD MATTERS: A GUIDE TO
CONSCIOUS EATING
Mark Bittman
Simon & Schuster, 2009
Bittman, a food writer for *The New
York Times*, changed his eating habits
because of health and environmental
concerns. Here he tears down the
accepted wisdom on health touted by
the American government and tackles
what is wrong with the American
(increasingly the global) diet.
Unputdownable.

WHAT TO EAT: FOOD THAT'S
GOOD FOR YOUR HEALTH,
POCKET AND PLATE
Joanna Blythman
Fourth Estate, 2012
Blythman, an investigative food
journalist, goes through every type of
food looking at its health properties
and the ethics around it. A brilliant
reference. I keep it in the kitchen.

FAT CHANCE: THE BITTER TRUTH
ABOUT SUGAR
Dr Robert Lustig
Fourth Estate, 2013
The most persuasive, frightening
book I read during my research.
You have to get your head round the
science, but persevere. And watch his
lecture online (see overleaf).

IN DEFENCE OF FOOD: AN EATER'S
MANIFESTO
Michael Pollan
Penguin, 2009

WHY WE GET FAT: AND WHAT TO
DO ABOUT IT
Gary Taubes
Anchor Editions, 2012

ESCAPE THE DIET TRAP
Dr John Briffa
Fourth Estate, 2013

EAT, DRINK, AND BE HEALTHY
Walter Willett
Free Press, 2003

wider reading

FOOD RULES, AN EATER'S MANUAL
Michael Pollan
Penguin, 2010

THE OMNIVORE'S DILEMMA
Michael Pollan
Bloomsbury Paperbacks, 2011

PURE, WHITE AND DEADLY
John Yudkin
Penguin, 2012

FOODS TO FIGHT CANCER
Richard Béliveau And Denis Gingras
Dorling Kindersley, 2007

ANTICANCER: A NEW WAY OF LIFE
Dr David Servan-Schreiber
Michael Joseph, 2011

THE DIET DELUSION
Gary Taubes
Vermilion, 2009

THE CHINA STUDY
Dr T Colin Campbell
Benbella, 2006

THE END OF OVEREATING
David A Kessler
Penguin, 2010

STUFFED AND STARVED
Raj Patel
Portobello Books, 2013

FAST FOOD NATION
Eric Schlosser
Penguin, 2002

NOT ON THE LABEL
Felicity Lawrence
Penguin, 2004

EAT YOUR HEART OUT
Felicity Lawrence
Penguin, 2008

THE REVOLUTION WILL NOT BE
MICROWAVED
Sandor Ellix Katz
Chelsea Green Publishing, 2006

WHY CALORIES COUNT: FROM
SCIENCE TO POLITICS
Marion Nestle And Malden Nesheim
University Of California Press, 2012

BAD SCIENCE
Ben Goldacre
Harper Perennial, 2009

THE FAST DIET
Dr Michael Mosley And Mimi Spencer
Short Books, 2013

THE DUKAN DIET
Dr Pierre Dukan
Hodder Paperbacks, 2010

DR ATKINS' NEW DIET REVOLUTION
Robert C Atkins
Vermilion, 2003

THE SPECTRUM
Dean Ornish
Ballantine Books, 2008

THE PALEO DIET
Loren Cordain
John Wiley, 2002

NUTRITIONISM: THE SCIENCE AND
POLITICS OF DIETARY ADVICE
Gyorgy Scrinis
Columbia University Press, 2013

SUSHI AND BEYOND: WHAT THE
JAPANESE KNOW ABOUT COOKING
Michael Booth
Vintage, 2010

GOOD TO THE GRAIN
Kimberley Boyce
Stewart, Tabori & Chang Inc,
2010

ANCIENT GRAINS FOR MODERN
MEALS
Maria Speck
Ten Speed Press, 2011

A COOK'S GUIDE TO GRAINS
Jenni Muir
Conran Octopus, 2002

ROOTS
Diane Morgan
Chronicle Books, 2012

VEGETABLE LITERACY
Deborah Madison
Ten Speed Press, 2013

JANE GRIGSON'S VEGETABLE
BOOK
Jane Grigson
Penguin Books, 1980

KNEAD TO KNOW: THE REAL
BREAD STARTER
The Real Bread Campaign
Grub Street, 2013

HOW TO BAKE BREAD
Emmanuel Hadjiandreou
Ryland Peters & Small, 2011

THE BREAKFAST BIBLE
Seb Emina and Malcolm Eggs
Bloomsbury, 2013

THE GREAT BRITISH BREAKFAST
Jan Read and Maite Manjon
Michael Joseph Ltd, 1981

JAPANESE COOKING: A SIMPLE ART
Shizuo Tsuji
Kodansha America Inc, 2012

THE JAPANESE KITCHEN
Kimiko Barber
Kyle Cathie, 2004

JAPANESE FARM FOOD
Nancy Singleton Hachisu
Andrews McMeel, 2012

WASHOKU
Elizabeth Andoh
Ten Speed Press, 2005

THE ENLIGHTENED KITCHEN
Mari Fujii
Kodansha America Inc, 2012

HOT SOUR SALTY SWEET
Naomi Duguid, Jeffrey Alford
Artisan, 2000

BURMA: RIVERS OF FLAVOR
Naomi Duguid
Artisan, 2012

THE INDIAN KITCHEN
Monisha Bharadwaj
Kyle Cathie, 2010

VEGETARIAN DISHES FROM THE
MIDDLE EAST
Arto Der Haroutunian
Grub Street, 2008

MIDDLE EASTERN COOKERY
Arto Der Haroutunian
Grub Street, 2010

CLASSIC VEGETARIAN COOKERY
Arto Der Haroutunian
Grub Street, 2011

THE SCANDINAVIAN KITCHEN
Camilla Plum
Kyle Cathie, 2010

THE NEW BOOK OF MIDDLE
EASTERN FOOD
Claudia Roden
Penguin, 1986

VIETNAMESE: FRAGRANT AND
EXOTIC
Ghillie Basan
Aquamarine, 2004

SECRETS OF THE RED LANTERN
Pauline Nguyen
Murdoch Books, 2007

THE ART OF SIMPLE FOOD
Alice Waters
Michael Joseph, 2008

broadcasts and internet

TRANSFATS
The Food Programme, BBC Radio
4, presented by Sheila Dillon,
transmitted 2011 (available on
BBC iPlayer)

SUGAR: THE BITTER TRUTH
Dr Robert Lustig
University Of California Television
(available on www.youtube.com)

THE SKINNY ON OBESITY (SERIES)
University Of California Televison
(available on www.youtube.com)

THE MEN WHO MADE US FAT
(SERIES)
BBC Television, reporter Jacques
Peretti, transmitted 2012

THE MEN WHO MADE US THIN
(SERIES)
BBC Television, reporter Jacques
Peretti, transmitted 2013

WWW.KELLIESFOODTOGLOW.COM
Website of health educationist
Kellie Anderson, who advises on
nutrition at Maggie's Cancer Caring
Centres, and offers fantastic food
that also happens to be good for you.
Delicious, colourful, plant-based
recipes and information about food's
relationship to health.

index

acknowledgements

For Miranda, with love.
Thank you for all the beautiful
books, and for so much else.

A Change of Appetite
by Diana Henry

First published in Great Britain in 2014
by Mitchell Beazley, an imprint of
Octopus Publishing Group Ltd
Endeavour House, 189 Shaftesbury Avenue
London WC2H 8JY
www.octopusbooks.co.uk

An Hachette UK Company
www.hachette.co.uk

Text copyright © Diana Henry 2014
Design and layout copyright © Octopus
Publishing 2014
Photography copyright © Laura Edwards 2014

ISBN 978 1 84533 784 1

A CIP catalogue record for this book is
available from the British Library

Printed and bound in China

10 9 8 7 6 5 4 3 2 1

Publisher: Denise Bates
Art Director: Jonathan Christie
Photographer: Laura Edwards
Design and Art Direction: Miranda Harvey
Editor: Lucy Bannell
Styling: Diana Henry and Miranda Harvey
Home Economist: Joss Herd
Assistant Production Manager: Caroline Alberti

All eggs are large unless otherwise stated.

My sons, Ted and Gillies, and my partner, Ben, ate rather a lot of 'new'
dishes while I was testing the recipes for this book (not all of them
successful, brown rice cooked in green tea was a particular low. And no, it
didn't make the cut). Thank you for patiently trying this different way of
eating. And thank you Ted and Ben (the scientists in my life) for helping
me to understand the material I had to digest while doing the research.
I'm glad you're all on whole grains now. But I also know you love bagels,
white bread, brioche… and Haribo Tangfastics. (You're a challenging lot.)

My good friend and fellow food writer Hattie Ellis gave me much guidance.
I found her help – and her book, *What to Eat* – invaluable. Thank you,
Hattie. Enormous thanks, too, to Kellie Anderson, who read several
chapters, kept me on the straight and narrow on various bits of science and
was extremely generous with her time and advice. Thanks also to Yotam
Ottolenghi, and to Chris Young from the Real Bread Campaign for various
bits of advice, to Yuki Sugiura for Japanese cooking lessons, and to Roopa
Gulati for lessons in lentils… Xanthe Clay, Brett Barnes, Darina Allen,
Roopa Gulati, Clare Henry and Levi Roots all kindly let me use recipes.
Thank you, guys.

Huge thanks to my publisher, Denise Bates at Mitchell Beazley, for
completely 'getting' what I was trying to do (she is so smart she can discern
this even when it's in embryo and I can barely articulate it) and for letting
me run with it, also for her unfailing support and fantastic judgement.

Thanks to Jonathan Christie, our talented and 'can-do' art director and to
the team who make sure the colour is right, the ribbons are of good quality
and the damned book gets printed. Sybella Stephens, Katherine Hockley
and Caroline Alberti, without all your work on the fundamentals and your
attention to detail my books wouldn't be nearly as good.

I'm very grateful to Amy Bryant from *The Sunday Telegraph* for additional
research on where to buy lots of healthy and hard-to-find stuff online.

Thanks also to Rachel Wood and Kathryn Morrissey who were total
troopers and fitted into the creative chaos of the shoot days.

My greatest debt goes to the team who were at the coal-face: designer
Miranda Harvey, photographer Laura Edwards, editor Lucy Bannell,
and cooks Joss Herd and Danny Maguire.

Laura, your photography is amazing, and you're developing so fast it leaves
Miranda and I breathless. We love working with you.

Joss, I don't know anyone who can produce food that is so alive, that has
such structure and movement. You are way more than a cook. You're also
like sunshine in the kitchen, always laughing, ever positive. Danny, rose
among thorns, we love you for being sane, a great cook, a good flirt and for
holding your own among us women. I hope we didn't shock you too often.

Lucy, you are, in my opinion, a genius editor. I can never see what you've
cut, you make my voice more elegant (without changing its spirit) and you
make each book as perfect as it can be. You're with me every inch of the
way. I can't thank you enough.

Miranda, we are now such a long-standing team we can finish each other's
sentences and completely understand each other's style. Working with you
is one of the most fulfilling parts of my life.

Thanks and love to all of you. It's been bloody good fun and a creative joy.